TALK

Spanish
Grammar

SUSAN DUNNETT
Series Editor: Alwena Lamping

Published by BBC Active, an imprint of Educational Publishers LLP, part of the Pearson Education Group, Edinburgh Gate, Harlow, Essex CM20 2JE, England.

© Educational Publishers LLP 2009

First published 2009.
6

ISBN 978-1-4066-7920-5

Cover design: Johanna Gale
Cover photograph: © iStock.com/rognar
Insides design and layout: BBC Active design team
Illustrations © Mark Duffin
Publisher: Debbie Marshall
Development editor: María L. Heredia-Fernández
Language consultant: Mike Thacker
Project editor: Emma Brown
Marketing: Fiona Griffiths
Senior production controller: Franco Forgione

Printed and bound in China (CTPSC/06).

The Publisher's policy is to use paper manufactured from sustainable forests.

Contents

introduction

Talk Spanish Grammar is the essential handbook for anyone setting out to learn Spanish, at home or in a class. With its straightforward approach and clear layout, it promotes a real understanding of how Spanish works and how it relates to English.

It's much more than an ordinary grammar book. Using the tried-and-tested principles of the bestselling **Talk Spanish** and **Talk Spanish 2**, it de-mystifies grammar and guides you through the key structures of Spanish in a way that's really easy to follow even if you have no experience at all of grammar and its terminology.

Its parallel focus is on building a large vocabulary – fast – for you to combine with an understanding of grammar to say whatever you want in Spanish, without having to rely on phrasebooks.

Among its special features you'll find:
- a summary of **the most significant differences** in the way Spanish and English work
- clear, **jargon-free explanations** of Spanish grammar, set out in units and illustrated by hundreds of **practical examples**
- **Word power** pages, tailored to individual units. Some of these focus on the fact that large numbers of Spanish and English words are easy to convert from one language to the other if you know what to look out for. **False friends** are highlighted too: words which look as though they might mean one thing but in fact mean something different.
- **learning tips and strategies**, positioned just where you need them
- **dictionary guidance**, with abbreviations and sample entries
- regular **Checkpoints** with practice activities to reinforce the language patterns and help you remember them. These are also useful as revision or as an aide-memoire.
- **verb tables**: the patterns for widely-used regular and irregular verbs
- a **glossary of grammar terms** with examples in English to make them crystal-clear
- a **comprehensive**, **easy-to-use index**.

Talk Spanish Grammar can be used successfully alongside any learning materials, and is also the perfect companion for both levels of **Talk Spanish**. The **Talk** series has online activities at www.bbc.co.uk/languages/spanish, and if you'd like to practise your grammar online, try out the grammar section of the **Steps** course at the same address.

How to use Talk Spanish Grammar

This book works on several levels – make it work for you!

New to language learning or forgotten everything you've learnt? Or perhaps you already know some Spanish words but have no structure to use them in?
Go to **Getting Started** on page 8, which gives you an overview of what grammar is about, introduces you to the keystones of grammar and provides a few short activities to help you recognise and remember them.

New to Spanish but understand the meaning of basic terms such as noun, adjective, verb?
Go to page 10, which prepares you for learning Spanish by highlighting the principal differences between Spanish and English.

Learning Spanish on your own or in a class and need extra support?
Choose the unit you want, work through it, then complete the **Checkpoint** at the end to see how much you've understood and remembered. You can select the units in the order that suits you because they're free-standing and they cross-reference to each other so that you can easily check things out if you need to.

Need a clear and comprehensive Spanish grammar reference book?
The index will show you where everything is. It uses key words in English and Spanish as well as grammar terms, making it easy for you to find what you're looking for quickly.

Want to brush up on your Spanish or do some revision?
The first page of each unit summarises the key points. Reading these and trying your hand at the **Checkpoint** activities will pinpoint any gaps in your knowledge so that you know what might be useful to spend some time on.

Just want to generally improve your Spanish, deepen your understanding and boost your vocabulary?
Dip into the book at random, reminding yourself of the structures, reading the examples, checking out the **Word power** pages and using the **Checkpoints**.

getting started

What is grammar?

When we talk we do more than just say words randomly; we use them in a specific order and they relate to one another. Grammar is the explanation of how that works: it provides definitions of the structures of a language and how they're used.

Can't I communicate without learning grammar?

Yes … if you're happy restricting yourself to phrases from a book or pidgin-type communication. You'll just about be able to make yourself understood, but conversation will be a strain and communication hit-and-miss. With relatively little knowledge of grammar, you can produce correct and unambiguous Spanish instead. You'll sound more articulate and it will be a much more constructive and satisfying experience.

How do babies cope without knowing about grammar?

It's true that children learn to talk without ever having heard of a verb or a noun. But if you listen to a toddler you'll often hear words like *hided, eated*, *sheeps* or *mans*, showing that the child has in fact absorbed the regular patterns of English and is applying them quite unconsciously – albeit not always correctly. As time goes on, irregularities get ironed out and the child, with no apparent effort, starts saying *hid* and *ate*, *sheep* and *men*.

It takes many months of constant exposure to a language to learn in this way. By the time the average child is starting to form sentences, they will have been hearing their mother tongue for around 4,500 hours over a period of 18 months or so.

Most adults want results more quickly than that. By consciously learning how Spanish is structured and how new words fit within sentences, you shortcut the process considerably. But you'll still experiment and make mistakes, just as children do, because that's part of the learning curve too.

How much grammar will I need?

At the start, you can get by comfortably with the basics. As you carry on with your Spanish, you'll gradually accumulate knowledge, and more pieces of the jigsaw will slot into place. There are some aspects of grammar that you might never need or want to know about – as with most things, there's a level that's largely of interest only to the professional or the enthusiast.

Where do I start?

It pays to become familiar with some of the terms used to describe how a language works because it allows you to make sense of statements that you might come across in course books, such as
The adjective usually goes after the noun or *The definite article is not used when …*

Focus first on the six main building blocks of a sentence. Read these descriptions, then see if you can pick them out in sentences.

- **Nouns** are the words for living beings, things, places and abstract concepts: *woman, son, doctor, Oliver, dog, table, house, Scotland, time, joy, freedom.*
- **Pronouns** are words used to avoid repeating a noun: *I, me, we, us, you, he/she, him/her, it, they, them.*
- **Articles** are *the, a/an* and *some.*
- **Adjectives** are words that describe nouns and pronouns: **good** *wine;* **strong red** *wine;* **my** *wine; I am* **tired**; *it was* **superb**.
- **Adverbs** add information to adjectives, verbs and other adverbs: **very** *good wine; you speak* **clearly**; *you speak* **really** *clearly.*
- **Verbs** are words like *go, sleep, eat, like, have, be, live, die,* that relate to doing and being.

---

1 Have a look at the underlined words and write N by the nouns, V by the verbs and ADJ by the adjectives.
   a) <u>Ana</u> works for a <u>glossy</u> <u>magazine</u>. She <u>organises</u> <u>interviews</u>, <u>hires</u> <u>professional</u> <u>models</u> and <u>photographers</u> and <u>travels</u> all over the <u>world</u>. Her <u>boyfriend</u> is a <u>well-known</u> <u>actor</u>.
   b) <u>My</u> <u>father</u> <u>comes</u> from <u>Salamanca</u> although he <u>lives</u> in <u>Madrid</u> because he <u>works</u> at the <u>central</u> <u>office</u> of a <u>large</u> <u>company</u>.
   c) They <u>prepared</u> a <u>fantastic</u> <u>meal</u> for us. We <u>ate</u> <u>grilled</u> <u>fish</u>, <u>fresh</u> <u>asparagus</u> and <u>new</u> <u>potatoes</u>, <u>drank</u> a <u>superb</u> <u>Spanish</u> <u>white</u> <u>wine</u> – and the <u>dessert</u> was absolutely <u>incredible</u>.

2 Now pick out the adverbs ADV and the adjectives ADJ.
   a) The house was <u>very</u> <u>reasonable</u> but it was <u>rather</u> <u>dilapidated</u> … and the garden was <u>really</u> <u>small</u> and <u>overgrown</u>.
   b) We played <u>superbly</u>. It wasn't our fault that the pitch was <u>terribly</u> <u>uneven</u> and the ref <u>deliberately</u> <u>unfair</u>.

How different are Spanish and English?
On the whole, Spanish grammar is similar to English, but there are a few aspects which are rather different. If you're prepared for these, you'll find that you get used to them very quickly.

Gender: masculine and feminine
Every single Spanish noun – not just the words for people and animals – is either masculine (m) or feminine (f). There's no sense of *it*, not even for things like cars, furniture, sport or days of the week – everything is *he* or *she*. Words linked to a noun, such as articles and adjectives, also have to be masculine or feminine.

The endings of nouns and adjectives
Many nouns and adjectives end in an -o or an -a. This is significant because it can show whether the word is masculine or feminine: generally speaking -o is masculine and -a is feminine – as you might expect from names like Antonio, Ricardo, Francisco; María, Ana, Ángela. Nouns with other endings can either be masculine or feminine, so it's best to learn them individually.

Articles
There are four words for *the* in Spanish. The one you use depends on whether the following noun is masculine or feminine, singular or plural. And there are two words for *a/an*, depending on whether the following noun is masculine or feminine.

Different versions of you
In English there's only one word for *you*; in Spanish there are four, depending on who you're talking to. **Tú** and **usted** convey different degrees of familiarity, friendliness and respect when you're talking to one person. When there's more than one person, you use either **vosotros/as** or **ustedes**.

Verb endings; I, we, you, he/she, they
In English a verb stays pretty much the same no matter who's carrying it out: *I eat, we eat, you eat, the cats eat, Joe eats*.
In Spanish, instead of using *I, you, she*, etc. you change the ending of the verb to show who's doing what.

Word order
On the whole, word order is similar to English. The most noticeable differences are adjectives, which come after nouns, not before them as in English: **música clásica** *classical music*. Also, words like *it* and *them* often come before a verb not after it.

What about vocabulary?

Learning a new language is a several-pronged process. Knowledge of grammar has a key place, with even a few simple structures going a long way towards making sure you're understood. Knowing how to use verbs and when to include words like **pero** *but* and **porque** *because* take you a big step further, letting you express more complex thoughts. But all these are of limited use without a good stock of words to slot into the structures – and the most obvious source of these is a dictionary.

What sort of dictionary is best?

When choosing your first English/Spanish dictionary, go for a medium-sized one. Too small and it won't give you enough information; too big and it will confuse you with too much. There are also dictionaries online, many of them free.

Why are dictionaries so full of abbreviations?

Some words are straightforward, with just one meaning: **preferir** *prefer* can only be a verb, **posible** *possible* can only be an adjective. Others are more complex, with the same word belonging in more than one grammatical category. *Mind* can mean what you think with (noun) and to look after (verb). *Book* can mean something you read (noun) and it can mean to reserve a place (verb). *Calm* can mean peaceful (adjective), peace (noun) and to soothe (verb).

To make sure you find the right category of word, each has an abbreviation next to it. The most common are:

art article	*adj* adjective	*adv* adverb
f feminine	*m* masculine	*n* noun
pl plural	*prep* preposition	*pron* pronoun
sing singular	*v* verb	

You may find slight variations in some dictionaries so it's worth checking with the introduction.

How do I make sure I choose the right translation?

Some words have more than one meaning even within the same grammatical category: the adjective *hard* can mean *solid* and it can mean *difficult*. The noun *habit* can be something a nun wears or it can be something you do on a regular basis. The verb *to press* can mean to iron clothes or to push down on something.

There's often an explanation or a phrase to guide you, but if you've looked up an English word and are still not sure which of the Spanish translations to use, look them all up and see what English translations are given.

hard *adj* **1.** duro, rígido: ~ *seat* asiento duro; ~ *surface* superficie rígida **2.** difícil: ~ *problem* problema difícil **3.** severo: ~ *father* padre severo; ~ *winter* invierno severo **4.** duro, vigoroso: ~ *match* partido duro **5.** ~ *shoulder* arcén *m*; *to learn the* ~ *way* aprender por experiencia

habit *n* **1.** hábito *m*, costumbre *f*: *by force of* ~ por costumbre; *bad* ~ vicio *m*; *drug* ~ adicción a las drogas, toxicomanía **3.** [*relig*] hábito *m*

press *v* **1.** apretar: *to* ~ *the right button* apretar el botón justo **2.** exprimir: *to* ~ *an orange* exprimir el zumo de una naranja **3.** planchar: *to* ~ *a shirt* planchar una camisa **4.** comprimir *to* ~ *down* **5.** estrujar *to squeeze* **6.** hacer acusaciones *to* ~ *charges* **7.** pedir insistentemente: *to* ~ *for an answer* pedir insistentemente que uno conteste a algo

What if I can't find the word I'm looking for?

This is where your knowledge of grammar comes in. The two main points to remember are that:

- adjectives in a dictionary are in the masculine singular
- verbs are in the infinitive, so you have to replace any other endings with -**ar**, -**er** or -**ir** before you look up a verb

If you still have a problem, it probably means that you've come across part of an irregular verb, the most common of which are written out in full on pages 197-247.

How else can I build up a wide vocabulary?

The most obvious source of Spanish outside Spain is the internet, where you can find information in Spanish on practically anything. Use a dictionary to find the key words relating to your interests then just browse. You'll be surprised at how much Spanish you absorb when words are in a familiar context that interests you.

Don't forget that you already have a huge latent vocabulary simply because, for historical reasons, Spanish and English have a lot of words in common. Some word groups are all but identical, others have moved apart slightly. These are the main focus of the **Word power** pages, which show you how to 'convert' from one language to the other. Not only will you find your vocabulary increasing dramatically, but you'll also have the knowledge and the confidence to make an educated guess at the meaning of new words.

Is it true that many English words are used in Spanish?

Over the years Spanish and English have borrowed and absorbed many words from each other. Most of them have stayed unchanged but a few have adapted to their adopted language. For example, **esnobismo** has become a Spanish noun from *snob*; **footing** is regularly used in Spain for *jogging,* and **chaqueta** for a *jacket*.

Similarly, the rules of English grammar are often applied to Spanish imported words: when talking about more than one **conquistador**, we don't say **conquistadores** as a Spaniard would but just add **-s** as we do for English words.

Do these shared words sound the same?

Many of them are recognisable for speakers of the other language – but many more are pronounced with a 'local' accent, whether Spanish or English. Some Spanish words routinely used in the UK are not said as a Spaniard would say them. And you'll be surprised when you hear, for example, *internet* or *windsurf* pronounced the Spanish way.

The key to good pronunciation is to assume that even words you recognise might sound different in Spanish, and to approach **Sounds and Spelling** on page 15 with a completely open mind.

Here are just a few of the Spanish words used in English:

adobe	macho
aficionado	margarita
albino	mosquito
alfalfa	paella
alpaca	patio
armada	piña colada
armadillo	plaza
bonanza	pronto
bronco	rodeo
canasta	salsa
cargo	siesta
chihuahua	silo
chocolate	tequila
conquistador	toreador
flotilla	tornado
junta	tortilla
machete	vigilante
machismo	

… and some English words regularly used in Spanish:

bádminton	márketing
bar	parking
biquini	penalti
CD	radio
email	sandwich
golf	taxi
hotel	web
internet	western
jersey	windsurf
kayak	zoo

Sounds and spelling

In English, letters sound different according to which word they're in.
a: c**a**rt, c**a**re, w**a**r, wom**a**n
e: b**e**d, **e**vil, en**e**my, blu**e**

This doesn't happen in Spanish, where the connection between a letter and its sound doesn't vary from one word to the next.
a is always pronounced like the **a** in h**a**t: c**a**sa, p**a**dre,
e is always pronounced like the **e** in h**e**n: b**e**bé, **e**legant**e**
This means that once you're familiar with a few straightforward rules, you'll know how to pronounce any new words that you come across.

As well as knowing those rules, the key to success lies in remembering never to pronounce Spanish words as if they were English, even when they look identical or have become accepted as English. For example:
chocolate is pronounced chohcoh<u>lah</u>teh
junta is pronounced <u>hoohn</u>tah
paella is pronounced pah<u>eh</u>lliah
plaza *square* is pronounced <u>plah</u>thah
vigilante *security guard* is pronounced beehee<u>lahn</u>teh

Finally, good pronunciation comes from listening at every available opportunity to native Spanish speakers, and practising new words and phrases by saying them out loud. At first, exaggerate your pronunciation and act Spanish: open your mouth more than you do for English and use the muscles of your face more.

pronunciation

vowels

Spanish vowel sounds are always short and clear. They're pronounced consistently, even in combinations where each vowel is pronounced individually. And they're never silent like the e in English words such as *make*, *some* or *file*.

They sound much as they do in these English words:

a	c**a**t
e	p**e**n
i	m**ee**t
o	p**o**t
u	c**oo**l

pairs of vowels

Of the five vowels, **a**, **e** and **o** are strong vowels and **i** and **u** are weak.

- Two strong vowels next to each other are pronounced as two distinct syllables, with the position of stress following the normal pattern (page 18):
  maestro *teacher*, **atraer** *to attract*
- A strong and a weak vowel together form a diphthong, which means that they're pronounced as one syllable. The stress falls on the stronger vowel and, if an accent is needed, it goes on the strong vowel:
  quiero *I want*, **bebéis** *you drink*
- Two weak vowels form a diphthong with the stress on the second vowel:
  viuda *widow*, **ruido** *noise*
- Any vowel combination that doesn't follow the above patterns has an accent, and the two vowels are pronounced as separate syllables:
  día *day*, **río** *river*

Double letters are less common in Spanish, although **cc**, **nn** and **rr** do exist. When **cc** and **nn** occur in a word they are pronounced as separate letters and according to the rules of pronunciation (see opposite). For example, **acción** is pronounced *akthyon*. **ll** exists as a single letter, pronounced as the *ly* in *only*.

consonants

Some consonants sound very similar in Spanish and English. The ones to look out for are **c**, **d**, **g**, **h**, **j**, **ll**, **ñ**, **q**, **r**, **v** and **z**.

	English	
c + e/i	th as in **th**read	**c**ero, **c**ine
c + all other vowels	c as in **c**one	**c**asa, **c**oche, **cu**atro
c + h + all vowels	ch as in **ch**ocolate	no**ch**e
d at the beginning of a word	d as in **d**ouble	**d**ios
d between vowels and at the end of a word	th as in o**th**er	ciu**d**ad
g + e/i	hh as in lo**ch**	**g**eneral, **g**imnasia
g + silent u + e/i	g as in **g**uild	**gu**erra, **gu**ía
g + other letters	g as in **g**o	**g**ato, **g**rande
h	is silent as in **h**onest	**h**oja
j	hh as in lo**ch**	**j**amón, **j**uego
ll	ly as in on**ly**	**ll**ave, Sevi**ll**a
ñ	ny as in o**ni**on	ma**ñ**ana, ni**ñ**o
q + silent u	k as in **k**it	**qu**eso, al**qu**iler
r at the beginning of a word and **rr**	are strongly rolled as in Scotland	**r**ojo, **R**ioja pe**rr**o, Co**rr**eos
r between vowels	is softer	pe**r**o, ca**r**o
v	b as in **b**ear	**v**aso, **v**ino
z	th as in **th**ick	**z**umo, **z**oo

Try saying these words out loud, remembering that they may not sound as they do when they're used in English. You can check your pronunciation on page 255.

- **Almería, Gijón, León, Sevilla, Tarragona, Valladolid**
- **armadillo, chihuahua, jaguar, llama, mosquito**
- **chocolate, flan, paella, piña colada, salsa, tortilla**

stress

- Words ending in a vowel or **n** or **s** are stressed on the second-to-last syllable: **casa**, **coche**, **libro**, **hermanos**, **escriben**.

- Words ending in a consonant other than **n** or **s** are stressed on the last syllable: **beber**, **ciudad**, **papel**, **tapiz**.

- Any word that deviates from these basic rules has an accent over the stressed vowel: **café**, **estación**, **difícil**, **lápiz**.

accents

There are three accents in Spanish:
- the acute accent **´**, which can be used over any vowel and which shows where the stress is in a word:
  frágil, diabético, título, conversación
  It also distinguishes between otherwise identical words:

como *as, like*	**cómo** *how*
el *the*	**él** *he*
esta *this*	**está** *it is*
mas *but*	**más** *more*
Papa *Pope*	**papá** *daddy*
si *if*	**sí** *yes*
tu *your*	**tú** *you*

- the tilde **~**, which is only ever found over the letter **n**. The letter **ñ** is a separate letter of the alphabet and is pronounced *ny*:
  España *Spain*

- the diaeresis **¨**, which is used over **u** when it's between **g** and **e/i** to show that it's pronounced separately where otherwise it would be silent:
  vergüenza *shame*
  lingüista *linguist*

the Spanish alphabet

Spanish uses the same alphabet as English, but with the addition of two unique letters: **ll** as in **lluvia** *rain* and **ñ** as in **español** *Spanish*.
When spelling words out, the letters of the alphabet sound like the imitated pronunciation in the third column below. The words listed in the right-hand column are used when clarification is needed, in the same way as the UK uses: *alpha, bravo, charlie … x-ray, yankee, zulu.*

a	**a**	ah	Antonio
b	**be**	be	Barcelona
c	**ce**	theh	Carmen
d	**de**	deh	Dolores, Daniel
e	**e**	eh	Enrique, España
f	**efe**	eh feh	Francia
g	**ge**	heh	Gerona
h	**hache**	aah cheh	historia
i	**i**	ee	Inés
j	**jota**	hota	José
k	**ka**	cah	kilo
l	**ele**	ele	Lorenzo
ll	**elle**	eh li eh	Llobregat
m	**eme**	eh meh	Madrid
n	**ene**	eh neh	Navarra, Navidad
ñ	**eñe**	eh ni eh	ñoño
o	**o**	oh	Oviedo
p	**pe**	peh	París
q	**qu**	cooh	querido
r	**ere**	eh reh	Ramón
s	**ese**	eh seh	sábado
t	**te**	teh	Tarragona, Teruel
u	**u**	ooh	Ulises
v	**uve**	ooh beh	Valencia
w	**uve doble**	ooh beh doh bleh	Washington
x	**equis**	eh kees	Xiquena
y	**i griega**	ee gree eh gah	Yagüe, yegua
z	**zeta**	theh tah	Zaragoza

spelling things out

Spelling out Brighton would sound like this:
beh, eh reh, ee, heh, aah cheh, teh, oh, eh neh

In Spanish, **dos** *two* is used for *double*, so Liverpool would be:
eh leh, ee, oo beh, eh, eh reh, peh, **dos** oh, eh leh

When using the words **Antonio, Barcelona**, etc. for clarification, the link
word is **de** *as/like*:
James: **jota de José, a de Antonio, eme de Madrid, e de Enrique, ese de
sábado**
Bond: **be de Barcelona, o de Oviedo, ene de Navarra, de de Dolores**

punctuation marks

. **punto**	@ **arroba**
, **coma**	* **asterisco**
; **punto y coma**	# **almohadilla**
: **dos puntos**	*ABC upper case* **mayúscula**
/ **barra**	*abc lower case* **minúscula**
\ **barra inversa**	*(in brackets)* **entre paréntesis**
- **guión**	*"in inverted commas"* **entre comillas**
_ **guión bajo**	*space* **espacio**

It's useful to know the Spanish for punctuation marks and keyboard symbols
if you want to spell out, for example, your **dirección de correo electrónico/
email** *email address*. And when spelling out **un sitio internet/sitio web**
website or **una página web** *web page*, you need *www*, which is pronounced
tres uve dobles or **uve doble, uve doble, uve doble**.
www.bbcactive.com would sound like this: **tres** ooh beh doh blehs **punto**,
beh, beh, theh, ah, theh, teh, ee, oo beh, eh, **punto** com
and if you add */languages*: **barra** eh leh, ah, eh neh, heh, ooh, ah, heh, eh, eh
seh. Have a go at saying it out loud, then your own name and email address.

One of the most striking features of written Spanish is the way
questions have an upside-down question mark at the beginning
as well as one the right way up at the end: **¿Cómo te llamas?**
What's your name? It's the same for exclamations: **¡Qué
lástima!** *What a pity!*

capital letters

Spanish uses **mayúsculas** *capital letters* less than English. They're used at the beginning of a sentence but they're not used for:

- titles of films, books, plays, etc, apart from the first word:
  La guerra de las galaxias ("Star Wars")

- titles followed by a surname:
  la señora García *Mrs García*; **el doctor López**

- names of days or months (see page 30):
  jueves *Thursday*, **marzo** *March*

- languages, peoples or adjectives of nationality:
  Hablo inglés. *I speak English.*
  los alemanes *the Germans*; **los irlandeses** *the Irish*
  Soy escocés. *I'm Scottish.* **un país europeo** *a European country*

- adjectives or nouns expressing religion:
  Mercedes es católica. *Mercedes is a Catholic.*
  Andrés estudia el hinduismo. *Andrés is studying Hinduism.*

Capital letters are used:

- for names of people and institutions:
  Pedro y Silvia viven aquí. *Pedro and Silvia live here.*
  Unión Europea *European Union*; **Cruz Roja** *Red Cross*

- abbreviations of titles followed by a surname:
  la Sra. García *Mrs García*; **el Dr. López** *Dr López*

- place names:
  continentes: **África, América del Norte/Sur** *North/South America*, **Asia, Antártida** *Antarctica*, **Australia, Europa**

  países *countries*: **Alemania** *Germany*, **Australia, Canadá, Escocia, Finlandia, Francia, Inglaterra, Irlanda, Irlanda del Norte, Italia, Nueva Zelanda, País de Gales, Portugal, Reino Unido** *UK*, **Rusia**

  ciudades *cities*: **Madrid, Londres, Bilbao, Córdoba, Edimburgo, Granada, Málaga, Santander**

word power

Spanish and English have a lot of words in common, and many of those that are not identical are very similar. You can easily convert many English words to Spanish if you take the following differences in spelling into consideration:

🇬🇧	🇪🇸	
ph	f	elephant **elefante**, emphasis **énfasis**, pharmacy **farmacia**, phonetics **fonética**, photo **foto**, phrase **frase**, physics **física**, physique **físico**, telephone **teléfono**
th	t	aesthetic **estético**, cathedral **catedral**, catholic **católico**, Thailand **Tailandia**, theatre **teatro**, theme **tema**, thesis **tesis**, throne **trono**
ff	f	affect **afectar**, affirm **afirmar**, decaffeinated **descafeinado**, difficult **difícil**, different **diferente**, effect **efecto**, efficiency **eficacia**, offensive **ofensivo**
ll	l	allergy **alergia**, collaborate **colaborar**, collection **colección**, dollar **dólar**, illegal **ilegal**, illuminate **iluminar**, illusion **ilusión**, illustration **ilustración**
mm	m	accommodate **acomodar**, comment **comentar**, communicate **comunicar**, community **comunidad**, inflammable **inflamable**, recommend **recomendar**
nn	n	annual **anual**, announce **anunciar**, connect **conectar**, connection **conexión**, manner **manera**, sonnet **soneto**, tennis **tenis**, tunnel **túnel**, tyranny **tiranía**
pp	p	apparatus **aparato**, apparent **aparente**, appetite **apetito**, appreciate **apreciar**, opportunity **oportunidad**
ss	s	assassinate **asesinar**, assault **asaltar**, commission **comisión**, fossil **fósil**, mission **misión**, passion **pasión**, possessive **posesivo**, Russia **Rusia**, session **sesión**

tt	t	attack ataque, attend (patient) atender, attention atención, attic ático, battle batalla, bottle botella, cassette casete, letter (of alphabet) letra, libretto libreto
y	i	analysis análisis, bicycle bicicleta, dyslexia dislexia, gymnasium gimnasio, hygienic higiénico, mystery misterio, physical físico, type tipo, typical típico
qu	cu, c	aquatic acuático, delinquent delincuente, eloquent elocuente, equator ecuador, equation ecuación, quadrant cuadrante, quadruple cuadruplicar, quality calidad, (of person) cualidad, quantity cantidad, quarter cuarto, quartet cuarteto, question cuestión, questionable cuestionable, questionnaire cuestionario, unquestionable incuestionable

- The following spelling changes occur at the beginning of words:

s	es*	scene escena, scorpion escorpión, snobbism esnobismo, spaghetti espagueti, sphere esfera, special especial, species especie, splendour esplendor, statue estatua, stupid estúpido
imm	inm	immediate inmediato, immense inmenso, immigration inmigración, immoral inmoral, immortal inmortal, immobile inmóvil, immune inmune
ps	(p)s	psalm salmo, psoriasis (p)soriasis, psychiatrist (p)siquiatra, psychic (p)síquico, psychoanalysis (p)sicoanálisis, psychology (p)sicología, psychotherapy (p)sicoterapia
un	in	unnecessary innecesario, unacceptable inaceptable, unaffected inafectado, unaltered inalterado, uncertainty incertidumbre, unnavegable innavegable

* before a consonant

checkpoint 1

1   These names illustrate the contents of this unit and are useful pronunciation practice. Work out where the stress will fall, say the names out loud and give the English equivalents:
Men: **Carlos, Felipe, Francisco, Guillermo, Juan, Pedro**
Women: **Alejandra, Beatriz, Elena, Cristina, Juana, Sara**
Countries: **Argentina, Belice, Filipinas, Grecia, Perú, Turquía**

2   Can you pronounce and work out the English for:
cuestión, misionero, atractivo, tailandés, geografía, teoría, pasivo, canibalismo

3   When spelling words out, which words are used as clarification for the letters **b** and **v**?

4   How do you pronounce **pingüino, general, gimnasio, guía, guerra?**

5   How do you say @ in an email address?

6   Which of the words in this sentence needs a capital letter:
tanzania es un país africano?

7   Which is the most common accent in Spanish?

8   **Papa** or **Papá**? Which is the Spanish for *Pope*?

9   Does **tu** or **tú** mean *you*? And does **si** or **sí** mean *yes*?

10 Without looking at page 21, name four western European countries in Spanish.

> Once you're comfortable with spelling out your own details, have a go at spelling out the names and email addresses of friends and family.

Numbers, time and date

Numbers aren't difficult to learn in Spanish if you look out for patterns.

- 1-10 have a flow and a rhythm to them, so that they're best learnt by repeating them out loud.
- 11-19 don't flow quite as smoothly, as 11-15 have a different pattern from 16-19.
- 20 and onwards are straightforward once you're familiar with 1-10, just as they are in English.

A crucial difference between the way numbers are used in Spanish and English is the punctuation. In Spanish:

- **punto** *full stop*, or a space, separates thousands, so *24,000* is written:
  24.000
  24 000
- **coma** *comma* is used for a decimal point:
  7,5 s**iete coma cinco** *7.5*
  0,4 cero coma cuatro *0.4*

Zero is **cero** in Spanish. If you look it up in a dictionary, you'll find it has the following English translations:

cero 1. nought, zero: *bajo* ~ below zero; *la hora* ~ zero hour; *partir de* ~ start from scratch **2.** *[sport]* nil: *ganar por dos a* ~ to win 2-0; **3.** *[tennis]* love: *treinta a* ~ thirty-love **4.** *[telephone]* o

The plural of **cero** is **ceros**: **dos ceros** *two noughts*.

cardinal numbers 1-99

1	uno	11	once	21	veintiuno
2	dos	12	doce	22	veintidós
3	tres	13	trece	23	veintitrés
4	cuatro	14	catorce	24	veinticuatro
5	cinco	15	quince	25	veinticinco
6	seis	16	dieciséis	26	veintiséis
7	siete	17	diecisiete	27	veintisiete
8	ocho	18	dieciocho	28	veintiocho
9	nueve	19	diecinueve	29	veintinueve
10	diez	20	veinte		

- **Uno** and numbers ending in **uno**, such as 21 or 61, change to agree with the following noun, like *a/an* (page 48). They drop the final -o before a masculine noun and have the feminine form **una**:
  un parque *park*, **un adulto**, **una persona**, **una idea**
  veintiún días *21 days*; **veintiuna sillas** *21 chairs*;
  treinta y un hombres *31 men*; **treinta y una mujeres** *31 women*

- 11-15 all end in **-ce**: **once** *11*, **doce** *12* etc.

- 16-19 have a different pattern, starting with **diez** *ten*. They were originally **diez y seis** *ten and six*, **diez y siete**, etc. but became contracted into one word: **dieciséis** *16* **diecisiete** *17*, etc.

- 21-29 are also contracted numbers, with the final **e** of **veinte** *twenty* changing to **i**: **veintiuno** *21* (from **veinte y uno** *twenty and one*).

- The following numbers have a written accent:
  dieciséis *16*, **veintidós** *22*, **veintitrés** *23*, **veintiséis** *26*.

30	treinta	60	sesenta	90	noventa
40	cuarenta	70	setenta		
50	cincuenta	80	ochenta		

- 30-90 all end in **-nta** and have **y** *and* between the tens and units:
  treinta y tres *33*, **cincuenta y seis** *56*, **setenta y cinco** *75*.

100 +

100	cien	900	novecientos
101	ciento uno	1.000	mil
102	ciento dos	1.100	mil ciento
110	ciento diez	1.500	mil quinientos
150	ciento cincuenta	2.000	dos mil
200	doscientos	10.000	diez mil
300	trescientos	100.000	cien mil
500	quinientos	500.000	quinientos mil
600	seiscientos	1.000.000	un millón
700	setecientos	2.000.000	dos millones
800	ochocientos	1.000.000.000	un billón

- Cien *100*, the shortened form of **ciento**, is used on its own, before another larger number, or in front of a noun. It never has **un** before it: **cien** *a hundred*, **cien mil** *100,000*, **cien metros** *100 metres*

- **Ciento**, not *cien*, is used before a number smaller than 100: **ciento ochenta** *180*

- **Ciento** adds -s in the plural, and **doscientos, trescientos ... novecientos** agree with their noun: **cuatrocientos gramos** *400 grammes*; **setecientas latas** *700 tins*

- There's no **y** *and* between hundreds and tens: **cuatrocientos veinte** *420*, **seiscientos treinta** *630*

- % is **por ciento**, and percentages start with **el** *the* or **un** *a*: **el/un treinta por ciento** *30%*

- **Mil** *1,000* never changes and never has **un** *a* before it: **mil** *a thousand*, **tres mil** *3,000*, **seiscientos mil** *600,000*

- **Un millón** *a million* and **un billón** *a billion* have regular plurals (**millones** and **billones**). They're followed by **de** when used alone before a noun: **un millón de euros** *1,000,000 euros* **cinco millones de libras esterlinas** *5,000,000 pounds* **siete billones de dólares** *7,000,000,000 dollars* but **un millón quinientos mil euros** *1,500,000 euros*.

ordinal numbers

1st	primero/primer*	1°	6th	sexto	6°
2nd	segundo	2°	7th	séptimo	7°
3rd	tercero/tercer*	3°	8th	octavo	8°
4th	cuarto	4°	9th	noveno	9°
5th	quinto	5°	10th	décimo	10°

*primero and tercero drop the o before a masculine singular noun:
el primer autobús *the first bus*; el tercer piso *the third floor*

- Be careful not to confuse cuarto *fourth* with cuatro *four*.

- From 11th onwards, ordinal numbers are rarely used. Cardinal numbers are used instead and normally go after the noun:
el piso quince *the fifteenth floor*

- Because they're adjectives, ordinal numbers agree with their noun and normally go before it:
primer amor *first love*; primeros platos *first courses*
Consequently, the little ° changes to ª in the feminine:
primera (1ª) clase *first class*; la tercera (3ª) vez *the third time*

- In relation to sovereigns or popes, ordinal numbers go after the name when spoken:
la reina Isabel segunda *Queen Elizabeth II*
el papa Benedicto dieciséis *Pope Benedict XVI*

- Unlike in English, ordinal numbers aren't generally used for dates (page 30).

umpteenth *adj* enésimo: *for the ~ time* por enésima vez

There's nothing like seeing Spanish words on a regular basis for them to become embedded in your memory. If you search on the web for **calendario** and the relevant year you'll find downloadable calendars which will provide a daily reminder of the days and months as well as lists of saint days and Spanish public holidays.

time

The main points to remember about time are:

- the use of the 24-hour clock is widespread in Spain especially for timetables and schedules
- there's no translation of *o'clock*
- to indicate *am* and *pm* it's usual to refer to the part of the day, e.g. **de la mañana/de la tarde** *in the morning/in the afternoon* after the time.
- before all times except **mediodía** *midday* and **medianoche** *midnight*, you include **la/las** *the*: **es la** *it's* with one o'clock and minutes past one, and **son las** with all other times
- **y** *and* is used for minutes past the hour and **menos** *less* for minutes to the hour; **y** isn't used between hours and minutes for the 24-hour clock.

¿Qué hora es? *What time is it?*
Es la una. *It's one o'clock*
Es la una y cuarto. *It's quarter past one.*
Son las dos, las tres … las once. *… It's two, three … 11 o'clock.*
Es mediodía/medianoche. *It's midday/midnight.*

Son … *It's*

09.05	**las nueve y cinco**
09.10	**las nueve y diez**
09.15	**las nueve y cuarto**
09.20	**las nueve y veinte**
09.25	**las nueve y veinticinco**
09.30	**las nueve y media**
09.35	**las diez menos veinticinco** or **las nueve y treinta y cinco**
09.40	**las diez menos veinte** or **las nueve y cuarenta**
09.45	**las diez menos cuarto** or **las nueve y cuarenta y cinco**
09.50	**las diez menos diez** or **las nueve y cincuenta**
09.55	**las diez menos cinco** or **las nueve y cincuenta y cinco**

¿A qué hora …? *(At) what time …?*
a la una *at one o'clock*
a las dos, a las tres … a las once *at two, three … 11 o'clock*
a las ocho y cuarto *at quarter past eight*
a las cinco y media *at half past five*
a las doce menos cuarto *at quarter to 12*
a mediodía/medianoche *at midday/midnight*

date: days, months, years

- **Los días de la semana son** *the days of the week are:*

lunes	*Monday*
martes	*Tuesday*
miércoles	*Wednesday*
jueves	*Thursday*
viernes	*Friday*
sábado	*Saturday*
domingo	*Sunday*

> The days are masculine. Like the months, they're written without a capital letter.

The word *on* isn't translated in Spanish:
el lunes *on Monday*   **los lunes** *on Mondays*

- **Los meses del año son** *the months of the year are*:

enero	*January*	**julio**	*July*
febrero	*February*	**agosto**	*August*
marzo	*March*	**septiembre***	*September*
abril	*April*	**octubre**	*October*
mayo	*May*	**noviembre**	*November*
junio	*June*	**diciembre**	*December*

* Both **septiembre** and **setiembre** are in current use.
Voy a las islas Canarias en abril. *I'm going to the Canaries in April.*

- **Las cuatro estaciones son** *the four seasons are:*

la primavera	*spring*	**el verano**	*summer*
el otoño	*autumn*	**el invierno**	*winter*

En verano voy a Francia. *In the summer I'm going to France.*

- For dates, you use **de** before the month and the year. **Primero** is used for the first of the month but cardinal numbers are used for all other dates. *On* isn't translated.
el primero de mayo de mil novecientos quince *(on the) 1st of May 1915*
el catorce de diciembre de dos mil ocho *(on the) 14th December 2008*

> When saying the year in Spanish, numbers aren't grouped in the same way as in English. You say *one thousand nine hundred and sixty-six* rather than *nineteen sixty-six*.

word **power**

¿cuándo? *when?*
a las tres en punto *at three o'clock on the dot*
a eso de las seis *about six o'clock*
a las once y pico *just after 11 o'clock*
de las nueve a la una *from nine o'clock to one o'clock*
antes/después de las tres *before/after three o'clock*
en/dentro de cinco minutos *in five minutes' time*

un cuarto de hora *a quarter of an hour*
tres cuartos de hora *three quarters of an hour*
media hora *half an hour*
una vez por hora *once an hour*
dos veces al día/a la semana/al mes *twice a day/week/month*
todos los días *every day*; **cada dos días** *every other day/two days*

hoy *today*
a las diez de la mañana *at ten o'clock in the morning*
a las cuatro de la tarde *at four o'clock in the afternoon*
a las siete de la tarde *at seven o'clock in the evening*
a las diez de la noche *at ten o'clock at night*

mañana *tomorrow*
mañana por la mañana/tarde/noche *tomorrow morning/afternoon*
el domingo por la mañana *on Sunday morning*
pasado mañana *the day after tomorrow*
el sabado que viene *next Saturday*
la semana próxima *next week*; **el año próximo** *next year*

ayer *yesterday*
ayer por la mañana/tarde *yesterday morning/afternoon or evening*
anoche *last night*; **anteayer** *the day before yesterday*
hace dos días/una semana *two days/a week ago*
la semana pasada *last week*; **el año pasado** *last year*
en los años sesenta *in the '60s*
en mil novecientos sesenta y seis *in 1966*
en el siglo XX (veinte) *in the 20th century*

1   What's the Spanish for a) *nil*, b) *0.5*

2   Is **ciento setenta y nueve** greater or smaller than **ciento sesenta y siete?**

3   Write down the Spanish for six, 16, 26 and 66.

4   Now write **dos millones cuatrocientos mil** in numbers, punctuating it the Spanish way.

5   What do these mean?
   a **Son las cinco.**
   b **a las siete de la tarde**
   c **después de medianoche**
   d **a las nueve anoche**
   e **a las tres y media**
   f **dos veces al día**
   g **Es la una y cuarto.**
   h **a las once de la noche**
   i **el sábado a las tres en punto veinte**
   j **el lunes a las dieciocho**

6   And how do you say these times in Spanish?
   a *It's 11 o'clock.*
   b *at ten am*
   c *at 12 noon*
   d *before 19.00*
   e *at about 09.00*
   f *at ten o'clock tomorrow*
   g *at 10.00 yesterday*
   h *Sunday at 16.00*
   i *just after seven o'clock*
   j *before three o'clock in the afternoon*

7   What's the missing word? **Septiembre tiene** *has* .... **días.**

8   How do you say *in the '70s* in Spanish?

9   In Spanish, write the date of New Year's Day, Christmas Day and New Year's Eve.

10 What does **el lunes por la tarde** mean?

11 What time is **el tren de las dieciséis cuarenta y tres** expected?

12 What comes between **cuatrocientos** and **seiscientos?**

13 In Spanish, which century is **mil ochocientos cincuenta y cuatro** in?

14 Does **primavera, verano, otoño** or **invierno** mean *spring?*

15 How do you say *75%* in Spanish?

Nouns

Nouns are the words for
- living beings: man, sister, doctor, lion, Antonio
- things: table, water, night, lesson, sport
- places: country, town, Spain, Seville
- concepts: beauty, freedom, time, democracy

Every single Spanish noun – not just the words for people – is either masculine (m) or feminine (f). This is its **gender**, and you need to know a noun's gender because words used with it, such as articles and adjectives, have corresponding masculine and feminine forms.

The ending of some nouns is a guide to their gender. For example, nouns that end in **-o** are generally masculine and nouns that end in **-a** are generally feminine. However, there's no foolproof way of predicting the gender of other nouns, which is why all nouns in a dictionary have *m* or *f* next to them. On the following pages, the definite article *(the)* is used instead – masculine nouns have **el/los** before them and feminine ones have **la/las**.

In an English–Spanish dictionary, abbreviations to look out for include *n* noun, *m* masculine, *f* feminine, *sing* singular, *pl* plural. If you look up *car* and *horse*, this is what you might find:

car *n* coche *m*, automóvil *m*: *by ~* en coche; *~park n* aparcamiento *m*, parking *m*

horse *n* caballo *m*, *[gym]* potro *m*: *~ racing* carreras *fpl* de caballos; *~ riding* equitación *f*; *Trojan ~* caballo de Troya; *Don't look a gift ~ in the mouth*. A caballo regalado no le mires el diente.

people: the family

Most of the nouns for people have corresponding masculine and feminine versions:

m		f	
el niño	*young boy*	la niña	*young girl*
el muchacho	*boy*	la muchacha	*girl*
el hombre	*man*	la mujer	*woman*
el señor	*Mr*	la señora	*Mrs*
el hijo	*son*	la hija	*daughter*
el hermano	*brother*	la hermana	*sister*
el padre	*father*	la madre	*mother*
el abuelo	*grandfather*	la abuela	*grandmother*
el tío	*uncle*	la tía	*aunt*
el primo	*cousin (male)*	la prima	*cousin (female)*
el sobrino	*nephew*	la sobrina	*niece*
el nieto	*grandson*	la nieta	*granddaughter*
el suegro	*father-in-law*	la suegra	*mother-in-law*
el cuñado	*brother-in-law*	la cuñada	*sister-in-law*
el hermanastro	*stepbrother*	la hermanastra	*stepsister*
el hijastro	*stepson*	la hijastra	*stepdaughter*
el padrino	*godfather*	la madrina	*godmother*
el ahijado	*godson*	la ahijada	*god-daughter*

When talking about a group of males and females, you use the plural of the masculine noun (add -s to a singular noun that ends in a vowel, page 39):
Los niños están en la escuela. *The children are in school.*
¿Tienes hermanos? *Do you have brothers and sisters?*
Mis primos llegan hoy. *My cousins arrive today.*
Tenemos tres hijos. *We have three children.*

Unexpectedly, there are nouns relating to people that have only one form, regardless of the gender of the person they refer to. They include **el bebé** *baby*, **la persona** *person*, **el personaje** *character*, **la víctima** *victim*, **el ángel** *angel* and **el ser** *being*.

... and the workplace

The words for many masculine occupations change their final vowel to a for the feminine, or add -a if they end in a consonant:

m	f	
el ministro	la ministra	*minister*
el médico	la médica	*doctor*
el cocinero	la cocinera	*cook*
el camarero	la camarera	*waiter/waitress*
el enfermero	la enfermera	*nurse*
el peluquero	la peluquera	*hairdresser*
el abogado	la abogada	*lawyer*
el profesor	la profesora	*teacher*
el director	la directora	*manager*
el escritor	la escritora	*writer*
el fontanero	la fontanera	*plumber*
el secretario	la secretaria	*secretary*
el mecánico	la mecánica	*mechanic*
el empleado	la empleada	*employee*
el funcionario	la funcionaria	*civil servant*

Exceptions: **el actor/la actriz** *actor/actress*

Some occupations use the same word for males and females:
- nouns ending in -a, -ta, -ista:
  el/la colega *colleague*   **el/la astronauta** *astronaut*
  el/la atleta *athlete*   **el/la dentista** *dentist*
  el/la periodista *journalist*   **el/la artista** *artist*
  el/la electricista *electrician*   **el/la recepcionista** *receptionist*
  el/la guía *guide* (**la guía** also means *guide book, telephone book*)

- most nouns ending in -e, -te, -ente:
  el/la contable *accountant*   **el/la gerente** *manager*
  el/la intérprete *interpreter*   **el/la estudiante** *student*

Exceptions: **el cliente/la clienta** *customer*; **el presidente/la presidenta** *president*; **el jefe/la jefa** *boss*; **el alcalde/la alcaldesa** *mayor/mayoress*

animals

The words for some animals are the same for the male and the female of the species:

m		f	
el delfín	*dolphin*	la ballena	*whale*
el tiburón	*shark*	la foca	*seal*
el cangrejo	*crab*	la culebra	*snake*
el pulpo	*octopus*	la tortuga	*tortoise*
el sapo	*toad*	la rana	*frog*
el ratón	*mouse*	la rata	*rat*
el hámster	*hamster*	la ardilla	*squirrel*
el gorila	*gorilla*	la cebra	*zebra*
el cocodrilo	*crocodile*	la jirafa	*giraffe*
el cuervo	*crow*	la gaviota	*seagull*

Animales domésticos *pets* and **ganado** *livestock* tend to have distinct masculine and feminine versions:

m	f	
el perro	la perra	*dog/bitch*
el gato	la gata	*cat*
el gallo	la gallina	*cockerel/hen*
el caballo	la yegua	*horse/mare*
el toro	la vaca	*bull/cow*
el carnero	la oveja	*ram/sheep*
el macho cabrío	la cabra	*billy/nanny goat*

As do these animals:

el oso	la osa	*bear*
el elefante	la elefante	*elephant*
el mono	la mona	*ape, monkey*
el zorro	la zorra	*fox*
el león	la leona	*lion/ess*
el tigre	la tigresa	*tiger*

... and everything else

With objects and abstract ideas, the ending of the word can be a clue to its gender.

-o Nearly all nouns ending in **-o** are masculine:

el zapato *shoe*
el vino *wine*

el supermercado *supermarket*
el viento *wind*

Exceptions include **la mano** *hand* and a few abbreviations of longer words: **la foto(grafia)** *photograph*, **la moto(cicleta)** *motorbike*, **la radio(fonía)** *radio* (in some parts of Latin America, **el radio** is used).

-a Nouns ending in **-a** are usually feminine:

la energía *energy*
la cerveza *beer*
la farmacia *pharmacy*

la montaña *mountain*
la casa *house*
la guitarra *guitar*

Exceptions include **el día** *day*, **el mapa** *map*, **el planeta** *planet*, **el sofá** *sofa*, **el tranvía** *tram*, and most nouns ending in **ma**:

el aroma, **el clima** *climate*, **el diagrama**, **el diploma**, **el drama**, **el enigma**, **el panorama**, **el problema**, **el programa**, **el sistema**, **el tema**

-e Some nouns ending in **-e** are masculine while some are feminine:

el cine *cinema*
el coche *car*
el nombre *name*
el pie *foot*

la carne *meat*
la calle *street*
la clase *class*
la noche *night*

However, you can presume the gender of most nouns with the following endings:

-aje, -ambre, -án, -ón, -or are usually masculine

el equipaje *luggage*, **el alambre** *wire*, **el azafrán** *saffron*, **el buzón** *letterbox*, **el amor** *love*

-ión, -dad, -tad, -tud, -ie, -ez, -iz, -sis, -umbre are usually feminine

la canción *song*, **la edad** *age*, **la amistad** *friendship*, **la virtud** *virtue*, **la serie** *series*, **la vejez** *old age*, **la matriz** *womb*, **la crisis** *crisis*, **la costumbre** *custom*

Exceptions include **el avión** *aeroplane*, **el camión** *lorry*, **el pie** *foot*, **el lápiz** *pencil*, **el tapiz** *carpet*, **el análisis** *analysis*, **el énfasis** *emphasis*, **el paréntisis** *parenthesis*.

The following categories of noun are masculine:

- cardinal numbers:
  el tres *three*, **el cinco** *five*

- colours:
  el blanco *white*, **el verde** *green*

- compound nouns, i.e. those which combine two words:
  el abrelatas, *can opener*, **el paraguas** *umbrella*

- days and months:
  un domingo relajante *a relaxing Sunday*
  un abril frío *a cold April*

- fruit trees:
  el manzano *apple tree*, **el cerezo** *cherry tree*

- languages:
  el español *Spanish*, **el italiano** *Italian*

- mountains, rivers and seas:
  el Everest, **el Támesis** *the Thames*, **el Mediterráneo** *the Mediterranean*

The following categories of noun are feminine:

- islands; countries and regions ending in **-a**:
  las (islas) Canarias, **Inglaterra**, **Andalucía**
  exception: **el Canadá**

- letters of the alphabet:
  la be, **la ce**

- tree fruit:
  la manzana *apple*, **la cereza** *cherry*

Given there are no hard and fast rules for gender, it's a good idea to learn each new noun with its article, **el** or **la**.

making nouns plural

When there's more than one of something:

- most nouns that end in a vowel add **-s**:
  la tía → las tías *aunts*
  la mesa → las mesas *tables*
  la pierna → las piernas *feet*
  el pasaporte → los pasaportes *passports*
  el hermano → los hermanos *brothers*
  el vino → los vinos *wines*

- most nouns that end in a consonant add **-es**:
  el árbol → los árboles *trees*
  el bar → los bares *bars*
  el reloj → los relojes *clocks*
  la ciudad → las ciudades *cities*
  la flor → las flores *flowers*

- nouns that end in **-z** change the z to **ces**:
  la cruz → las cruces *crosses*
  el lápiz → los lápices *pencils*
  una vez → dos veces *twice*
  la voz → las voces *voices*

- nouns that end in **-án, -én, -és, -ín, -ión, -ón, -ús** lose their accent:
  el alemán → los alemanes *Germans*
  el andén → los andenes *platforms*
  el irlandés → los irlandeses *Irish*
  el maletín → los maletines *small cases, briefcases*
  el camión → los camiones *lorries*
  el buzón → los buzones *letterboxes*
  el autobús → los autobuses *buses*

- nouns that end in unstressed **-en** add an accent to the preceding syllable to maintain the correct stress:
  la imagen → las imágenes *pictures*
  el joven → los jóvenes *young people*

irregular plurals

The endings of these two groups don't change in the plural:

- most nouns ending in -s, if the last syllable is unstressed:

  el/los paracaídas *parachute/s*   el/los tocadiscos *record player/s*
  el/los lunes *Monday/s*   el/los martes *Tuesday/s*
  la/las crisis *crisis/crises*   la/las dosis *dose/s*
  la/las tesis *thesis/theses*   el/los cactus *cactus/cacti*

- and surnames:

  los García   los Sánchez

For compound nouns (formed with two nouns), the plural ending is added to the first noun only:

la ciudad jardín → las ciudades jardín *garden cities*
el coche cama → los coches cama *sleeping cars*
la fecha límite → las fechas límite *deadlines*
el hombre rana → los hombres rana *frogmen, divers*

Nouns from foreign words which end in a consonant just add -s to form the plural:

los bistecs *steaks*   los clubs* *clubs*
los carnets *ID cards, licences*   los coñacs *cognacs*
los jerseys *jerseys*   los pubs *pubs*

* You will also see **los clubes** in common use.

Some nouns are plural in English but singular in Spanish:

- nouns referring to a collective group or certain items of clothing:

  el billar *billiards*   **el bosque** *woods*
  el pijama *pyjamas*   **la ropa** *clothes*

- nouns which end in -ics in English (the Spanish equivalent is usually -ica):

  la física *physics*   **la política** *politics*

adding endings to nouns

Endings such as **-ito/a** or **-ón/ona**, added to a noun without its final vowel, are called suffixes. They alter the noun's meaning and are often used instead of an adjective. Some refer to size, but others reflect the speaker's emotions, whether it's affection or antipathy.

- **-illo/a, -ito/a** *little, small, cute*

la campana *bell*	la campanilla *small bell*
el chico *boy*	el chiquillo/ chiquito *small boy*
el palo *stick*	el palillo *small stick, toothpick*
el pan *bread*	el panecillo *bread roll*
la abuela *grandmother*	la abuelita *granny*
la casa *house*	la casita *little house, cottage*
Jaime *James*	Jaimecito *Jim, Jimmie*
Pedro *Peter*	Pedrito *little Peter, Pete*
el perro *dog*	el perrito *puppy*
el pueblo *village*	el pueblecito *little village, hamlet*

- **-azo/a** (also means *a blow with*), **-ón/ona**, **-ote/ota** *big, large, clumsy, ugly*

la bala *bullet*	el balazo *shot, bullet wound*
la gripe *flu*	el gripazo *really bad bout of flu*
el perro *dog*	el perrazo *brute of a dog*
el puño *fist*	el puñetazo *punch*
la casa *house*	la casona *big house*
el hombre *man*	el hombrón *big man*
la silla *chair*	el sillón *armchair*
la palabra *word*	la palabrota *swearword*

- **-ucho/a, -acho/a, -uzo/uza, -uco/uca, -(z)uelo/a** *bad, poor, horrible*

el cuarto *room*	el cuartucho *poky little room*
la gente *people*	la gentuza *scum*
la ventana *window*	la ventanuca *poky little window*
el autor *writer*	el autorzuelo *hack*

Adding a suffix is regularly used in Spanish to great effect. The difficulty for learners is that there are no absolute and consistent rules; not all nouns can be modified, and meaning often depends on the attitude of the speaker.

word **power**

There are hundreds of English nouns which you can convert to Spanish if you know the endings to look out for. Don't forget to factor in any consonant changes (pages 22-23).

🇬🇧	🇪🇸	
-nt	-nte	la consonante, el restaurante, el/la elefante, el/la paciente, el presidente
-ism	-ismo	el comunismo, el fascismo, el realismo, el socialismo, el turismo
-ist	-ista	el/la dentista, el/la terrorista, el/la optimista, el/la pesimista, el/la pianista
-nce/ ncy	-ncia	la distancia, la emergencia, la independencia, la inocencia, la existencia
-ologist	-ólogo	el arqueólogo, el astrólogo, el ginecólogo, el patólogo, el psicólogo
-(s)sion	-sión	la confusión, la impresión, la ocasión, la pasión, la televisión
-tion	-ción	la ambición, la atención, la petición, la solución, la estación
-ction	-cción	la acción, la introducción, la producción, la infección, la reacción
-ty	-dad	la capacidad, la enormidad, la posibilidad, la universidad, la cualidad
-y	-ía/ia	la categoría, la economía, la perfumería, la industria, la historia

false friends

Not all nouns mean what they appear to mean:

el **conductor** means *driver*	*conductor* is **el director**
la **decepción** means *disappointment*	*deception* is **el engaño**
la **fábrica** means *factory*	*fabric* is **el tejido, la tela**
el **éxito** means *success*	*exit* is **la salida**
el **grillo** means *cricket (insect)*	*grill* is **la parrilla**
la **librería** means *bookshop*	*library* is **la biblioteca**
el **mayor** means *adult*	*mayor* is **el alcalde**
la **ostra** means *oyster*	*ostrich* is **el avestruz**
el **pan** means *bread*	*pan* is **la cacerola**
los **parientes** means *relatives*	*parents* is **los padres**
el **pie** means *foot*	*pie* is **el pastel**
el **preservativo** means *condom*	*preservative* is **el conservante**
la **ropa** means *clothes*	*rope* is **la cuerda**
el **váter** means *toilet*	*water* is **el agua**

Look out too for nouns which have entirely different meanings depending on whether they end in **-o** or **-a**:

m	f
el **caso** *case*	la **casa** *house*
el **libro** *book*	la **libra** *pound*
el **modo** *way, manner*	la **moda** *fashion*
el **plato** *plate*	la **plata** *silver*
el **puerto** *port*	la **puerta** *door*

and these nouns, which are identical apart from their gender:

el **capital** *money*	la **capital** *capital city*
el **coma** *comma*	la **coma** *coma*
el **cometa** *comet*	la **cometa** *kite*
el **corte** *cut*	la **corte** *court*
el **cura** *priest*	la **cura** *cure*
el **editorial** *editorial*	la **editorial** *publishing house*
el **final** *ending*	la **final** *sports final*
el **frente** *front*	la **frente** *forehead*
el **orden** *order* (in a sequence)	la **orden** *order (command)*
el **Papa** *the Pope*	la **papa** *potato*
el **pendiente** *earring*	la **pendiente** *slope, hillside*
el **policía** *police officer*	la **policía** *police force*

checkpoint 3

1   Write m, f, or m/f in the boxes depending on whether the noun is masculine, feminine or could be either?

vino ☐   dentista ☐   problema ☐

cura ☐   amor ☐   estación ☐

pendiente ☐   mano ☐   casa ☐

mapa ☐   calle ☐   ciudad ☐

2   What are these in the plural (include the article)?

ministra ....   conversación ....

delfín ....   gorila ....

café ....   cocinero ....

noche ....   profesor ....

ciclista ....   catalán ....

cualidad ....   ratón ....

excursión ....   cine ....

dificultad ....   dirección ....

paréntesis ....   virtud ....

foto ....   telegrama ....

3   How do you say *aunts and uncles* in Spanish?

4   Think of a noun that's feminine even when it refers to a man.

5   **león, oso, rana**: which is the odd one out and why?

6   Are **moto, avión** and **lápiz** masculine or feminine?

7   What's the plural of **el pez** *fish*?

8   Is the plural ending added to the first or the second noun of the compound noun **el coche cama**?

9   What's the plural of **el carnet**?

10 Can you work out the Spanish, with its gender, for a) *biology*, b) *fascist*, c) *probability*, d) *difference*, e) *nation*, f) *direction*, g) *feminism*?

11 Does **la casita** or **la casona** mean *little house*?

12 Given that **el campeón** is *champion* (male) and **la campeona** is *champion* (female), what is the female equivalent of **el bailarín** *ballet dancer* (male)?

Articles: the, a, some

An **article** is used with a noun to show whether you're talking about something which is specific or defined: ***the*** *house,* ***the*** *houses,* or something which is not: ***a*** *house,* ***some*** *houses.*

Grammatically, articles fall into three categories:
- the definite article: the
- the indefinite article: a/an
- the partitive article: some/any

Articles are very different in English and Spanish. In Spanish, they change according to whether the following noun is masculine or feminine, singular or plural. Whilst in English there is one definite article: *the*, in Spanish there are four: **el**, **la**, **los**, **las**.

The indefinite articles **un** or **una** are used for *a/an* and their plural form **unos** or **unas** for *some/any*.

There's a difference too in the way articles are used. Spanish uses the definite article when English doesn't, and vice versa. For example, the definite article is used when generalising: **el vino español** *Spanish wine*, but isn't used when talking about royal titles: **Isabel segunda** *Elizabeth the Second*.

In Spanish the indefinite article is not used in sentences where it's used in English such as *He's a doctor* or *She's a Catholic* or after certain verbs such as **tener** *to have* or **llevar** *to wear*.

the: el, la, los, las

Whereas English has one word for *the*, Spanish has four:
el, la, los, las.

Which one you use depends on two things:
- the gender of the noun that's with the article;
- whether that noun is singular or plural.

masculine

The words for *the* with masculine nouns are **el** and **los**:

- **el** before singular nouns:
  el jardín *the garden*; **el director** *the manager*

- **los** before plural words:
  los jardines *the gardens*; **los directores** *the managers*

feminine

The words for *the* with feminine nouns are **la** and **las**:

- **la** before singular nouns:
  la playa *the beach*; **la marea** *the tide*

- **las** before plural nouns:
  las playas *the beaches*; **las mareas** *the tides*

But if the feminine singular noun starts with a stressed **a** or **ha**, **el** is used
instead of **la** as this avoids having two 'a' sounds next to each other and
makes it easier to pronounce:
El agua está muy clara. *The water is very clear.*
Luchan contra el hambre en el tercer mundo. *They are fighting hunger in
the Third World.*

a, de + el

When **el** comes after **a** *to/at*, they combine to form **al** *to the/at the*. And
when **el** comes after **de** *from/of*, they combine to form **del** from *the/of the*:
Voy al mercado. *I'm going to the supermarket.*
Está cerca del banco. *It's near the bank.*

... and when to use them

Like *the* in English, **el, la, los, las** are used before a noun referring to a specific person or thing.

In Spanish they're also needed:
- when making generalisations:
  Los leones comen la carne. *Lions eat meat.*
  Evita las grasas. *Avoid fatty foods.*

- with abstract nouns:
  El amor es ciego. *Love is blind.*
  No pierdas la esperanza. *Don't lose hope.*

- when talking about someone and referring to them by their title but not when talking to them:
  La señora Ramos no está. *Mrs Ramos isn't here.*
  Buenos días, señora Ramos. *Hello, Mrs Ramos.*

- with some countries (including all those with an adjective):
  la India; El Salvador; el Reino Unido *the United Kingdom;* **la República Dominicana; la soleada España** *sunny Spain*

- with languages, except after **aprender** *to learn,* **hablar** *to speak,* **saber** *to know* and **en** *in:*
  Me gusta el italiano. *I like Italian.*
  ¿Hablas alemán? *Do you speak German?*

- to say *on* with days of the week and dates, and with times and seasons:
  el sabádo *on Saturday;* **los sábados** *on Saturdays*
  el catorce de diciembre *on 14th December*
  la una y diez *ten past one;* **el invierno** *winter*
  but not after **en** *in:* **En verano hace calor.** *In summer it's hot.*

- with parts of the body, where in English you would use the possessive adjective (my, his/her, your, etc.):
  Me duele la cabeza. *My head hurts.*

- with institutions:
  en la cárcel *in prison;* **en el colegio** *at school;* **en la iglesia** *at church;* **en el tribunal** *at court;* **en la universidad** *at university;* **en el hospital** *in hospital*

a: un, una

Like English, Spanish has two forms of the indefinite article in the singular.
However, in English the use of *a* or *an* depends on the sound beginning
the following word, whereas in Spanish the use of **un** or **una** depends on
whether the noun with the article is masculine or feminine.

masculine
The word for *a/an* with all masculine singular nouns is **un**:

un hombre *a man*
un niño *a boy*
un euro *a euro*
un vaso de vino *a glass of wine*

feminine
The word for *a/an* with all feminine singular nouns is **una**:

una mujer *a woman*
una amiga *a (female) friend*
una casa *a house*
una botella de vino *a bottle of wine*
una buena idea *a good idea*
But if the feminine singular noun starts with a stressed **a** or **ha**, **un** is used
instead of **una** to avoid having two 'a' sounds next to each other:
Es un águila. *It's an eagle.*

... and when not to use them

Un and **una** are used in pretty much the same circumstances as *a/an* in
English, i.e. before a noun referring to a non-specific person or thing.

However, unlike English, they're *not* used:
- with nouns of occupation, nationality or religion after **ser** *to be* or
  hacerse *to become*:
  Soy estudiante. *I'm a student.*
  Laura se hizo abogada. *Laura became a lawyer.*
  Mi tío es cocinero. *My uncle's a cook.*
  Eres australiano? *Are you (an) Australian?*
  Ana es católica. *Anna's (a) Catholic.*
  unless those nouns have additional information with them:
  Soy una estudiante trabajadora. *I'm a hard working student.*
  Mi tío es un muy buen cocinero. *My uncle's a very good cook.*

- after **buscar** *to look for*, **comprar** *to buy*, **llevar** *to wear*, **tener** *to have* and **usar** *to use* when talking about something you would normally only have one of:
  Busco empleo. *I'm looking for a job.*
  Lleva falda. *She's wearing a skirt.*
  No tiene coche. *He doesn't have a car.*
  unless the noun includes extra information:
  Busco un empleo interesante. *I'm looking for an interesting job.*
  Lleva una falda muy de moda. *She's wearing a very fashionable skirt.*
  Tiene un coche negro. *He has a black car.*

- before **mil, cien, medio**:
  Lo he dicho mil veces. *I've said it a thousand times.*
  Hay cien personas. *There are a hundred people.*
  un kilo y medio de manzanas *a kilo and a half of apples*

- before **cierto, otro, semejante, tal**:
  cierto libro *a certain book*
  otra cerveza *another beer*
  semejante falda *a similar skirt*
  tal cosa *such a thing,* but **un tal Señor Prados** *a certain Mr Prados*

- after **qué** in exclamations:
  ¡Qué buena idea! *What a good idea!*
  ¡Qué susto! *What a fright!*
  ¡Qué mala suerte! *What bad luck!*
  ¡Qué pena! *What a shame!*

- after **como** *as*, **con** *with* (except when it means *accompanied by*), **sin** *without*:
  Isabel trabaja como camarera. *Isabel works as a waitress.*
  Escribe con bolígrafo. *He's writing with a biro.*
  Salí sin impermeable. *I went out without a raincoat.*

some/any

The plural of **un** and **una** is **unos** and **unas**. Their basic meaning is *some* or *a few*, and they're often used in Spanish when they're not needed in English:
Comimos unos helados en el parque. *We ate (some) ice creams in the park.*
Cuesta sólo unas libras. *It only costs a few pounds.*
In a list, you use the article before each noun:
unos limones y unas peras *some lemons and pears*

They're also used to mean *approximately*:
unos veinte niños *about twenty children*
...and they're used when in English we would say *a pair of*:
unas tijeras *a pair of scissors*; **unas gafas** *a pair of glasses*

There are other ways besides **unos/unas** of translating *some* and *any*:

- **cualquier** + noun *any ... at all*:
  Puedes coger cualquier autobús. *You can take any bus.*
  ¿Puedo comer cualquier manzana? *Can I eat any apple?*
  If **cualquier** is put after the noun, it adds **-a**:
  Hoy no es un día cualquiera. *Today isn't any old day.*

- **algún, alguna, algunos, algunas** *some*:
  Volverá algún día. *He'll come back some day.*
  ¿Tiene alguna pregunta? *Do you have any questions?*
  Tienen algunos problemas. *They have some problems.*
  Alguno, alguna can be used in a negative sentence to mean *at all*:
  No tiene inteligencia alguna. *He has no intelligence at all.*

- *any* in a negative sentence is **ningún, ninguna**. They're used with a singular noun even though the English translation is plural:
  No lo veo en ninguna parte. *I can't see it anywhere.*
  No tenemos ningún problema. *We don't have any problems.*

Some/any are not translated into Spanish:
- before a singular noun:
  Quiero leche. *I'd like some milk*; **Necesito azúcar.** *I need some sugar.*

- in questions where *any* can be left out in English:
  ¿Tiene hijos? *Do you have (any) children?*
  ¿Hay tiendas por aquí? *Are there (any) shops around here?*

---

lo

Lo is a neuter article, i.e. neither masculine nor feminine, which is not used with nouns.

Instead, it can be used:

- with a masculine singular adjective or past participle (page 153) to form an abstract noun:
  Lo interesante es que funciona bien. *The interesting thing is that it works well.*
  Lo bueno es que no me vio. *The good thing is that he didn't see me.*
  Visto lo ocurrido tienes suerte. *In view of what has happened, you're lucky.*

- with an adjective or adverb followed by **que** to intensify the phrase. The adjective agrees with the noun:
  ¿Has visto lo alta que es? *Have you seen how tall she is?*
  Veo lo seriamente que estudias. *I see how seriously you study.*

- as part of many useful phrases:
  por lo general *generally*; **a lo lejos** *in the distance*
  a lo mejor *maybe*; **por lo menos** *at least*
  por lo tanto *therefore*; **por lo visto** *apparently*

Lo is also used with **de**, as an indefinite pronoun, to refer to something already known about:
Lo de la semana pasada no es grave. *What happened last week is not serious.*

... and with **que**, as a relative pronoun, meaning *what*:
Lo que más me interesa es leer. *What interests me most is reading.*

checkpoint 4

1 Choose **un** or **una** for these nouns. If in doubt about what gender they are, check with pages 34-38:

tapiz	análisis	tigre
noche	actriz	avión
amor	dificultad	virtud
televisión	jersey	ratón
programa	madre	crisis

2 Put **los**, **las** or both in front of these plural nouns:

sistemas	lápices	estudiantes
acciones	contables	camiones
mapas	nombres	costumbres
manos	series	terroristas
colegas	clases	universidades

3 Fill the gaps with **el, la, un, una, unos, unas**. Not all the gaps need filling:

a **Me gusta ___ chocolate.** *I like chocolate.*

b **Juan es ___ profesor, ___ muy buen profesor.** *Juan is a teacher, a very good teacher.*

c **Trabaja sin ___ ordenador.** *He works without a computer.*

d **Quiero ir a ___ India.** *I want to go to India.*

e **___ japonés es difícil.** *Japanese is difficult.*

f **Lleva ___ chaqueta.** *He's wearing a jacket.*

g **___ doctor García es amable.** *Dr García is kind.*

h **___ viernes no trabajo.** *On Fridays I don't work.*

i **¡Qué ___ mujer!** *What a woman!*

j **Necesitamos ___ mil libras.** *We need a thousand pounds.*

4 Which words could go in this sentence to mean *some*?
Leo ___ libros. *I read some books.*

5 Complete the following sentence using the correct article:
Siempre busca ___ imposible. *He's always looking for the impossible.*

Adjectives

Adjectives are words that describe nouns and pronouns:
We have a **small** garden.
The film was **superb**.
She is **Spanish**.
Take the **second** turning.
I prefer **red** wine.

There are two major differences in the way Spanish and English adjectives are used:

- **Position**
  Spanish adjectives generally – though not always – go after the noun: **el Parlamento Europeo** *the European Parliament*; **la Alianza Atlántica** *the Atlantic Alliance*; **el servicio militar** *military service*; **la guerra fría** *the Cold War*

- **Agreement**
  The ending of a Spanish adjective varies depending on the noun/pronoun it's describing; it has to be masculine or feminine, singular or plural to agree with, i.e. match, that noun/pronoun: **Reino Unido** *United Kingdom*; **Estados Unidos** *United States*.

The dictionary abbreviation for *adjective* is *adj*. If you look up *clear*, this is what you might find:

clear *adj* **1.** claro, transparente, despejado **2.** manifiesto, evidente: *as ~ as day* más claro que el sol **3.** neto: *~ profit* ganancia neta **4.** tranquilo: *with a ~ conscience* con la conciencia tranquila

word power

There are hundreds of English adjectives which you can easily convert to Spanish when you know the endings to look out for. But, although they look similar they won't sound the same and the stress on many of them will be in a different place. Check with page 18 if you're not sure of the rules on stress.

🇬🇧	🇪🇸	
-ary	-ario	contrario, culinario, disciplinario, extraordinario, hereditario, imaginario, incendiario, literario, mercenario, monetario, ordinario, primario, solitario, temporario, voluntario
-ct	-cto	abstracto, compacto, correcto, directo, exacto, imperfecto, incorrecto, indirecto, inexacto, intacto, perfecto
-ic(al)	-ico	clásico, diplomático, erótico, geográfico, islámico, microscópico, político, realístico, típico and many more adjectives ending in *-ological*: arqueológico, astrológico, cardiológico, geológico, ginecológico, ideológico, psicológico, radiológico
-ist(ic)	-ista	capitalista, evangelista, materialista, moralista, naturalista, optimista, pacifista, realista, socialista
-ive	-ivo	agresivo, comunicativo, excesivo, impulsivo, inclusivo, intensivo, ofensivo, positivo
-nt	-nte	diferente, excelente, elegante, frecuente, importante, paciente, permanente, persistente
-ous	-oso	ambicioso, curioso, delicioso, espacioso, famoso, generoso, glorioso, melodioso, nervioso, numeroso, religioso, pomposo
-ute	-uto	absoluto, astuto, bruto, irresoluto, resoluto

The consonants in some Spanish adjectives differ in a predictable way from their English equivalent (page 22):
farmacéutico *pharmaceutical,* **fenomenal** *phenomenal,* **físico** *physical,* **flemático** *phlegmatic,* **fotogénico** *photogenic* **imposible** *impossible,* **masivo** *massive,* **posesivo** *possessive* **católico** *catholic,* **matemático** *mathematical,* **patológico** *pathological,* **homeopático** *homeopathic*

Many adjectives are identical in Spanish or so close that you'll recognise them instantly:

- artificial, central, digital, federal, final, general, informal, local, musical, natural, normal, original, personal, social

- incompatible, inevitable, noble, probable, tolerable

- cándido, espléndido, estúpido, flórido, frígido, mórbido, pálido, rápido, sórdido, tímido, tórrido

- agnóstico, artístico, doméstico, drástico, fantástico, materialístico, plástico, honesto, modesto

- italiano, americano, australiano

false friends

Look out for these adjectives:

aventurado means *risky*	*adventurous* is **aventurero**
casual means *random*	*casual* is **informal**
constipado means *to have a cold*	*constipated* is **estreñido**
decepcionado means *disappointed*	*deceptive* is **engañoso**
destituido means *dismissed*	*destitute* is **indigente**
disgustado means *upset*	*disgusted* is **indignado**
embarazada means *pregnant*	*embarassed* is **avergonzado**
emocionante means *exciting*	*emotional* is **emocional**
fútil means *insignificant*	*futile* is **inútil**
largo means *long*	*large* is **grande**
quieto means *still; calm*	*quiet* is **callado**
sensible means *sensitive*	*sensible* is **sensato**
sucesivo means *consecutive*	*successful* is **exitoso**

adjective endings and agreement

In a dictionary, adjectives are listed in the masculine singular. Their endings change, depending on whether the noun being described is masculine or feminine, singular or plural.

- Adjectives that end in -o have four possible endings:

-o	m sing	el tren moderno *the modern train*
-a	f sing	la ciudad moderna *the modern town*
-os	m pl	los pisos modernos *the modern flats*
-as	f pl	las estaciones modernas *the modern stations*

- Adjectives that end in -e have only two possible endings:

-e	m sing	el momento importante *the important moment*
	f sing	la victoria importante *the important victory*
-es	m pl	los detalles importantes *the important details*
	f pl	las fechas importantes *the important dates*

- Adjectives that end in -l and -s add -es in the plural and have no separate feminine forms:

m sing	un vestido azul *the blue dress*
f sing	una falda azul *the blue skirt*
m pl	los zapatos azules *the blue shoes*
f pl	las blusas azules *the blue blouses*

- Adjectives that end in -án, -ín, -ón add -a in the feminine singular, -es in the masculine plural and -as in the feminine plural. There's no accent in the feminine or the plural:

m sing	el niño charlatán *the talkative boy*
f sing	la abuela charlatana *the talkative grandmother*
m pl	los padres charlatanes *the talkative fathers*
f pl	las tías charlatanas *the talkative aunts*

If the adjective ends in -n with an unstressed vowel, such as **joven** *young*, it has no separate feminine form; **joven** gains an accent in the plural to keep the stress in the same place: **jóvenes**.

- Adjectives that end in **-or** add **-a** for the feminine singular, **-es** for the masculine plural and **-as** for the feminine plural:

m sing	**el Partido Conservador** *the Conservative Party*
f sing	**la ropa conservadora** *conservative dress*
m pl	**los colores conservadores** *conservative colours*
f pl	**las ideas conservadoras** *conservative ideas*

  However, adjectives of comparison (page 69) ending in **-or**: **mayor** *greater*, *larger*, **menor** *smaller*, *fewer*, *less*, **mejor** *better* and **peor** *worse*, don't have a feminine form.
  una habitación mayor *a larger room*

- Adjectives of nationality and region add **-a** for the feminine singular, **-es** for the masculine plural and **-as** for the feminine plural. Unlike English, they're not written with a capital letter.

m sing	**el jerez español** *the Spanish sherry*
f sing	**la naranja española** *the Spanish orange*
m pl	**los quesos españoles** *the Spanish cheeses*
f pl	**las tortillas españolas** *the Spanish omelettes*

  If the masculine singular ends in **-z**, it changes to **-c** in the masculine plural:
  el sol andaluz *the Andalusian sun*
  los caballos andaluces *Andalusian horses*

- Adjectives ending in the stressed vowels **-í** and **-ú** add **-es** in the plural and have no separate feminine forms:

m sing	**el clima israelí** *the Israeli climate*
f sing	**la fruta israelí** *the Israeli fruit*
m pl	**los aguacates israelíes** *the Israeli avocados*
f pl	**las ciudades israelíes** *the Israeli cities*

- An adjective describing more than one noun has the masculine plural ending except when both the nouns are feminine:
  Juan y Pedro son españoles.
  María y Pedro son españoles.
  María y Julia son españolas.

position of adjectives

When adjectives and nouns are next to each other, the adjective usually goes after the noun:

un ruido sorprendente *a surprising noise*
la música clásica *classical music*
los precios altos *high prices*
las atracciones fatales *fatal attractions*

Some adjectives **always** go after the noun:

- colour   **un gato negro** *a black cat*
            los vinos rojos *red wines*

- shape   **una mesa redonda** *a round table*
            un pastel cuadrado *a square cake*

- nationality   **la cocina española** *Spanish cooking*
            la bandera americana *the American flag*

- an adjective with an adverb, e.g. *very, too, fairly*
  un lugar muy tranquilo *a very quiet spot*
  una casa bastante pequeña *a fairly small house*

A few adjectives always go before the noun:

- numbers: **una pera** *one pear*
            cuatro ciruelas *four plums*
            la primera vez *first time*
            el tercer mundo *Third World*

- other adjectives relating to quantity: **ambos** *both*, **bastante** *enough*,
  demasiado *too much*, **mucho** *much/many*, **poco** *little/few*, **tanto** *so much/so many*, **todo** *each/every/all*
  bastantes patatas *enough potatoes*
  demasiada pimienta *too much pepper*
  muchos tomates *many tomatoes*
  poco sal *little salt*

- possessive and demonstrative adjectives:
  mi madre *my mother*
  tu padre *your father*
  este jersey/esa chaqueta *this jersey/that jacket*

Adjectives which normally go after the noun can be put before it for emphasis:
el sorprendente ruido *the surprising noise*
el horrible animal *the horrible animal*

Some adjectives actually change their meaning depending on whether they go before or after the noun:
un antiguo hospital *a former hospital*; **un hospital antiguo** *an ancient hospital*
diferentes/varios problemas *various problems*; **problemas diferentes/varios** *different problems*
un gran hombre *a great man*; **un hombre grande** *a big man*
media hora *half an hour*; **la mujer media** *the average woman*
la misma cosa *the same thing*; **la cosa misma** *the thing itself*
una nueva casa *a new house*; **una casa nueva** *a brand new house*
un país pobre *a poor country*; **¡pobre María!** *Poor Maria!*
la pura verdad *the plain truth*; **el aire puro** *clean air*
un viejo amigo *an old friend*; **un amigo viejo** *an elderly friend*

When two adjectives are used to describe the same noun:
- if both are of equal importance, they come after the noun and are separated by **y** *and*:
  un coche grande y rojo *a big red car*

- if one is less closely connected to the noun, it's placed before it:
  una hermosa casa española *a beautiful Spanish house*

- if one adjective normally comes before the noun, it still does:
  varias películas interesantes *various interesting films*

In English we use the word *one(s)* with adjectives to avoid repeating a noun:
Which car? The red one./The big one.
Which cars? The red ones./The big ones.

In Spanish you simply use the adjective as a noun, preceded by *the*. It agrees in the usual way:
¿Qué coche? El rojo./El grande.
¿Qué coches? Los rojos./Los grandes.

irregular adjectives

There are shortened forms of some common adjectives when they're used before the noun:

- these drop the final **-o** before a masculine singular noun:

bueno *good*	**buen tiempo** *good weather*
malo *bad*	**mal tiempo** *bad weather*
alguno *some*	**algún* bar** *some bar*
ninguno *no*	**ningún* cambio** *no change*
uno *one*	**un bolso** *one handbag*
primero *first*	**el primer piso** *the first floor*
tercero *third*	**el tercer mundo** *the third world*

  ***algún** and **ningún** have an accent in this shortened form only.

- **grande**, which means *great* in front of a noun, is shortened to **gran** in the singular:
  Es un gran hombre. *He's a great man.*
  Es una gran mujer. *She's a great woman.*

  After the noun, **grande** means *big*:
  Es un hombre grande. *He's a big man.*
  Es una mujer grande. *She's a big woman.*

- **Santo** *Saint* is shortened to **San** in front of masculine singular saints' names, unless they begin with **Do** or **To**:
  San Miguel, Santo Domingo
  Female saints are **Santa: Santa Teresa**

- **cualquiera** *any* drops the final **-a** before m and f nouns:
  cualquier mes *any month*
  cualquier semana *any week*

Adjectives ending in **-a**, e.g. **hipócrita** *hypocritical* and **-ista** e.g. **egoísta** *selfish*, are the same in both the masculine and feminine singular. They add **-s** for the plural:
un hombre hipócrita y egoísta *a hypocritical and selfish man*;
una mujer hipócrita y egoísta *a hypocritical and selfish woman*
hombres y mujeres hipócritas y egoístas *hypocritical and selfish men and women*

Colours are not always straightforward:

- Some behave normally:
  el Mar Rojo *the Red Sea*; **una chaqueta negra** *a black jacket*

- But colours which are nouns, or which are words borrowed from other languages, are invariable, i.e. have only one possible ending:
  café *coffee*, **malva** *(mallow) mauve*, **naranja** *orange*, **rosa** *(rose) pink*, **turquesa** *turquoise*, **violeta** *violet*
  un vestido rosa *a pink dress*
  los calcetines violeta *the purple socks*

- **Marrón** *(chestnut) brown* is different in that it becomes **marrones** (without an accent) in the plural:
  La camiseta marrón *the brown tee-shirt*
  Los abrigos marrones *the brown coats*

- Colours using a combination of two words are invariable too:
  una camisa verde claro *a light green shirt*
  las cortinas amarillo oscuro *the dark yellow curtains*
  los pantalones azul marino *the navy blue trousers*

There are a few other invariable adjectives:
cada *each/every*, **macho** *male*, **hembra** *female*, **monstruo** *monster*, **modelo** *model*, **tabú** *taboo*
cada día *every day*; **cada semana** *every week*
las cebras macho *the male zebras*; **las cebras hembra** *the female zebras*
... and words borrowed from other languages:
las páginas web *the web pages*

In English you can put two nouns together, with one of them acting as an adjective: *a football match, the geography teacher.* You can't do this in Spanish, you use **de** *of* instead: **un partido de fútbol** lit. *a match of football*; **la profesora de geografía** lit. *the teacher of geography.*

You also use **de** to say what something is made of: **una silla de madera** *a wooden chair*; **un vestido de seda** *a silk dress.*

checkpoint 5

1   Put the correct ending on the adjectives and work out or guess
    what the phrases mean:
    a el primer__ ministro   b la Casa Blanc__
    c los juegos olímpic__   d los gases contaminant__
    e el turismo verd__   f escrito en tercer__ persona
    g el País Vasc__   h las Comunidades Autónom__
    i segund__ clase   j el sistema universitari__
    k los recursos natural__   l el hombre materialist__

2   What's the opposite of these adjectives?
    a impaciente   b antipático
    c formal   d negativo
    e lento   f innecesario
    g posible   h inteligente

3   Work out the Spanish for these – remembering to include
    accents where necessary:
    a informative   b ecological
    c voluntary   d rigid
    e generous   f American
    g arrogant   h evident
    i rustic   j theological

4   If malsano means *unhealthy* and maleducado means *rude*,
    what do sano and educado mean?

5   How would you say in Spanish:
    a) *the white one* (wine); *the big ones* (houses); *the old one*
    (a man); *the dark green one* (jacket); b) *the silk shirt*; *the Madrid
    train*; *the French omelette*; *the wooden table*

Adverbs and comparisons

Adverbs are words that add an extra dimension to:

- adjectives   Our garden is **very** small.
        I'm **really** tired, **too** tired to go out.
- verbs   They cooked it **well/perfectly**.
        They live **nearby/far away**.
        I'd like to leave **now/shortly**.
- other adverbs They cooked it **absolutely** perfectly.
        He's walking **extremely** quickly.
- whole sentences **Unfortunately** we have to leave.
        They would be here **otherwise**.
        She's arriving **today**.

Spanish adverbs are easy to use because they correspond so closely to English adverbs:

- Many end in **-mente**, just as many English ones ends in -*ly*.
- Their endings never change.
- They go before adjectives and other adverbs.
- They usually go after verbs – although they can also go first if they're being emphasised. However, they don't usually go between the subject and its verb as they do in English; for example in a sentence like *Ana often works*, the order in Spanish is *Ana works often*.

The dictionary abbreviation for *adverb* is *adv*. If you look up **clearly** and **nicely**, this is what you might find:

clearly *adv* **1.** claramente, distintamente, con claridad **2.** *[obviously, without doubt]* evidentemente, obviamente, decisivamente

nicely *adv* **1.** bien: *she paints* ~ pinta bien **2.** *[politely, kindly]* cortésmente, gentilmente **3.** *[in a pleasant way]* agradablemente

word **power**

- Many adverbs are formed by adding **-mente** to the feminine singular of an adjective:

afortunado *fortunate*	afortunadamente *fortunately*
completo *complete*	completamente *completely*
exacto *exact*	exactamente *exactly*
fabuloso *fabulous*	fabulosamente *fabulously*
fantástico *fantastic*	fantásticamente *fantastically*
inmediato *immediate*	inmediatamente *immediately*
justo *just*	justamente *justly*
necesario *necessary*	necesariamente *necessarily*
perfecto *perfect*	perfectamente *perfectly*
tranquilo *quiet*	tranquilamente *quietly*
verdadero *true, real*	verdaderamente *truly, really*

- Adjectives without a separate feminine form just add **-mente**:

difícil *difficult*	difícilmente *with difficulty*
eficaz *efficient*	eficazmente *efficiently*
especial *special*	especialmente *especially*
fácil *easy*	fácilmente *easily*
frecuente *frequent*	frecuentemente *frequently*
igual *equal*	igualmente *equally*
increíble *incredible*	increíblemente *incredibly*
natural *natural*	naturalmente *naturally*
normal *normal*	normalmente *normally*
particular *particular*	particularmente *particularly*
regular *regular*	regularmente *regularly*
simple *simple*	simplemente *simply*

Take care with the pronunciation of adverbs ending in **-mente**. In English they're pronounced with the stress in the same place as the adjectives they come from: n<u>a</u>tural, n<u>a</u>turally. This isn't the case in Spanish, where, unless there is an accent, the stress is on the first syllable of m<u>e</u>nte: natur<u>a</u>l, naturalm<u>e</u>nte.

- There are many adverbs that don't end in -**mente**:
  muy *very*, **tan** *so*, **más** *more*, **menos** *less*, **bien** *well*, **mal** *badly*,
  así *like this*, **ahora** *now*, **pronto** *early, soon*, **tarde** *late*,
  ya *already*, **delante** *in front*, **detrás** *behind*, **cerca** *near*, **lejos** *far*
  aquí *here*, **allí** *there*

- Phrases are often used as alternatives to adverbs:
  con cuidado *carefully*; **con éxito** *successfully*
  de manera triste *sadly*; **de modo elegante** *stylishly*
  de prisa *hastily/in haste*; **de repente** *suddenly, all of a sudden*
  sin entusiasmo *unenthusiastically*

- Just as in English, some Spanish adjectives are used as adverbs.
  They don't change their ending when they're adverbs. These
  include **caro** *expensive(ly)*; **barato** *cheap(ly)*; **alto** *high, loudly*;
  bajo *low, quietly*; **fuerte** *hard, loudly*; **claro** *clear(ly)*; **despacio**
  slow(ly); **rápido** *fast, quickly*; **demasiado** *too much*; **mucho**
  much, many, a lot of; **poco** *not very much, little*; **tanto** *so much*.
  Me gustan <u>mucho</u>. *I like them a lot* (adverb).
  Había <u>muchas</u> **personas en el parque.** *There were a lot of*
  (adjective)*people in the park.*
  La casa se vende <u>barato</u>. *The house is going cheap* (adverb).
  Busco una casa <u>barata</u>. *I'm looking for a cheap* (adjective) *house.*

  Recién is used instead of **recientemente** *recently* in
  expressions such as **recién casado** *newly-wed*; **recién hecho**
  newly-made; **recién nacido** *newborn*; **recién puesto** *newly-laid*.

false friends

actualmente *currently*	*actually* is **realmente**
bizarramente *bravely*	*bizarrely* **extrañamente**
desgraciadamente *unfortunately*	*disgracefully* **vergonzosamente**
eventualmente *possibly, by chance*	*eventually* **finalmente**
ocasionalmente *accidentally, by chance*	*occasionally* **de vez en cuando**
sensiblemente *perceptibly*	*sensibly* **sensatamente**
simpáticamente *nicely*	*sympathetically* **con compasión**
últimamente *recently*	*ultimately* **a la larga**

más and menos

Más and **menos** are used in several ways.

- *plus* and *minus*, with numbers:
  dos más dos son cuatro *2 + 2 = 4*
  tres menos uno son dos *3 - 1 = 2*
  más de 500 *500+*

- *more* and *less/fewer*, followed by a noun. Although **más** and **menos** are used as adjectives here, they don't agree with the noun.
  Tienes más paciencia que yo. *You have more patience than me.*
  Tienen más dinero que nosotros. *They have more money than us.*
  Tengo menos hambre hoy. *I'm less hungry today.*
  Hay menos restaurantes aquí. *There are fewer restaurants here.*

- *more* and *less*, followed by **de** + noun:
  hace más de dos días *more than two days ago*
  Hay más de cien razones para no hacerlo. *There are more than a hundred reasons for not doing it.*
  en menos de una semana *in less than a week's time*
  vacaciones para menos de quinientos euros *holidays for less than 500 euros*

They also feature in many everyday phrases:
al menos/a lo menos/por lo menos *at least*
a lo más tarde *at the latest*
a lo mejor *probably, maybe*
cada vez más caro *more and more expensive, dearer and dearer*
cada vez menos contento *less and less happy*
diez veces más grande *ten times bigger*
lo menos posible *as little as possible*
más o menos *more or less*
¡Menos mal! *Just as well/Thank goodness!*
nada más *nothing more*
nunca más *never again*

comparisons

When making comparisons – using adjectives, adverbs or nouns – **más** and **menos** are the key words. There's no equivalent of the English -er ending for adjectives, as in *faster, cheaper, nicer* or *bigger*.

Este método es más fácil. *This method is easier (more easy).*
¿Quiere adelgazar más fácilmente? *Do you want to lose weight more easily?*
El curso es menos intensivo. *The course is less intensive.*
Hoy he estudiado menos intensivamente. *Today I studied less intensively.*
Sara trabaja menos que Juan. *Sara works less than Juan.*
Sara tiene más libros que Juan. *Sara has more books than Juan.*

Than is either **de** or **que**:

- **De** before numbers. If the sentence is negative, **que** can mean *only*:
  Gana más de 10.000 euros. *She earns more than 10,000 euros.*
  No ganas más que 10.000 euros. *She only earns 10,000 euros.*

- **Que** in all other cases – which usually involve comparing two nouns, adjectives, adverbs, verbs or phrases.
  Tienen más dinero que gusto. *They have more money than taste.*
  Me gusta más Londres que París. *I like London more than Paris.*
  Es más astuto que inteligente. *He's more cunning than clever.*
  Más vale tarde que nunca. *Better late than never.*
  Prefiero salir que quedarme aquí. *I'd rather go out than stay here.*
  Hace más calor en Andalucía que en Galicia. *It's hotter in Andalucia than in Galicia.*

as ... as

With both adjectives and adverbs, *as ...as* is **tan ... como**:
El té no es tan bueno como el café. *The tea isn't as good as the coffee.*
No hago ejercicio tan regularmente como mis amigos. *I don't exercise as often as my friends.*

With nouns, you use **tanto/tanta/tantos/tantas ... como**:
No tenemos tanto dinero como nuestros vecinos. *We don't have as much money as our neighbours.*
Felipe no tiene tantos coches como Carlos. *Felipe doesn't have as many cars as Carlos.*

superlatives: el más, el menos

- To say *the most/least* … you use **el/la/los/las** + **más/menos** + adjective or adverb. There's no equivalent of the English *-est* ending for adjectives as in *fastest*, *cheapest* or *biggest*.

- If you want to follow the superlative with *in* …, you use **de**, which becomes **del** when followed by **el**.

  Éste es el plato más rico del mundo. *This is the tastiest/most tasty dish in the world.*
  Es la habitación menos cara del hotel. *It's the least expensive room in the hotel.*
  Son los más interesantes de nuestros amigos. *They're the most interesting of our friends.*

-ísimo

- You can also express an ultimate degree of something by adding **-ísimo** to an adjective without its final vowel and any accent it might have. Some words change their spelling to keep the sound the same: **co** changes to **qu**, **go** to **gu** and **z** to **c**.

  La ciudad es hermosa, ¿verdad? *Isn't the town beautiful?*
  Es hermosísima. *It's really beautiful.*
  ¿Los exámenes son difíciles? *Are the exams difficult?*
  Son dificilísimos. *They're incredibly difficult.*
  Beatriz quiere hacerse rica … riquísima. *Beatriz wants to become rich … ultra rich.*
  ¿Tenéis un viaje largo? *Do you have a long journey?*
  Es un viaje larguísimo. *It's a really long journey.*
  El perro es feroz, es ferocísimo. *The dog is fierce, extremely fierce.*

- A few **-ísimo** forms are irregular:
  antiguo *ancient* **antiquísimo**; **amable** *kind* **amabilísimo**
  joven *young* **jovencísimo**; **malo** *bad* **pésimo**
  nuevo *new* **novísimo**

  Las iglesias son antiquísimas. *The churches are extremely old.*

mejor/peor, mayor/menor

- In English *better/best* and *worse/worst* can be adjectives or adverbs, and the same is true of **mejor** and **peor** in Spanish. As you'd expect, when they're adjectives they agree with the noun – they don't have a separate feminine form but they add -**es** in the plural.

adjectives

bueno *good*	**mejor** *better*	**el mejor** *the best*
malo *bad*	**peor** *worse*	**el peor** *the worst*

Es la mejor profesora. *She's the best teacher.*
Son los peores vecinos. *They're the worst neighbours.*

adverbs

bien *well*	**mejor** *better*	**mejor** *best*
mal *badly*	**peor** *worse*	**peor** *worst*

Está mejor que ayer. *He's feeling better than yesterday.*
¿Es posible jugar peor? *Is it possible to play worse?*
Él lo hace mejor. *He does it better/(the) best.*

- **Mayor** and **menor** are comparative adjectives with a variety of English translations. They don't have a separate feminine form but they add -**es** in the plural:
mi hermano mayor *my older brother*
mi hija menor *my youngest daughter*
las personas mayores *adults*
un número mayor de 50 *a number greater than 50*
en grado menor *to a lesser degree*
la tonalidad mayor/menor *major/minor key* (music)
el delito menor *minor offence*; **daños menores** *minor damages*
Es su mayor éxito. *It's his greatest success.*
Tiene menor valor hoy en día. *It has less value these days.*
Esto tiene la mayor importancia. *This has the greatest importance.*
Eso tiene la menor importancia. *That has the least importance.*

Even though **mayor** and **menor** mean bigger and smaller, when talking about size you often use **más pequeño** and **más grande**:
Este coche es más pequeño. *This car is smaller.*
Es la más grande que tenemos. *It's the biggest we have.*

checkpoint 6

1   What's the masculine singular of the adjective these adverbs come from?

a absolutamente .... b velozmente ....

c simplemente .... d raramente ....

e típicamente .... f normalmente ....

g profundamente .... h misteriosamente ....

i severamente .... j dulcemente ....

2   And what's the adverb from these adjectives?

a paciente .... b fundamental ....

c científico .... d extraordinario ....

e regular .... f económico ....

g extremo .... h indiferente ....

i relativo .... j lógico ....

3   Find the opposites of these adverbs. They're all in this unit.

a desafortunadamente .... b injustamente ....

c difícilmente .... d cerca ....

e ineficazmente .... f peor ....

4   Make four pairs from these adverbs. There's one left over – what does it mean?

   honestamente obviamente finalmente cruelmente despacio
   evidentemente sinceramente lentamente brutalmente

5   Fill in these gaps.

a Ese coche es .... que el otro. *That car is worse than the other one.*

b Ana es .... que María. *Ana is older than Maria.*

c Estos bombones son .... de todos. *These chocolates are the worst of all.*

d ¡Nuestro gato es .... que tu perro! *Our cat is bigger than your dog!*

e Carmen es .... de la clase. *Carmen is the smallest in the class.*

f Esta película es .... de todas. *This film is the best of all.*

g María es .... que Ana. *Maria is younger than Ana.*

Demonstratives and possessives

Whereas English has two demonstrative adjectives: *this* and *that*, Spanish has three: **este** *this*, **ese** *that* and **aquel** which also means *that* but which conveys the sense of something further away than **ese**. They're adjectives, used with a noun, and like other adjectives they have feminine and plural forms to agree with that noun.

Demonstrative pronouns are used instead of a noun, to avoid repeating it. In English you add the word *one(s)* to the demonstrative adjective; in Spanish you add an accent to it: **éste** *this one*, **ése** *that one*, **aquél** *that one over there*. Although they're not used with a noun, they still have to agree with the noun they refer to.

The English possessive adjectives are *my*, *your*, *his*, *her*, *its*, *our*, *their*. In Spanish there are two alternatives:
- the short forms **mi**, **tu**, **su**, **nuestro**, **vuestro**, which go before their noun
- the full forms **mío**, **tuyo**, **suyo**, **nuestro**, **vuestro**, which go after their noun.

The full forms are also used with **el/la/los/las** to translate the possessive pronouns *mine*, *ours*, *yours*, *his*, *hers*, *its*, *theirs*.

Both the adjectives and the pronouns have feminine and plural forms to agree with the noun they describe or represent.

este and ese

Este *this* and **ese** *that* are demonstrative adjectives, which:
- go in front of the noun they describe,
- change their ending to agree with that noun,
- must be used with each noun in a list.

Este (m) changes to **esta** (f), **estos** (m pl), **estas** (f pl):
este año *this year*
esta tarde *this afternoon*
estos meses *these months*
estas semanas *these weeks*

No puedo ayudarte en este momento. *I can't help you at the moment.*
¡Qué bonita es esta casa! *How lovely this house is!*
¿Has probado estos vinos? *Have you tried these wines?*
Nunca me olvidaré de estas palabras. *I'll never forget these words.*

Ese (m) changes to **esa** (f), **esos** (m pl), **esas** (f pl):
De ese modo *(in) that way;* **en ese momento** *at that moment*
esa casa *that house;* **esa semana** *that week*
esos vinos *those wines;* **esos meses** *those months*
esas palabras *those words;* **esas mesas** *those tables*

You can use **este** and **ese** with other adjectives or with numbers:
este sitio web inútil *this useless website*
esta gran pasión *this great passion*
ese sitio tranquilo *that quiet place*
esa otra aventura *that other adventure*
estas dos semanas *these two weeks*
esos últimos días *those last days*

Use **ese** *that* when the noun in question is further away from the speaker and nearer to the listener. When it's at a distance from both listener and speaker, use **aquel** (page 74):
¿Puede darme ese abrigo y ese paraguas, por favor?
Could you give me that coat and umbrella, please?

éste and ése

Éste and **ése** are pronouns i.e. they're used on their own without a noun, translating *this (one)*, *that (one)*, *these (ones)*, *those(ones)*.

To distinguish them from **este** *this* and **ese** *that*, they're written with an accent. Apart from the accent, they have the same feminine and plural forms as **este** and **ese**, and they agree with the noun they represent:
Ésta es facilísima. *This one's really easy.*
¿Te gustan ésos? *Do you like those (ones)?*

- **Éste** is often used in introductions:
  Éste es mi marido. *This is my husband.*
  Ésta es mi mujer. *This is my wife.*
  Éstos son mis amigos. *These are my friends.*
  Éstas son nuestras hijas. *These are our daughters.*

- **Éste** and **ése** are used for comparing and contrasting:
  Aquí tienes las habitaciones – ésta es más grande que ésa.
  Here are the bedrooms – this one's bigger than that one.
  Me llevo ésos en el escaparate – no me gustan éstos.
  I'll take those in the window – I don't like these.

- You can use **éste** and **ése** with other pronouns:
  Prefiero éste otro. *I prefer this other one.*
  Me gustan ésos negros. *I like those black ones.*

esto and eso

Esto *this* and **eso** *that* are neuter, i.e. they're neither masculine nor feminine. They're used when you're referring to an idea or a situation rather than to a specific noun. **Esto** and **eso** are singular and they never change.

¡Esto es absurdo! *This is ridiculous!*
Eso me sorprende. *That surprises me.*
Esto no tiene nada que ver contigo. *This has nothing to do with you.*
No obstante esto, ganaré. *In spite of this, I'll win.*
¡Eso es! *That's it!*
por esto/eso *for this/that reason*
esto/eso de tu madre *this/that business about your mother*

aquel/aquél

Aquel *that* and **aquél** *that one* are used for things which are further away in distance or time than **ese** *that* and **ése** *that one*. **Aquel** is used with a noun as an adjective and **aquél** is used on its own as a pronoun.

The adjective **aquel**:
- goes in front of the noun it describes
- has the four forms **aquel** (m), **aquella** (f), **aquellos** (m pl), **aquellas** (f pl) to allow it to agree with its noun
- must be used with each noun in a list.

en aquel momento at that moment
aquella casa that house
aquellos vinos those wines
aquellas mesas those tables

Aquellos hombres y aquellas mujeres son miembros de la familia real. *Those men and women are members of the royal family.*

The pronoun **aquél**:
- has an accent to distinguish it from the adjective **aquel**
- has the four forms **aquél**, **aquélla**, **aquéllos**, **aquéllas** to agree with the noun it stands for.

No me gusta ese coche, me gusta aquél. *I don't like that car, I like that one over there.*
No me gusta esa casa, me gusta aquélla. *I don't like that house, I like that one over there.*
No me gustan esos coches, me gustan aquéllos. *I don't like those cars, I like those over there.*
No me gustan esas casas, me gustan aquéllas. *I don't like those houses, I like those over there.*

Aquél can be used to mean the former and **éste** the latter when referring to two or more things in a previous sentence: **Belén y Carmen son hermanas; aquélla es alta y ésta es baja.** *Belén and Carmen are sisters; the former is tall and the latter is short.*

aquello

Like **esto** and **eso**, **aquello** *that (one)* is a neuter form used when you're referring to an idea or situation rather than to a specific noun. **Aquello** is singular and never changes.

Aquello no tiene urgencia. *That's not urgent.*

checkpoint 7

1   Which form of **éste** would you use to introduce
    a   your sister   b   two colleagues (male)
    c   your boyfriend   d   your father
    e   your daughter   f   two aunts?

2   Put the correct form of **ese** before these nouns:
    a _____ **chef**   b _____ **casa**
    c _____ **mujeres**   d _____ **hoteles**
    e _____ **hombre**   f _____ **parque**

3   Put the correct form of **aquel** before these nouns:
    a _____ **señoras**   b _____ **bares**
    c _____ **cama**   d _____ **coche**
    e _____ **señor**   f _____ **silla**

4   When referring to an idea or situation rather than a specific noun, how would you say *this one*, *that one* and *that one (over there)*?

5   Complete the answer to the question with the appropriate demonstrative pronouns:
    ¿Qué libros has leído? He leído _____ (*these*), **pero no he leído** _____ (*those*), **tampoco** _____ (*those over there*).

possession

When you're talking about possession in Spanish, these are the key points to remember.

- There's no equivalent of the English apostrophe -s ('s) as in *Raúl's house* or *the company's address*. Nor is there the equivalent of two nouns together as in *company address*. Instead, you always say *the house of Raúl*, *the address of the company*. *Of* is **de**, changing to **del** when followed by **el** (page 46).
  la casa de Raúl *Raúl's house*
  la dirección de la empresa *the company's address*
  el coche del director *the manager's car*

- There are two sets of possessive adjectives, i.e. two ways of saying *my*, *our*, *your*, *his/her*, *its*, *their*. There's a short form which goes before the noun and a full form which goes after the noun.

- The possessive pronouns, i.e. *mine*, *yours*, *his*, *hers*, *ours*, *its*, *theirs* are identical to the full form of the possessive adjectives and are used with **el/la/los/las**:
  el coche mío *my car*, **el mío** *mine* (referring to the car).

- All possessive adjectives and pronouns agree with what's owned, not with the owner. *My car* is **mi coche** or **el coche mío** regardless of whether the person talking is a man or a woman.

- Spanish possessive adjectives are used less often than in English. When it's clear who the owner is, e.g. when you're talking about parts of the body or articles of clothing, you use *the* instead of a possessive adjective:
  El estudiante levantó la mano. *The student raised his hand.*
  Te lavas la cara. *You wash your face.*
  Me puse el abrigo. *I put on my coat.*

 Possessive adjectives are used in formal correspondence:
Muy señora mía *Dear Madam*; **Muy señores míos** *Dear Sirs*

possessive adjectives

These are the two sets of possessive adjectives. The short form is used more often than the full form.

short forms

singular		plural		
m	f	m	f	
mi	mi	mis	mis	*my*
tu	tu	tus	tus	*your* tú
su	su	sus	sus	*your* usted *his, her, its*
nuestro	nuestra	nuestros	nuestras	*our*
vuestro	vuestra	vuestros	vuestras	*your* vosotros
su	su	sus	sus	*your* ustedes *their*

full forms

singular		plural		
m	f	m	f	
mío	mía	míos	mías	*my*
tuyo	tuya	tuyos	tuyas	*your* tú
suyo	suya	suyos	suyas	*your* usted *his, her, its*
nuestro	nuestra	nuestros	nuestras	*our*
vuestro	vuestra	vuestros	vuestras	*your* vosotros
suyo	suya	suyos	suyas	*your* ustedes *their*

These two sets mean the same thing:
mi nombre, el nombre mío *my name*
tus llaves, las llaves tuyas *your keys*
tus responsabilidades, las responsabilidades tuyas *your responsibilities*
su llave, la llave suya *his key, her key, your key*
nuestros nombres, los nombres nuestros *our names*
vuestra casa, la casa vuestra *your house*
su dirección, la dirección suya *their address*
sus direcciones, las direcciones suyas *their addresses*

There's more about **su** and its various meanings on page 79.

possessive pronouns

Possessive pronouns are identical to the full form of possessive adjectives (previous page), used after *the* **el/la/los/las**.

- They're used without a noun but they agree with the noun they represent:
  El mío está aquí. *Mine's here* (referring to something masculine).
  La mía está aquí. *Mine's here* (referring to something feminine).
  ¿Los pasaportes? Aquí está el mío. ¿Dónde está el tuyo? *Passports? Here's mine. Where's yours?*
  ¿Y las maletas? Las nuestras están con las suyas. *And the cases? Ours are with theirs.*

- When possessive pronouns follow the verb **ser** *to be*, **el/la/los/las** are usually left out, although they can be retained for emphasis:
  Estas llaves son mías. *These keys are mine.*
  Estas llaves son las mías. *These keys are mine.*

- When **a** and **de** come before the possessive pronoun, they combine with **el** to become **al** and **del** (page 46):
  Prefiero el mío al tuyo. *I prefer mine to yours.*
  Su apartamento está cerca del nuestro. *Their apartment is close to ours.*

Possessive pronouns can act as nouns if used in the singular masculine form with the neuter article **lo**:
Lo mío es tuyo. *What's mine is yours.*
Cada uno a lo suyo. *Each to his own.*

The masculine plural used after **los** is often used to mean family:
Voy de vacaciones con los míos. *I'm going on holiday with my family.*
Habla con los tuyos. *Talk to your family.*

su

Su and all its variations have several meanings:

- the adjectives **su**, **sus** and **suyo/a**, **suyos/as**
  can **all** mean:
  his
  her
  its
  your (**usted**)
  their
  your (**ustedes**)

- the pronouns **el suyo, la suya, los suyos, las suyas**
  can **all** mean:
  his
  hers
  yours (**usted**)
  theirs
  yours (**ustedes**)

Roberto conduce su coche/el coche suyo, el suyo. *Roberto drives his car, his.*
Elena conduce su coche/el coche suyo, el suyo. *Elena drives her car, hers.*
Usted conduce su coche/el coche suyo, el suyo. *You drive your car, yours.*
Los padres de Mariano conducen su coche, el suyo. *Mariano's parents drive their car, theirs.*

Because **su coche** can mean *his car*, *her car*, *your car*, *their car*, the sentence **Roberto conduce su coche** has several possible meanings. Context is usually enough to make the meaning clear but if ever there's potential ambiguity, you can use the following after the noun instead of using **su/suyo**:
de él *his*, **de ella** *her*, *hers*
de ellos (m), **de ellas** (f) *their*, *theirs*
de usted (sing), **de ustedes** (pl) *your*, *yours*

Me encanta su casa. *I love his/her/your/their house.*
Me encanta la casa de ella. *I love her house.*
Esta casa es suya. *This house is his/hers/yours/theirs.*
Esta casa es de él. *This house is his.*

checkpoint 8

1   Underline the right possessive adjective.
    a [su, sus] casas
    b [nuestro, nuestra, nuestros, nuestras] coche
    c [su, sus] perro
    d [tu, tus] tías
    e [mi, mis] abuelos
    f [vuestro, vuestra, vuestros, vuestras] gato
    g [su, sus] hermanos

2   Write the answer to the questions in Spanish.
    a ¿De quién es este perro? Es _____ [mine]
    b ¿De quién son estos zapatos? Son _____ [his]
    c ¿De quién es esta maleta? Es _____ [hers]
    d ¿De quién son estas chaquetas? Son _____ [ours]
    e ¿De quién son estos juguetes? Son _____ [yours, tú]
    f ¿De quién es este libro? Es _____ [yours, usted]
    g ¿De quién es esta casa ? Es _____ [theirs]

3   What are the three ways of saying your passport using the short
    form of the possessive adjective? How would you say yours
    (referring to the passport)?

4   Give all the possible meanings of Es su vida (life).

5   Change this sentence to make it clear you're talking about
    finding **her** keys: He encontrado sus llaves.

6   Translate the following phrases:
    The company car _____
    My mother's house _____
    Dear Sir _____

Personal pronouns

Pronouns are words like *I*, *she*, *we*, *us*, *him*, *them*, *your*, *mine*, *those*, which you use to save repeating a noun:
The plumber called – **he**'s going to be late.
Have you seen **the children**? I can't find **them**.
Where's **my key**? Have you seen **it**?

Personal pronouns can be:
- the subject of a verb: *I*, *we*, *you*, *he*, *she*, *they*;
- the direct object of a verb: *me*, *us*, *you*, *him*, *her*, *them*;
- the indirect object of a verb: *(to/for) me*, *(to/for) us*, *(to/for) you*, *(to/for) him*, *(to/for) her*, *(to/for) them*. Spanish has single words for these.

There are differences in the way personal pronouns are used in English and Spanish:
- Subject pronouns are used far less often – you don't need them to tell you who's doing what because that information in carried in the ending of the verb.
- Object pronouns usually go before the verb, not after it – except in certain circumstances.

For demonstrative pronouns (e.g. *this one*, *those*) see pages 73-75;
for possessive pronouns (e.g. *mine*, *yours*) see pages 78-79.

subject pronouns

yo *I*	**nosotros/as** *we* (m/f)
tú *you*	**vosotros/as** *you* (m/f)
él *he*	**ellos** *they* (m)
ella *she*	**ellas** *they* (f)
usted *you*	**ustedes** *you*

- Unlike *I* in English, **yo** isn't written with a capital letter, except when it starts a sentence.

- **tú** *you* and **él** *he* have accents to distinguish them from **tu** *your* and **el** *the*.

- There are four words for *you*, each using a different verb ending:
  tú: someone you call by their first name
  usted: someone you don't know well, someone older than you.
  In writing, it's usually abbreviated to **Ud**. or **Vd.**, and the verb with it has the same ending as for **él/ella** *he/she*
  vosotros/as: more than one person in a familiar situation
  ustedes: more than one person in a formal situation. In writing, it's usually abbreviated to **Uds.** or **Vds.** and the verb with it has the same ending as for **ellos/ellas** *they*. In Latin America **ustedes** is used rather than **vosotros/as**.

- *We* can be the masculine **nosotros** or the feminine **nosotras**, depending on who's talking. Similarly, depending on who's being addressed, the familiar plural *you* can be **vosotros** or **vosotras**. When these words relate to a mixed group of men and women, the masculine forms are used. The same is true of **ellos** *they*.

- Spanish subject pronouns usually go before the verb, but in questions they go after it: **¿Pagan ellos?** *Are they paying?*

- When *it* is used as the subject and when *they* refers to things, you never use a subject pronoun in Spanish:
  Es un cachorro. *It's a puppy.*
  Son botellas de vino tinto. *They're bottles of red wine.*
  There is a word for *it*: **ello**, but **ello** refers to a whole idea rather than to a noun and is mainly used only in formal written texts.

- Subject pronouns are used much less than in English because the verb ending clearly shows who's doing something. So they tend to be used mainly for contrast, emphasis or to avoid ambiguity.
  Él trabaja en Barcelona ... _He works in Barcelona_ ...
  ... mientras yo trabajo aquí. ... _while I work here._
  Nosotros no podemos ir pero tú sí. _We can't go but you can._
  ¿Cómo se llama usted? _What's your name?_
  ¿Cómo se llama él? _What's his name?_

- For even greater emphasis, you can add **mismo/a/os/as**:
  Yo mismo creo que ... _I myself believe that_ ...
  ¿Lo ha escrito ella misma? _Did she write it herself?_
  Vosotros mismos la habéis visto. _You yourselves saw her._

- Subject pronouns are also used in phrases like these:
  Soy yo. _It's me._
  ¿Quién, yo? _Who, me?_
  ¡Es él! ¡Es ella! _It's him! It's her!_
  Nosotros también. _Us too./So are/have/did we._
  Yo tampoco. _Nor me./Neither am/have/did I._
  and when making comparisons:
  Silvia es más lista que tú. _Silvia is cleverer than you._
  Silvia no es tan lista como yo. _Silvia is not as clever as me._

se: undefined subject

When the subject of a verb is nobody in particular, **se** is often used.
The English equivalent is _one, you, we, they, people._

- The verb with **se** is in the third person singular, i.e. it has the same ending as _he/she._
  ¿Se puede aparcar aquí? _Can you park here?_
  ¿Cómo se dice ... en español? _How do you say ... in Spanish?_
  ¿Cómo se escribe? _How do you write it? How is it written?_
  se cree/dice/espera que _it is believed/said/hoped that_

- When there's a direct object (page 84) after **se** + verb, that verb is singular with a singular object and plural with a plural object:
  Se come mucho ajo. _People eat a lot of garlic._
  Se comen tartaletas de cerdo. _People eat pork pies._

object pronouns

Object pronouns (*me, us, you, him, her, it, them*) can either be:

- the direct object of a verb: *Anna knows <u>me</u>, The children saw <u>him</u>, I've invited <u>them.</u>*
- or the indirect object of a verb: *Anna writes <u>to me</u>, The children listened <u>to him</u>; I've made a cake <u>for them</u>.*

In Spanish, there's no distinction made between these four direct and indirect object pronouns:

me *me, to/for me*   **te** *you, to/for you* (**tú**)
nos *us, to/for us*   **os** *you, to/for you* (**vosotros**)

Ana me/nos conoce. *Anna knows me/us.*
Ana me/nos escribe. *Anna writes to me/to us.*

However, the pronouns *him, her, it, them, you* (**usted**) are entirely different words from *to/for him, to/for her, to/for them, to/for you*:

direct	**indirect**
lo *him, it* (m), *you* (**usted** m)	**le** *to him/her/you* (**usted** m/f)
la *her, it* (f), *you* (**usted** f)	
los *them* (m), *you* (**ustedes** m)	**les** *to them/you* (**ustedes** m/f)
las *them* (f), *you* (**ustedes** f)	

Ana lo/la conoce. *Anna knows him/her/you.*
Ana le escribe. *Anna writes to him/to her/to you.*
Los/las he invitado. *I've invited them/you* (pl.).
Les he hecho una tarta. *I've made a cake for them/you* (pl.).

- **Los** is used when *them* refers to a mixed male and female group:
  ¿Ana y Jorge? Los conozco bien. *Anna and Jorge? I know them well.*
- **Le** *to him, to her, to you* (**usted**) and **les** *to them, to you* (**ustedes**) are the same words for both masculine and feminine. If clarification is needed, **a él, a ella** etc. are added:
  Le explico a él. *I explain to him.* **Le explico a ella.** *I explain to her.*
- When the object of a sentence comes before the verb, the corresponding object pronoun must be used as well:
  La ciudad no la conocemos bien. *We don't know the city well.*
- **Le** and **les** are sometimes used instead of **lo** and **los** to refer to male people. This is known as **leísmo**: **Le vi** (instead of **lo vi**). *I saw him.*

direct or indirect object?

In general, the same verbs take a direct or indirect object in English and Spanish. However, there are some to look out for.

- With some verbs it's not immediately obvious that the object is indirect because there are two ways of using them in English – with or without a preposition before the pronoun:
  ¿Puede usted enviarles esto?
  Can you send them this?/Can you send this to them?
  Le he dado un regalo.
  I've given him/her a present./I've given a present to him/her.

  Similar verbs include **contar a** *to tell*, **dar a** *to give*, **decir a** *to tell*, **enviar a**, **mandar a** *to send*, **ofrecer a** *to offer, give*, **prestar a** *to lend*, **servir a** *to serve*, **traer a** *to bring*, **regalar a** *to give a present*.

- Unlike English, the following have an indirect object in Spanish:
  contestar a *to answer*   **doler a** *to hurt* (page 181)
  gustar a *to please* (page 180)   **preguntar a** *to ask (a question)*

  No le contestaron la pregunta. *They didn't answer your question.* lit. *They didn't answer to you the question.*
  Le duele la cabeza. *His head hurts.* lit. *His head is painful to him.*
  Les gusta el vino. *They like wine.* lit. *Wine is pleasing to them.*
  Le pregunté la hora. *I asked her the time.* lit. *I asked to her the time.*

- In English, these verbs are followed by a preposition before a noun whereas in Spanish they have a direct object:
  escuchar *to listen to*   **pedir** *to ask for*
  esperar *to wait for*   **buscar** *to look for*
  mirar *to look at*

  Prefiero escuchar la música pop. *I prefer to listen to pop music.*

Take care not to confuse the personal **a** (page 99) with the indirect object in sentences such as **Conozco a María** *I know María*. Here María is the direct object of **conozco**, and would therefore be replaced by the direct object pronoun **la**: **La conozco.** *I know her.*

position of object pronouns

- Object pronouns, direct and indirect, generally go before a verb:
  ¿Me entiendes? *Do you understand me?*
  Te creo. *I believe you.*
  Os escribiré una carta. *I'll write you a letter.*
  ¿La viste? *Did you see her?*

- In the perfect tense (page 154), they go before **haber**:
  Tu padre nos ha visto. *Your father has seen us.*
  Lo he terminado. *I have finished it.*
  ¿Me has enviado el libro? *Have you sent the book to me?*

- When the verb is an infinitive (ending in **-ar**, **-er** or **-ir**) or a gerund
  (ending in **-ando** or **-iendo**), pronouns follow it, attaching themselves
  to it. When a pronoun is attached to a gerund, an accent is added to
  maintain the position of the stress:
  Es difícil creerte. *It's difficult to believe you.*
  Pensándolo, he decidido no salir. *Thinking it over, I've decided not
  to go out.*

  If the infinitive or gerund follows another verb, pronouns can either
  attach themselves to the end of the infinitive/gerund or they can go
  before the first verb:
  ¿Puedo mostrarte la casa? ¿Te puedo mostrar la casa? *Can I show the
  house to you?*
  Tienes que escribirme. Me tienes que escribir. *You have to write to me.*
  Estamos bebiéndolo. Lo estamos bebiendo. *We're drinking it.*

- When the verb is an imperative (pages 166-167) telling someone to do
  something, pronouns follow it, attaching themselves to it. A written
  accent is added to maintain the position of the stress:
  Perdóneme. *Excuse me.*
  Póngame un kilo de patatas. *Give me a kilo of potatoes.*
  Tráiganos más pan, por favor. *Bring us more bread, please.*

  When the verb is an imperative telling somebody ***not*** to do something,
  pronouns go before it:
  No lo hagas. *Don't do it.*
  No los abráis. *Don't open them.*

reflexive pronouns

The infinitive of reflexive verbs ends in **se**: **casarse** *to get married*, **lavarse** *to wash*; **llamarse** *to be called*. **Se** is a reflexive pronoun, meaning *oneself*, so **lavarse** literally means *to wash oneself*, **llamarse** *to call oneself*.

When reflexive verbs have a subject, they lose the infinitive ending **-arse**, **-erse**, **-irse** and use the same endings as non-reflexive verbs. But they always have to have one of the following reflexive pronouns with them, and it's always the one that matches the subject of the verb.

me	*myself*
te	*yourself*
se	*himself, herself, yourself* (**usted**)
nos	*ourselves*
os	*yourselves*
se	*themselves, yourselves* (**ustedes**)

Although their literal meaning is *myself, himself*, etc. most of the time they're not translated into English at all:
Nos divertimos mucho en Madrid. *We really enjoyed ourselves in Madrid.*
Se vistió. *He dressed (himself)/got dressed.*
Me levanto a las ocho. *I get up at eight o'clock.*
¿Cuándo se casaron? *When did they get married?*

Nos, os and **se** (plural) can mean *each other* or *one another*:
Nos vemos cada día. *We see each other every day.*
¿Os conocéis desde hace mucho tiempo? *Have you known each other long?*
Se ayudan mucho. *They help one another a lot.*

Reflexive pronouns follow the same rules as other pronouns (see opposite). The key thing to remember is that a reflexive pronoun must always match the subject of the verb, even when it's at the end of an infinitive or an imperative (page 167):
Voy a vestirme. *I'm going to get dressed.* lit. *I'm going to dress myself.*
Siéntate. *Sit (yourself) down.*

double object pronouns

When two object pronouns are used in the same sentence, the indirect object pronoun comes before the direct object pronoun:

Me la dio. *He gave it to me.*
Te lo digo. *I'll tell you (it).*
Te los enviaré. *I will send them to you.*
Nos los consiguió un amigo. *A friend got them for us.*

The indirect pronouns **le** and **les** change to **se** when they're followed by **lo, la, los** or **las** to avoid two pronouns beginning with **-l** being used together:

Se lo regalé. *I gave it to him.*
Se las enviaron. *They sent them to her.*
Se los he comprado. *I bought them for him.*
Voy a comprárselos. *I'm going to buy them for him.*

Some double object pronouns have several possible meanings:
se lo mando can mean *I send it to him, I send it to her,*
I send it to you (**usted/ ustedes**), *I send it to them.*
It rarely causes confusion because context usually makes the meaning obvious. But if there's any potential ambiguity, you can add **a él, a ella, a usted, a ellos/ellas, a ustedes**:

Se lo mando a él/a ella. *I send it to him/to her.*
Se lo mando a ellos. *I send it to them.*
Se lo mando a usted. *I send it to you.*

Spanish has a lot of object pronouns, many of which look very similar. This can make them seem confusing at first, but the more you make a point of using them the easier they become. The main points to remember are that:

- they generally go before a verb, not after it (except for infinitives, imperatives and gerunds).
- they're doubled up quite regularly: **A mí no me gusta** *I don't like it.*
- they're used in instances where we would leave them out in English: **No lo sé.** *I don't know.* **No lo comprendo.** *I don't understand.*
- and **se** has many different uses; as a reflexive pronoun (**se presenta** *he introduces himself*), as a passive form (**¿se puede?** *can we?*), as an indirect pronoun before **lo, la, los** or **las.**

pronouns after prepositions

The following pronouns are generally used after prepositions (page 97):

mí *me*	**nosotros/as** *us*
ti *you*	**vosotros/as** *you*
él/ella *him/her*	**ellos/ellas** *them* (m/f)
usted *you*	**ustedes** *you*

Para mí, un vino blanco. *For me, a white wine.*
Vivimos cerca de ti. *We live near you.*

- These pronouns are often used in addition to other object pronouns for emphasis or to make sure the meaning is absolutely clear:
  A ti te gusta pero a mí no. *You like it but I don't.*
  Se lo di a usted. *I gave it to you.*
  Se lo prometimos a él. *We promised it to him.*

- **Yo** and **tú** are used instead of **mí** and **ti** after **entre** *between*, **excepto/ menos/ salvo** *except*, **hasta** *even*, **según** *according to*.
  Entre tú y yo ... *Between you and me ...*

- **Con** *with* combines with **mí** and **ti** to form **conmigo** *with me* and **contigo** *with you*:
  ¿Vienes conmigo? *Are you coming with me?*
  María quiere ir contigo. *Maria wants to go with you.*

- Unlike **conmigo** and **contigo**, **consigo** means *with himself/herself/ themselves*.
  Conchita está enfadada consigo. *Conchita is annoyed with herself.*
  If you want to talk about *himself/herself/themselves* with any other preposition, you use **sí**:
  Él compra las flores para sí. *He's buying the flowers for himself.*
  Alternatively, you can use the pronouns listed above and add the word for *self/selves* **mismo/a/os/as** (page 83).
  Conchita está enfadada con ella misma.
  Él compra las flores para él mismo.

Mismo also means *same* or *identical* and changes to agree with the noun it's describing:
Vivimos en la misma calle y vamos al mismo colegio. *We live in the same street and go to the same college.*

checkpoint 9

1   How would you say *Hi, it's me* in Spanish?

2   Would you use **tú**, **vosotros/as**, **usted** or **ustedes** for:
    a a six-year-old child?   **b** an elderly neighbour?
    c two female friends?   **d** some new clients to your office?
    e a student friend?   **f** the person on the hotel reception desk?

3   What do these mean?
    a **Se lo regalo a ella.**   b **Te lo preparo.**
    c **No la conocemos.**   d **Le llamo a usted.**
    e **Se afeita. (él)**   f **No las he visto.**
    g **Perdónenos.**   h **No te lo dio. (ella)**

4   Fill the gap with the correct pronoun.
    a ¿Qué quiere _____ ? *What would you like?*
    b _____ **veo**. *I see you.* (**tú**)
    c _____ **lo explicas.** *You explain it to him.*
    d _____ **laváis.** *You wash.*
    e ¿Son _____ ? *Is it them?* (m)
    f _____ **lo han dado.** *They have given it to us.*
    g _____ **he comido.** *I have eaten it.* (f)
    h _____ **gusta.** *They like it.* (**ustedes**)

5   Replace **el café** and **los billetes** with *it* and *them*. There are two possible ways of arranging the words.
    ¿Quieres probar el café?
    Tengo que comprar los billetes.

6   Translate these into Spanish. If you need to check up on prepositions, they're on page 98-106.
    a *with himself*   **b** *for you* (**tú**)   **c** *near me*
    d *of them* (f)   **e** *to him*   **f** *even you* (**tú**)

7   What do you think **Aquí se habla inglés** means?

8   To emphasise that you've made something yourself, what could you add to **Lo he hecho yo**?

9   What do the English translations of **escuchar**, **esperar** and **buscar** have in common?

10   In *I offer them a drink*, what's the Spanish for *them*?

Sentence structure

The more Spanish you learn, the more you'll progress from simple, short phrases to longer sentences which express your needs and opinions in more detail. The two main things to consider when constructing more complex sentences are word order and how to join together the various parts of the sentence.

- Word order is broadly similar in English and Spanish although there are some fundamental differences, such as the position of adjectives after nouns, and the position of pronouns (e.g. *us*, *him*, *them*) before verbs in Spanish.

- To join together the various elements of what you want to say, you can use conjunctions – words like *and*, *but*, *since*, *so*, *however*. You also need words that save you having to repeat nouns or phrases when you're giving additional information about them: words like **que** and **quien** *who*, *which*, *that*. These are called relative pronouns as they relate one part of a sentence to the other.

Progressing isn't simply about more and more grammatical rules. If you listen to native speakers of any language, you'll find that they use words like *well then*, *let's see*, *anyway*, *furthermore*, which bring a sense of continuity to what they say and take it beyond the strictly functional. When you learn a new language, it's an effort at first to remember to use these words as well as everything else – but when you get used to them you'll find not only that they make you sound more fluent but also that they give you useful thinking time when you're stuck for a word.

word order

Word order in Spanish is more flexible than in English and there are a number of key differences between the two languages:

- When a noun and an adjective are used together, the adjective often goes afterwards in Spanish (pages 58-59): **una decisión importante** *an important decision.*

- As in English the verb usually follows the subject in a statement. However, it can also come before the subject to emphasise it: **Murió su madre el año pasado.** *Her mother <u>died</u> last year.* **Viene Paco a la fiesta.** *Paco <u>is coming</u> to the party.*

- To ask a question, English brings in words like *do/does*: *Does your wife work here?* Spanish doesn't use these extra words, so the same question looks like this: **¿Trabaja tu mujer aquí?** The order of the subject and verb are reversed. In questions using words like **cuándo** *when*, **por qué** *why*, the question word goes at the beginning of the question: **¿Cuándo empieza el partido?** *When does the match start?*

- When the object of a verb is a pronoun (*me, us, you, him, her, it, them*) it generally goes in front of the verb (page 86): **Me llama cada día.** *She phones <u>me</u> every day.*

- In Spanish the preposition always goes before the word it modifies. Unlike in English, a Spanish sentence can never end in a preposition (pages 97-108):
  ¿Con quién vas al teatro? *Who are you going to the theatre with?* lit. *With whom are you going to the theatre?*

- In negative sentences (page 123) **no** *not* goes before the verb. If there are any object pronouns in front of the verb it goes before them. **Mi amiga no vino al cine.** *My friend didn't come to the cinema.* **No me lo dio.** *He did not give it to me.*

making conversation flow

Words that help the flow of conversation, such as *well*, are difficult to translate exactly – making it more effective to focus on the context they're used in.

- **Entonces** can convey *Well then…, So …, Right then…* at the start of a sentence. Other words used in the same way include **bien, bueno**.
- **Pues**, also meaning *well*, suggests a bit of uncertainty or hesitation.
- **¡Bah!** shrugs something off, conveying *I don't really care! Whatever!*
- **En general** is used where English might use *all in all, on the whole*.
- **De hecho** *in fact, indeed,* **en realidad** *actually* and **de todos modos** *in any case, anyway* could reinforce what you're saying.
- **¡Anda!** meaning *Go on! Well!* is used to convey surprise.
- **¡Caramba!** can be used to convey surprise as in *Good gracious!* or annoyance as in *For crying out loud!*
- **¡Ojalá!** is a word of Arabic origin used where English might use *If only (it were so)! Some hope!*

opinions

When giving your opinion, you can start with **según yo, a mi parecer** or **para mí** *in my view*. To strengthen your argument you can use **claramente** *clearly* or **evidentemente** *obviously*.

As you get into your stride you can punctuate what you're saying with **en primer lugar** *first of all* and **en segundo lugar** *secondly*, and summarise with **en resumen** *in short*. And you can show that you're coming to a conclusion with **por lo tanto** *therefore* or **así** *so*, **por último** or **finalmente** *finally*.

¿Qué piensas tú?/¿Qué piensa usted? or **¿Qué opinas tú?/¿Qué opina usted?** *What do you think about it?* bring others into the discussion. Or you can use **en tu/su opinión** *in your opinion* instead.

To agree with someone you can say **estoy de acuerdo** *I agree* or **tienes/ tiene usted razón** *you're right*, and when you disagree you use **no estoy de acuerdo**.

joining parts of a sentence

- Draw things together with **y** *and* (**y** becomes **e** before words beginning with **i** or **hi**), **también** *also* or **tampoco** *nor, neither*.

- Express reservation with **sin embargo** or **no obstante**, both meaning *however,* or **pero** *but* (**sino** after a negative).

- Introduce alternatives with **o** *or* (**o** becomes **u** before words beginning with **o** or **ho**), **de otra manera** *otherwise* or **en cambio** *instead*.

- Contrast two elements with **por una parte** *on the one hand* and **por otra parte** *on the other hand*.

- Show you're about to infer a conclusion with **por lo tanto** *therefore* and **así** *so*.

- Reinforce or clarify what you've said with **es decir** *that is, i.e.* or **por ejemplo** *for example*.

- Provide detail with **donde** *where*, **cuando** *when* and **mientras** *while, whereas*.

- Introduce an explanation with **porque** *because*, **ya que** or **puesto que**, both meaning *since*, or **dado que** *given that*.

- Show there's a consequence with **entonces** or **pues**, both meaning *then*, or **por consiguiente** *as a result*.

- Introduce a condition with **si** *if*.

which, who, whom, whose, that

These words are used to join together parts of a sentence and save having to repeat a noun or a phrase when you're giving additional information about it. Grammatically they're known as **relative pronouns**, and the one used most in Spanish is **que**.

- **Que** has several different meanings and uses (pages 49, 67 and 128). One of these is as a relative pronoun meaning *who, whom, which, that*. **Que** is never left out of a sentence as *who, whom, which, that* very often are in English.

  mi hermano, que vive conmigo *my brother, who lives with me*
  el hombre que tú no conoces *the man (whom) you don't know*
  las fotos que te he prometido *the photos (which) I've promised you*
  las botas que compré *the boots (which) I bought*

  Note that in a question, *who/whom* is **quién** (page 129).

- After a preposition, you use **el/la/los/las que** or **quien/quienes** instead of **que**. These agree with what they're referring to.
  El/la/los/las que are used to refer to people or things but **quien/quienes** can only be used with people.
  el hombre con el que/quien vivo *the man I live with*
  la casa en la que vivo *the house I live in*
  los directores para los que/quienes trabajo *the managers I work for/for whom I work*
  las casas de las que hablaba *the houses I was talking about*

  When **a** and **de** come before **el que**, they combine as **al que** and **del que**.
  el cliente al que/a quien escribo *the customer I'm writing to*
  el actor del que/de quien te hablo *the actor I'm talking to you about*

- **El que, la que, los que, las que** also mean *the one(s) who/which* or *those who/which*.
  Esa actriz es la que quiero ver. *That actress is the one (who) I want to see.*
  Estos zapatos son los que voy a llevar. *These shoes are the ones/those (which) I'm going to wear.*

- **El cual, la cual, los cuales, las cuales** can be used instead of **el que, la que, los que, las que** but their use is confined mainly to more formal language and literary texts.
  la casa en la cual vivo *the house I live in (in which I live)*
  las colegas con las cuales trabajo *the colleagues I work with*

- **Lo que** *which* is used when you're referring to an idea rather than to a particular noun. It sometimes conveys *and this*.
  Dice que es imposible, lo que no es verdad. *He says it's impossible, which isn't true.*
  El alojamiento es lujoso, lo que se refleja en el precio. *The accommodation is luxurious, and this is reflected in the price.*

- **Cuyo, cuya, cuyos, cuyas** mean *whose* and agree with the noun that follows:
  El hombre cuya mujer es inglesa quiere conocerte. *The man whose wife is English wants to meet you.*
  Éste es el tío en cuya casa me quedaba. *This is the uncle in whose house I used to stay.*
  Es la florista cuyas rosas son magníficas. *It's the florist whose roses are magnificent.*

checkpoint 10

1   Which of these would you use:

estoy de acuerdo   según yo   ¡Caramba!
¡Bah!   entonces   de hecho

   a to reinforce what you've just been saying?
   b to say you agree with someone?
   c if you don't know and don't much care?
   d when offering your opinion?
   e to express annoyance?
   Which one is left over and what does it mean?

2   What's the English for que, quien and cual in the following?
   a la fruta que he comprado   b el hombre que vive aquí
   c ¿Quién trabaja allí?   d el año en el que nací
   e los chicos, la mayoría de los cuales llevaban uniforme
   f una persona a quien puedo decir todo
   g Mi amiga llega hoy, lo que me alegra mucho.

3   Do you need cuyo, cuya, cuyos or cuyas in the gap?
   He hablado con Laura, _____ hijos conocen a Andrés.

4   Fill these gaps with cuyas, la cual, el que, que, quiénes, cuáles.
   a ¿Con _____ queréis ir al parque?
   b Este es el carnicero _____ chuletas son ricas.
   c La hermana de Felipe, _____ vive cerca de aquí, es
      muy guapa.
   d Pienso _____ no voy a salir esta tarde.
   e El perro de mi hija, _____ tiene cinco años, es un poco
      travieso.

5   What's the opposite of por una parte?

6   How do you say in my opinion in Spanish?

7   Which of these means the same as sin embargo: de hecho,
   entonces, no obstante?

Prepositions

Prepositions are words like *at*, *in*, *on*, *of*, *with*, *to*, *between*:
- I'm **at** home.
- He's going **to** Spain, **with** her.
- It's **in** the office, **by** the phone.

In Spanish they usually have a noun or a pronoun after them; they never go at the end of a sentence or question as they often do in English:
¿Con quién vas? *Who are you going with?* lit. *With whom are you going?*
¿Para qué banco trabajas? *Which bank do you work for?* lit. *For which bank do you work?*

A few Spanish and English prepositions correspond directly: **con** *with*, **contra** *against*, **durante** *during*, **sin** *without*. But this isn't the case for the widely used **a**, **de**, and **en**. For example:
- Spanish **en** is used where English uses *in*, *on*, *at* and *into*. **De** can mean *from* as **de Málaga** *from Malaga* but it also has other meanings, such as **de mi hermano** *my brother's*, **de plástico** *(made) of plastic*.

- Certain verbs are always followed by **a** or **de**. These are not translated into English; they're simply part of that verb: **jugar al tenis** *to play tennis*; **salir de la casa** *to leave the house*.

It's therefore more effective to associate a preposition with the way it's used rather than look for a straight translation.

a

A, which becomes **al** when followed by **el** *the*, is used for:

- *to* + a person:
  He escrito ... *I've written ...*
  ... a María. *... to Maria.*
  ... a mi padre. *... to my father.*
  ... al director. *... to the manager.*
  ... a la profesora. *... to the teacher.*
  ... a los estudiantes. *... to the students.*

- *to* + places and destinations:
  Se ha ido al aeropuerto. *He's gone to the airport.*
  Voy a Alicante. *I'm going to Alicante.*

- *at* + place but only when motion is implied, otherwise use **en** (page 104):
  Llegó tarde a la oficina. *He arrived late at the office.*
  Te busco al hotel. *I'll pick you up at the hotel.*

- *at* + time:
  ¿A qué hora llega/sale? *What time does it arrive/leave?*
  a mediodía/medianoche *at 12 noon/midnight*
  a la una *at one o'clock*
  a las diez *at ten o'clock*

- *at/a* + prices and rates:
  a cuatro euros el kilo *at four euros a kilo*
  a cien kilómetros por hora *at 100 kph*
  tres veces al día *three times a day*
  a diario *daily*

- *from/off* + a person after verbs such as **comprar** *to buy*, **confiscar** *to confiscate*, **quitar** *to take away*, **robar** *to rob*:
  Compré mi coche a un amigo. *I bought my car from a friend.*
  Le robaron el dinero al turista. *They stole the tourist's money.*

- *on* followed by an infinitive translated in English as *-ing* (page 114):
  al terminar el vino *on finishing the wine*
  al salir del teatro *on leaving the theatre*

A is also used:

- when talking about direction, distance and location:
  la primera a la derecha/la izquierda *the first on the right/left*
  Está a dos kilómetros/dos horas. *It's two kilometres/three hours away.*
  Segovia está al norte de Madrid. *Segovia is north of Madrid.*

- to indicate manner or means:
  a caballo *on horseback;* **a pie** *on foot*
  a lápiz *in pencil;* **a mano** *by hand*
  a la americana *(in) the American way*
  a escape *at full speed;* **a solicitud** *on request*
  dos a dos *two by two;* **cocina a gas** *gas stove*

- to describe food and drink:
  calamares a la romana *fried squid rings in batter*
  champiñones al ajillo *mushrooms with garlic*
  gambas a la plancha *grilled prawns*
  dorada al horno *baked sea bream*

- after certain adjectives:
  dispuesto a salir *ready to go out*
  obligado a irse *obliged to leave*
  parecido a su padre *similar to his father*

- after certain verbs (pages 190-192):
  Aprendo a nadar. *I'm learning to swim.*
  Empieza a llover. *It's starting to rain.*

- between a verb and its direct object when that object is a specific person or a pet. This is called the personal **a** and it's not translated in English:
  Quiero a mi marido. *I love my husband.*
  La niña adora a su cachorro. *The little girl adores her puppy.*
  Exception: **tener** *to have* is not followed by the personal **a**:
  Tengo un hijo y dos hijas. *I've got one son and two daughters.*

de

De, which becomes **del** when followed by **el** *the*, is used for:

- *from* + time, distance, origin:
  de lunes a viernes *from Monday to Friday*
  del diecisiete al veintisiete de mayo *from the 17th to 27th of May*
  Está lejos del mar. *It's a long way from the sea.*
  ¿Cuánto hay de aquí a Toledo? *How far is Toledo from here?*
  ¿De dónde eres? *Where are you from?*
  Soy de Londres. *I'm from London.*
  Tengo una carta de mi tía. *I've got a letter from my aunt.*

- *of*
  una taza de té *a cup of tea;* **un kilo de tomates** *a kilo of tomatoes*
  un niño de cinco años *a child of five;* **cada uno de vosotros** *each of you*

- *(made) of*
  una camisa de seda *a silk shirt;* **botas de piel** *leather boots*
  puertas de madera *wooden doors*
  ¿Es de lana? ¿De algodón? *Is it wool? Cotton?*

- *as a*
  De estudiante era deportista. *As a student he was sporty.*
  De niño tenía un gato. *When I was little I had a cat.*
  Va vestida de hombre. *She's dressed as a man.*

- *about*
  Hablan de política. *They're talking about politics.*
  Se queja de la lluvia. *He's complaining about the rain.*

- *than* with numbers (pages 26-27).
  Tienes más de cien euros. *You've got more than 100 euros.*
  Tengo menos de cincuenta euros. *I've got less than 50 euros.*

- *in* after superlatives
  Es el hombre más alto del mundo. *He's the tallest man in the world.*
  Es la ciudad más grande de España. *It's the largest town in Spain.*
  and with some expressions relating to time:
  a las siete de la mañana *at seven in the morning*
  a las tres de la tarde *at three in the afternoon*

- when attaching a price or value to a noun:
  un sello de noventa céntimos *a 90-cent stamp*
  el menú de cuarenta euros *the 40-euro menu*
  una casa de cinco millones *a five million (euro) house*

- to indicate purpose, followed by a noun or a verb:
  gafas de sol *sunglasses*
  un reloj de pulsera *a wristwatch*
  una máquina de coser *a sewing machine*
  una máquina de escribir *a typewriter*

- when describing a person:
  el muchacho del pelo largo *the boy with the long hair*
  el hombre de la barba negra *the man with the black beard*
  la chica de los ojos azules *the girl with the blue eyes/the blue-eyed girl*

- where English uses *'s*:
  el periódico de hoy *today's paper*
  la llegada del tren *the train's arrival*
  la casa de Felipe *Philip's house*
  los hijos de la dueña *the landlady's children*

- where English uses two nouns together:
  un helado de fresa *a strawberry ice cream*
  una casa de campo *a country house*
  una película de guerra *a war film*
  una revista de noticias *a news magazine*
  la cáscara de limón *lemon peel*
  los números de teléfono *phone numbers*
  el tren de las once y cinco *the 11.05 train*

- after some adjectives:
  cubierto de nieve *covered in snow*
  contento de estar aquí *pleased to be here*
  cansado de viajar *tired of travelling*
  fácil/difícil de hacer *easy/difficult to do*

- after some verbs (page 193):
  Nos mudamos de casa pronto. *We're moving house soon.*
  Acabo de cenar. *I've just had dinner.*

por

- *for, because of, on behalf of, for the sake of, on account of:*
  Le quiero por su sentido del humor. *I love him for his sense of humour.*
  Por el mal tiempo no podemos salir. *Because of the bad weather we can't go out.*
  Lo hago por él. *I do it for him/on his behalf.*
  Gracias por tu apoyo. *Thanks for your support.*
  Me lo regaló por mi cumpleaños. *He gave it to me for my birthday.*

- *for* meaning *in exchange for:*
  Lo compré por quinientos euros. *I bought it for 500 euros.*
  Quisiera cambiar esta camisa azul por ésta negra. *I'd like to change this blue shirt for this black one.*

- *for* to express duration
  Fuimos a España por dos semanas. *We went to Spain for two weeks.*
  Voy a Madrid por un mes. *I'm going to Madrid for a month.*

- *through, along, around, by (means of):*
  Pasé por Málaga. *I passed through Malaga.*
  Andan por la calle. *They're walking along the street.*
  Está por aquí. *It's around here.*
  por correo *by post;* **por cheque** *by cheque*
  por teléfono *by phone;* **por escrito** *in writing*
  freight: **por tren** *by train;* **por barco** *by boat*

- *per*
  Conduce a ochenta kilómetros por hora. *He's driving at 80 kph.*
  Hay dos entradas por persona. *There are two tickets per person.*

- *by* (in the context of done/made/created by somebody):
  La casa fue construida por mi amigo. *The house was built by my friend.*
  El poema fue escrito por Lorca. *The poem was written by Lorca.*

- with parts of the day:
  No trabaja por la tarde. *She doesn't work in the afternoon.*

- followed by other prepositions to express movement:
  Tienes que pasar por delante de la catedral. *You have to go past the cathedral.*

para

- *for* with time, destination or purpose:
  ¿Estará listo para las ocho? *Will it be ready for eight o'clock?*
  Quisiera una habitación para tres noches. *I'd like a room for three nights.*
  Salieron para Francia ayer. *They left for France yesterday.*
  Las flores son para ti. *The flowers are for you.*
  Estudia para médica. *She's studying to be a doctor.*
  No sirve para nada. *It's no use for anything.*

- *in order to* + infinitive – often translated in English simply as *to*:
  Trabajo para sobrevivir. *I work (in order) to survive.*
  He venido para hablar contigo. *I've come in order to talk to you.*
  Y para concluir … *And to finish …*

- *for* as comparison
  Maria lee bien para su edad. *Maria reads well for her age.*

por or para?

When you're translating *for* into Spanish, you need to be clear when to use **por** and when to use **para**. They're not interchangeable, and using the wrong one could lead you to say something different from what you really mean – as shown in these two sentences.

Compró el coche para su mujer. *He bought the car for his wife.*
The car is intended for his wife as a present.
Compró el coche por su mujer. *He bought the car for his wife.*
He bought it on behalf of his wife because she couldn't.
Lo dejaré para ti. *I'll leave it for you* (as a gift to you).
Lo dejaré por ti. *I'll leave it for you* (on account of you, because you want me to).

When talking about time, **para** carries the idea of purpose or finality, whereas **por** is concerned with the duration of time:
Quisiera una habitación para dos noches. *I'd like a room for two nights.* **Tengo que hacerlo para mañana.** *I've got to do it for tomorrow.*
Voy a España por dos meses. *I'm going to Spain for two months.*

en

- *in/into* + place:
  una casa en el campo *a house in the country*
  Están en las montañas. *They're in the mountains.*
  Se encuentra en el sur de España. *It's in the south of Spain.*
  Viven en Australia. *They live in Australia.*
  Entran en la iglesia. *They go into the church.*

- *in* + years, months, seasons:
  Fui allí en 2009. *I went there in 2009.*
  Voy en agosto. *I'm going in August.*
  en primavera/en otoño *in spring/in autumn*
  en verano/en invierno *in summer/in winter*

- *at:*
  Trabajo en casa. *I work at home.*
  Mis hijas están en el colegio. *My daughters are at school.*
  Esperamos en la parada de autobús. *We're waiting at the bus stop.*
  Estudias en la universidad. *You study at university.*

- *on:*
  Las llaves están en la mesa. *The keys are on the table.*
  Vivís en el primer piso. *You live on the first floor.*
  El gato está sentado en una silla. *The cat is sitting on a chair.*
  La ropa está en el suelo. *The clothes are on the floor.*
  ¿Dónde está en el mapa? *Where is it on the map?*

- *by* + means of transport (for passengers, not freight – see page 102):
  en avión *by plane;* **en barco** *by boat*
  en bicicleta *by bike;* **en autocar** *by coach*
  en coche *by car;* **en tren** *by train*

- after certain verbs (see page 194 for a list):
  Confío en mis amigos. *I trust my friends.*
  Elena insiste en bailar. *Helen is insisting on dancing.*
  Pensamos en él. *We're thinking about him.*

- after some adjectives:
  Marta es buena en matemáticas. *Marta is good at maths.*
  Pepe fue el primero en felicitarla. *Pepe was the first to congratulate her.*

word power

There are many everyday expressions with **a**, **de**, **en**, **por** and **para**:

al final in the end; **a tiempo** on time
al máximo at the most; **al menos** at least
al contrario on the contrary; **a la larga** in the long run
a veces sometimes; **a menudo** often
a la puerta at the door; **a orillas del mar** by the seaside
al aire libre in the open air; **a oscuras** in the dark
al sol in the sun; **a la sombra** in the shade
poco a poco little by little; **a mi ver** in my opinion
a fines del mes at the end of the month
a lo lejos in the distance; **al teléfono** on the phone
a decir verdad to tell the truth

de acuerdo okay; **de cierta manera** in a certain way
de moda in fashion; **de pie** standing
de prisa in a hurry; **de todas formas** in any case
de vacaciones on holiday; **de veras** really
de vez en cuando from time to time
fuera de lo común out of the ordinary
fuera de temporada out of season

en aquella época at that time; **en este momento** at this moment
en cambio on the other hand; **en cuanto** as soon as
en seguida immediately; **en voz baja** in a low voice
en voz alta in a loud voice; **lavar en seco** to dry clean

por favor please; **por excelencia** par excellence
por ejemplo for example; **por casualidad** by chance
por lo menos at least; **por fin** finally, at last
por supuesto of course; **dos por cinco** 2 x 5
por un lado/por una parte on the one hand
por otro lado/por otra parte on the other hand
cien por cien 100%; **el diez por ciento** 10%

para empezar to start with; **leer para sí** to read to oneself
para siempre for ever

other common prepositions

ante *before, faced with*
con *with*
desde *from (time, place), since*
entre *between, among*
hacia *towards, around (time)*
según *according to, depending on*
sobre *on, about, over*

bajo *under, below*
contra *against*
durante *during, for*
excepto *except*
hasta *until, as far as*
sin *without*
tras *after*

Ante el juez, hay que mostrar respeto. *Before the judge, one must show respect.*
Ante esta situación, no podemos hacer nada. *Faced with this situation, we can do nothing.*
Hay polvo bajo la cama. *There's dust under the bed.*
Estamos a veinte grados bajo cero. *It's twenty degrees below zero.*
Un café con leche, por favor. *A coffee with milk, please.*
Jugaron contra el mejor equipo. *They played against the best team.*
Vamos a ir en tren desde Madrid hasta Sevilla. *We're going to go by train from Madrid to Seville.*
Nieva desde el viernes. *It's been snowing since Friday.*
Cantó durante dos horas. *He sang for two hours.*
La farmacia está entre la panadería y la carnicería. *The pharmacy is between the bakery and the butcher's.*
No hay fumadores entre ellos. *There are no smokers amongst them.*
Fueron al bar, excepto yo. *They all went to the bar, except me.*
Tienes que ir hacia la estación. *You have to go towards the station.*
Debéis estar allí hacia las dos. *You should be there around two o'clock.*
Hasta mañana. *See you tomorrow.* lit. *Until tomorrow.*
Siga todo recto hasta los semáforos. *Go straight on as far as the lights.*
Según el pronóstico del tiempo va a hacer sol. *According to the weather forecast, it's going to be sunny.*
Según la película vamos al cine. *Depending on the film, we're going to the cinema.*
Prefiero el té sin azúcar. *I prefer tea without sugar.*
Hay tenedores sobre la mesa. *There are forks on the table.*
Vienen sobre las tres. *They're coming at about three.*
Es un programa sobre la economía. *It's a programme on/about the economy.*
Volamos sobre Barcelona. *We're flying over Barcelona.*
Día tras día llueve. *It rains day after day.*

compound prepositions

Some prepositions are two words, the second of which is **a** or **de**.

debido a *due to, owing to, because of*
con rumbo a *in the direction of, on the way to*
en cuanto a *as regards*
en torno a *round, about*
frente a *faced with, in front of*
junto a *next to*
pese a *in spite of*

Debido al trabajo, vuelve tarde. *Because of work, he comes home late.*
Su vida gira en torno a su familia. *Her life revolves around her family.*
Pese al tiempo, van a jugar al fútbol. *In spite of the weather, they're going to play football.*

a causa de *because of;* **a pesar de** *in spite of*
a través de *across, through;* **acerca de** *about, concerning*
al final de *at the end of;* **al lado de** *next to*
al pie de *at the foot of;* **aparte de** *apart from*
cerca de *near to;* **debajo de** *beneath*
dentro de *inside, within, in … minutes'/days' etc. time*
después de *after;* **detrás de** *behind*
en vez de *instead of;* **enfrente de** *opposite*
fuera de *outside*

He llegado después de usted. *I arrived after you.*
Estaba detrás de ti. *She was behind you.*
¿Quería té en vez de café? *Would you like tea instead of coffee?*
Está enfrente de la estación. *It's opposite the station.*
Vive fuera del pueblo. *He lives outside the village.*
Dentro de una semana vamos a Mallorca. *In a week's time we're going to Mallorca.*

Without the **de** many of the prepositions can be used as adverbs.

cerca de *near to*	**cerca** *near*
lejos de *far from*	**lejos** *far*
delante de *in front of*	**delante** *in front*
encima de *on top of*	**encima** *on top*

Está cerca del cine. *It's near the cinema.*
El banco está cerca. *The bank is near.*

checkpoint 11

1. Choose a preposition from the box to fill the gap. Each can only be used once.
   a. Llegamos ___ aeropuerto.
   b. Carmen es la mujer ___ pelo rubio.
   c. Lo hacemos ___ ella.
   d. Las flores son ___ tu madre.
   e. ¿Quiere usted algo ___ comer?
   f. El tren sale ___ las siete.
   g. Mi hermano vive ___ Alemania.

a
del
de
por
al
en
para

2. What's the English for all these houses?
   a. una casa a orillas del mar
   b. una casa de treinta y cinco millones de euros
   c. la casa de mi tío
   d. una casa para las vacaciones
   e. una casa de madera
   f. una casa de campo
   g. una casa en las Canarias
   h. una casa al pie de los Pirineos
   i. una casa al lado del parque
   j. la casa de mis abuelos
   k. una casa de tres pisos
   l. una casa entre dos calles

3. What are these phrases in Spanish?
   a. *Paco's car*
   b. *a phone number*
   c. *orange peel*
   d. *each of us*
   e. *at the end of the film*
   f. *my mother's cousin*
   g. *the doctor's address*
   h. *the 09.55 train*

4. How would you say *to wait for* in Spanish?

5. In **la más grande reserva marina del mundo**, what does **del** mean?

6. What are **zapatos de tenis, zapatos de cuero**, and **zapatos de tacón**?

7. How do you say *It's behind the bank* in Spanish?

8. Decide which prepositions are missing from ___ **moto** *by motorbike*, ___ **vía aérea** *by airmail;* ___ **las dos** *for/by two o'clock;* **pintado** ___ **Picasso** *painted by Picasso*.

Verbs: overview

Verbs are the words we use to say

- what people and things are and have: *be, exist, have*
- what happens to them: *live, die, become, change, break*
- what they do physically: *breathe, eat, run, wait, arrive*
  … and mentally: *like, believe, decide, respect, dream, analyse*

In a dictionary you find the **infinitive** of a verb. In English, this is the basic verb, which can have *to* in front of it: *(to) invite, (to) depend, (to) decide*. In Spanish, infinitives are identified by their ending, which can be **-ar**, **-er** or **-ir**: **invitar**, **depender**, **decidir**. When you remove **-ar**, **-er**, **-ir**, you're left with the stem of the verb: **invit-**, **depend-**, **decid-**. A range of other endings can now be added to this stem, each of them conveying precise information about

- how the verb is being used = **mood**
- when it's happening: present, past or future = **tense**
- who/what is doing it = **person**

Each of the **-ar**, **-er** and **-ir** verb groups has sets of regular endings, and most verbs use these endings. However, some verbs are irregular and need to be learnt individually.

Some verbs have **-se** *oneself* at the end of the infinitive. Called reflexive verbs, many – but not all – of these include *oneself* or *get* in the English translation: **casarse** *to get married*, **lavarse** *to wash (oneself)*, **divertirse** *to enjoy oneself*.

When they're not in the infinitive, reflexive verbs have the same endings as other verbs but they also have to be accompanied by a reflexive pronoun e.g. **me**, **te**, **se** (page 117).

moods and tenses

Modo *mood* refers to how the verb is being used.

Infinitive	the name of the verb, i.e. the basic dictionary form: *(to) work*.
Indicative	indicating that facts are being talked about: *I work, they were working, he doesn't work, do you work?*
Conditional	referring to a hypothetical situation, often involving conditions: *we would work if… /but….*
Subjunctive	conveying that the verb is not fact but is subject to opinion, speculation, attitude or emotion: *if you were to work, should I ever work, if only I'd worked.*
Imperative	giving an instruction: *Work! Let's work!*

Tiempo *tense* refers to when the verb is happening: in the past, present or future. Tenses have names, e.g. present, perfect, imperfect. English has

- two simple one-word tenses: I work, I worked

- many compound tenses which use extra words with the basic verb, e.g. *I am working, I will work, I was working, I have worked, I have been working, I had worked*

Spanish too has simple and compound tenses but, as you see from the table opposite, the balance is different. In Spanish there are far more simple tenses, where the ending of the verb supplies all the necessary information without the need for any extra words.

You'll find it much easier to use Spanish tenses correctly if you make a point of remembering that the only extra words you'll use relate to *have* and *had*.

You can then concentrate on endings. Even if you think these look complicated at first, you'll find that you soon start to make subconscious associations. For example, you'll associate endings with a distinctive **r** sound with *will/would do something*.

Infinitive	cantar *to sing*	
stem	cant	

Indicative

Present	canto	*I sing, I'm singing*
Future	cantaré	*I will/shall sing*
Imperfect	cantaba	*I was singing, I used to sing*
Preterite	canté	*I sang*
Perfect	he cantado	*I have sung, I sang*
Future perfect	habré cantado	*I will have sung*
Pluperfect	había cantado	*I had sung*

Conditional

Present	cantaría	*I would sing*
Perfect	habría cantado	*I would have sung*

Subjunctive

Present	cante	*I sing*
Imperfect	cantara/cantase	*I sang*
Perfect	haya cantado	*I have sung, I sang*
Pluperfect	hubiera/hubiese cantado	*I had sung*

Imperative

	¡Canta! ¡Cantad!	*Sing!*
	¡Cantemos!	*Let's sing!*

Verbs also have:

Past participle	cantado	*sung*
Gerund	cantando	*singing*

person

The person of a verb refers to who/what is making the verb happen.

A verb has three persons in the singular and three in the plural:

1st person singular	**yo**	*I*
2nd person singular	**tú**	*you*
3rd person singular	**él, ella, usted**	*he, she, you, it*

1st person plural	**nosotros/as**	*we* (m/f)
2nd person plural	**vosotros/as**	*you* (m/f)
3rd person plural	**ellos/ellas, ustedes**	*they* (m/f), *you*

This is the order verbs are set out in, with each group of verbs (**-ar**, **-er** and **-ir**) having a specific ending for each of these six persons in each of the various moods and tenses.

The precise information transmitted by verb endings is the reason why **yo, tú, él, ella, usted, nosotros/as, vosotros/as, ellos/ellas, ustedes** aren't always needed and why they're omitted more often than not. They're only really used for emphasis (page 83) or to make it clear who the third person singular is (i.e. *he, she, it* or *you*).

In English there's only one word for *you*, while Spanish has four:
tú: someone you call by their first name
usted: someone you don't know well, someone older than you
vosotros/as: more than one person you're on familiar terms with
ustedes: more than one person you don't know well
Tú and **vosotros/as** are called the *familiar* or *informal you* and **usted/ustedes** the *formal you*.

Nosotros, vosotros and **ellos** are used for males and mixed groups; **nosotras, vosotras** and **ellas** are used for females.

verb groups and irregular verbs

Many English verbs follow predictable patterns. These verbs are called regular verbs and once you know the patterns you can apply them to all regular verbs:

to work	*I work*	*I worked*	*I have worked*
to believe	*I believe*	*I believed*	*I have believed*

Irregular verbs are verbs that deviate from the regular patterns.

to be	*I am*	*I was*	*I have been*
to go	*I go*	*I went*	*I have gone*
to hide	*I hide*	*I hid*	*I have hidden*

Spanish verbs divide into three groups, according to whether the infinitive ends in **-ar**, **-er** or **-ir**. Each group has sets of endings for each of the tenses and moods; and once you know a set of endings you can apply them to all the regular verbs in that group.

Each group also includes some irregular verbs which have to be remembered separately.

In Spanish and English, some of the most widely used verbs, such as **ser** *to be* and **ir** *to go*, are irregular. But a verb that's irregular in English isn't necessarily irregular in Spanish, and vice versa.

One ending for each of six persons in each of the moods and tenses sounds like a huge number of endings to learn – but in reality you'll find that the various endings for each person have a similarity across the tenses that makes most of them instantly recognisable. For example, the first person plural ending in the present, imperfect, preterite, future, conditional and subjunctive all end in **-mos**.

the infinitive

The infinitive is the basic form of a verb that you find in a dictionary, ending in -ar, -er or -ir: **visitar** *visit*, **beber** *drink*, **dormir** *sleep*.

The infinitive corresponds to both *to* ... and ... *ing* in English; it's used:

- after another verb, sometimes separated by **a** or **de** (page 190-193):
  Quiero ir solo. *I want to go alone.*
  Prefiero ir solo. *I prefer to go/going alone.*
  Empecé a ir solo. *I started to go alone.*
  Traté de ir solo. *I tried going alone.*

- after adjectives, either directly or linked by **de** or **para**:
  Es inútil ir. *It's no use going.*
  Es tan difícil creerlo. *It's so difficult to believe it.*
  ¿No es posible reservar? *Isn't it possible to book?*
  Está cansado de trabajar. *He's tired of working.*
  Estoy harto de esperar. *I'm fed up of waiting.*
  ¿Estás lista para salir? *Are you ready to go out?*

- after all prepositions:
  en vez de emigrar *instead of emigrating*
  además de tener miedo *besides being afraid*
  antes de ir *before leaving*
  Se fue sin llamarme. *He left without phoning me.*

- as a noun, with or without *the*, where in English we use ... *ing*.
  Vivir aquí es un privilegio. *Living here is a privilege.*
  El fumar es malo para la salud. *Smoking is bad for the health.*
  Bostezar es contagioso. *Yawning is contagious.*
  El esquiar es como ir en bicicleta. *Skiing is like riding a bike.*
  Viajar ensancha la mente. *Travelling broadens the mind.*

Spanish does have a verb form called the gerund, which also translates as -*ing*, but don't be tempted to use it in any of the circumstances listed opposite. See pages 162-164.

The infinitive can also used be used for orders and instructions, instead of the imperative (page 167):
Empujar. *Push.* **Tirar.** *Pull.*
Abrocharse el cinturón de seguridad. *Fasten your safely belts.*
Rellenar el cuestionario. *Complete the questionnaire.*
No pulsar este botón. *Don't press this button.*
Mezclar todos los ingredientes … *Mix all the ingredients* …
… **y calentar.** … *and heat up.*

verbs in a dictionary

In a dictionary, *v* stands for **verbo** *verb*. Next to the *v*, you'll find further information:
irr: irregular
pp: past participle, if this is irregular
rfl: reflexive
i: intransitive, needing only a subject; does not have a direct object: *go, laugh*
t or *tr* : transitive, needing a subject and a direct object: *give, use*
Many verbs can be both transitive and intransitive: *he's reading, he's reading a book; I continued, I continued the story.*

If you look up *change*, this is what you might find:

change 1. *vt* cambiar, transformar: *to ~ the topic* cambiar de asunto **2.** *vi* cambiar: *his voice ~d* su voz ha cambiado **3.** *v rfl* cambiarse: *to get ~d* cambiarse de ropa **4.** *n* cambio *m*, transformación *f* **5.** *[money]* suelto *m*, sencillo *m* **6.** *the ~ [of life]* la menopausia *f*

reflexive verbs: infinitives

Reflexive verbs have -**se** at the end of the infinitive. There's no consistent English equivalent, although many reflexive verbs include *get* or *oneself* in the translation:

aburrirse *to get bored*
acostarse *to go to bed*
acostumbrarse *to get used to*
afeitarse *to shave (oneself)*
alegrarse *to be glad*
cansarse *to get tired of*
casarse *to get married*
bañarse *to bathe (oneself)*
despertarse *to wake (oneself) up*
divertirse *to enjoy oneself*
dormirse *to fall asleep*
ducharse *to shower (oneself)*
emborracharse *to get drunk*
enamorarse *to fall in love*
equivocarse *to be wrong*
lavarse *to wash (oneself), to get washed*
levantarse *to get (oneself) up*
llamarse *to be called,* lit. *to call oneself*
quejarse *to complain*
acordarse *to remember,* lit. *to remind oneself*
sentirse *to feel*
vestirse *to get dressed*

Se means *oneself*, so when you want to say *myself, yourself, ourselves*, etc., you need to replace **se** with one of the other reflexive pronouns – **me, te, se, os, nos** or **se** (page 87):
Me acuesto a las diez. *I go to bed at ten.*
Quiero enamorarme. *I'd like to fall in love.*
¿Vas a levantarte temprano? *Are you going to get up early?*
Comenzamos a aburrirnos. *We were beginning to get fed up.*

… and various tenses

levantarse *to get up* lit. *to raise oneself*

present	**me levanto** *I get up*
	te levantas *you get up*
	se levanta *he, she/you get(s) up*
	nos levantamos *we get up*
	os levantáis *you get up*
	se levantan *they get up*
future	**me levantaré** *I will get up*
conditional	**me levantaría** *I would get up*
imperfect	**me levantaba** *I used to get up*
preterite	**me levanté** *I got up*

In compound tenses, reflexive verbs use *haber*:

perfect	**me he levantado** *I got up*
pluperfect	**me había levantado** *I had got up*
future perfect	**me habré levantado** *I will have got up*
past conditional	**me habría levantado** *I would have got up*

Reflexive verbs are often used with parts of the body, without the need for a possessive adjective (page 77):
Me lavo el pelo. *I wash my hair.*
Se lava los dientes. *He cleans his teeth.*

Some reflexive verbs can also be used without a reflexive pronoun as non-reflexive verbs:
Me levanté a las ocho. *I got up at eight.*
Levanté a mi hija a las ocho. *I got my daughter up at eight.*

word **power**

While hundreds of verbs are very similar in English and Spanish, there's a vital difference in the position of the stress. In English verbs it varies: _imitate_, _imagine_, _control_ – but it doesn't move from that syllable. In Spanish verbs, the stress on the infinitive is always on the ending: **imitar**, **imaginar**, **controlar** but this changes when the verb has other endings: **controlo** / _control_, **controlaré** / _will control_ (see page 18 for more on stress).

Notice how these Spanish verbs correspond to their English equivalents when you remove or change the verb ending.

🇬🇧	🇪🇸	
_	-ar	abandonar, calmar, confesar, consultar , controlar, costar, depositar, detestar, importar, informar, insultar, inventar, presentar, protestar, telefonear, visitar
-e	-ar	acusar, adorar, basar, causar, combinar, comparar, conservar, continuar, curar, examinar, imaginar, invitar, notar, preservar, usar, votar
-ate	-ar	celebrar, colaborar, comunicar, crear, cultivar, dedicar, educar, elevar, eliminar, emigrar, implicar, indicar, interrogar, iluminar, nominar, penetrar
-ise	-izar	antagonizar, fraternizar, idealizar, industrializar, marginalizar, materializar, modernizar, monopolizar, naturalizar, neutralizar, organizar, pulverizar, realizar, socializar, vaporizar, utilizar but not _apologise_ disculparse, _fantasise_ fantasear, _idolise_ idolatrar or _recognise_ reconocer
ify	-ficar	amplificar, certificar, clasificar, falsificar, gratificar, identificar, modificar, notificar, pacificar, petrificar, simplificar, significar, solidificar, unificar, verificar but not _horrify_ horrorizar or _terrify_ aterrar

- While the meaning of many Spanish verbs is immediately obvious (e.g. **copiar, programar, digitalizar**) others can be deduced from related English words:
  escribir *to write (scribe),* **lanzar** *to throw (lance),* **odiar** *to hate (odious),* **permanecer** *to remain (permanent),* **pensar** *to think (pensive),* **respirar** *to breathe (respiration),* **valer** *to be worth (value).*

Don't forget to take predictable letter changes into account in verbs such as **aceptar, acompañar, acumular, acusar, especializarse, especificar, estimular, estrangular, estudiar, expresar, progresar, fotocopiar, fotografiar, recomendar, respetar.** If you're not sure what any of them mean, check with pages 22-23.

false friends

apuntar means *to write down*
asistir a means *to attend*
contestar means *to answer*
importar means *to be important*
introducir means *to introduce something*
pretender means *to claim, to intend*
realizar means *to realise a dream/project*
recordar means *to remember*
soportar means *to put up with*
suspender means *to fail (exam)*
tranquilizar means *to calm down/ reassure*

to appoint is **nombrar**
to assist is **ayudar**
to contest is **refutar**
as well as *to import*
to introduce someone is **presentar**
to pretend is **fingir**
to realise (become aware) is **darse cuenta**
to record is **grabar**
to support is **apoyar**
as well as *to suspend*
as well as *to tranquillise*

checkpoint 12

1   Two of these words are not verbs. Can you identify them?*
    know, negotiate, applaud, arrival, disintegrate, play, depend, deep, realise, depart.

2   Which of these words can be a verb and a noun in English?
    disturb, describe, deny, distribute, deliver, dream.

3   What are the infinitive endings for the three groups of Spanish verbs?

4   Does *mood* or *tense* refer to the time something takes place?

5   In Spanish who's doing something when a verb is in the first person singular? And the third person plural?

6   In Spanish how many words are there for *you* and what are they?

7   In Spanish, how do you say *smoking* when it's used as a noun e.g. *Smoking kills?*

8   If you saw **Tirar** on a door, would you push or pull?

9   What does *v irr* signify next to a word in a dictionary? And *v rfl*?

10 What's the English for **pretender**?

11 Taking into account the rules for double letters (pages 22-23) work out the Spanish for *to accelerate, to illustrate, to separate* and the English for **comercializar, caramelizar** and **paralizar**.

12 Given that the prefix **des-** can signify an opposite meaning, and that the prefix **re-** is often the equivalent of *re-/again* in English, guess what these verbs mean: **desconectar, desfigurar, desinfectar, desmoralizar, recomenzar, reciclar, recrear.**

*If ever you're not sure, remember that you can put *to* in front of a verb and *the* in front of a noun.

Negatives and questions

There are two structural differences in the way English and Spanish negatives are formed:

- In Spanish, unlike English, both **no** *no*, *not* and a negative word like **nada** *nothing* or **nunca** *never* can be used in the same sentence.
- In the simple (one-word) tenses, English uses the words *do*, *does*, or *did*. These have no equivalent in Spanish, which just inserts **no** before the verb:
  Vivo aquí. *I live here.*
  No vivo aquí. *I do not live here.*

English also uses *do*, *does* and *did* to ask questions, or it reverses the order of the subject and verb: *Do you live here? Is she ill?* Spanish simply reverses the order of the subject and the verb, but this is sometimes not obvious when the subject of the sentence is contained within the verb: **¿Vives aquí?** *Do you live here?* **¿Está enferma?** *Is she ill?* **¿Han llegado tus amigos?** *Have your friends arrived?*

Question words, i.e. words like **cuándo** *when*, **cómo** *how*, **dónde** *where*, **por qué** *why*, have an accent to distinguish them from the same words used in statements. They go at the beginning of the question and the verb comes straight after:
¿Cuándo empieza el partido? *When does the match start?*

Most question words don't change. But **cuál** *which* has a plural form, and **cuánto** *how much* agrees with the noun it relates to.

no

To say something negative in Spanish the key word is **no** *no/not*, which you put before the verb. You don't translate the English words *do*, *does* or *did*.

Soy español. *I'm Spanish.*
No soy español. *I'm not Spanish.*
Hablo español. *I speak Spanish.*
No hablo español. *I do not/don't speak Spanish.*
Laura no habla español. *Laura does not/doesn't speak Spanish.*
¿No habla Laura español? *Doesn't Laura speak Spanish?*
Tienen dos hijos. *They have two children.*
No tienen hijos. *They don't have children./They haven't got children.*

- In compound (two-word) tenses, **no** goes before **haber** or **estar**:
  He terminado. *I've finished.*
  No he terminado. *I haven't finished.*
  Ha llegado. *She's arrived.*
  No ha llegado. *She hasn't arrived.*
  Habíamos pagado. *We had paid.*
  No habíamos pagado. *We hadn't paid.*
  Estamos comiendo. *We're eating.*
  No estamos comiendo. *We're not eating.*

- **No** normally goes before pronouns (see page 86):
  No me gusta el café. *I don't like coffee.*
  No se puede negar que … *One can't deny that …*
  No te creo. *I don't believe you.*
  ¿No le has escrito? *Haven't you written to her?*
  ¿No te levantas a las siete? *Don't you get up at seven o'clock?*
  No me lo has dado. *You haven't given it to me.*

> **No** is also the Spanish for *No*, which means that you often have the word repeated: **No, no me lo has dado**, *No, you haven't given it to me.*

position of negative words

Unlike English, Spanish uses double negatives. You always need **no** in the same sentence as a negative word like the following:

nadie *nobody/not ... anybody*
nada *nothing/not ... anything*
nunca/jamás *never/not even*
tampoco *not either*
ni … ni *neither … nor*
ni siquiera *not even*
más *no longer/not any more:*

- With simple (one-word) tenses, the word order is:
  no + verb + negative word:
  No veo a nadie aquí. *I don't see anyone here.*
  Luisa no come nada. *Luisa isn't eating anything.*
  No entienden nada. *They understand nothing.*
  No como nunca carne. No como jamás carne. *I never eat meat.*
  No me gusta tampoco. *I don't like it either.*
  No como ni carne ni pescado. *I don't eat meat or fish.*
  ¿No comes ni siquiera los huevos? *Don't you even eat eggs?*
  No vivo más en España. *I no longer live in Spain.*

- With compound (two-word) tenses, negative words go after the past participle. Unlike in English, **nunca** *never* cannot go in between *have/has* and the past participle:
  No he ido <u>nunca</u> a la India. *I have <u>never</u> been to India.*
  No ha venido nadie. *Nobody has come.*
  Luisa no ha comido nada. *Luisa hasn't eaten anything.*
  No han entendido nada. *They haven't understood anything.*
  No he comido ni carne ni pescado. *I haven't eaten meat or fish. I've eaten neither meat nor fish.*
  No ha llamado ni siquiera. *He hasn't even rung.*

use of negative words

No + verb + **ninguno/ninguna** + noun *no/not … any*.
When using **ninguno**, you need to remember:

- it's only used with a singular noun – even though the English translation might be plural
- it's an adjective and so agrees with the noun
- it drops the **-o** in front of a masculine singular noun (page 33) and adds an accent
- it gives a stronger negative meaning than just using **no**:
  No tengo ningún problema. *I have no problems.*
  No hay ningún error. *There's no mistake.*
  No respeta ninguna regla. *He doesn't respect any rules.*
  No hay ninguna otra solución. *There's no other solution.*

Alguno/alguna after the noun can be used instead of **ninguno** to give a more emphatic negative meaning:
No hay error alguno. *There's no mistake at all/whatsoever.*

Nada generally means *nothing* but can also be used for *not at all:*
No me gusta nada. *I don't like it at all.*

Nunca and **jamás** both mean *never*, but **jamás** is stronger and is used less. They can be used together to reinforce each other:
No quiero verte nunca jamás. *I don't ever want to see you again.*

When **nadie** *nobody* is the object of the verb it's preceded by the personal **a** (page 99):
No he visto a nadie. *I've seen nobody. I haven't seen anybody.*

Ni on its own can mean *not even, not a single:*
Ni saca la basura. *He doesn't even take the rubbish out.*
No hay ni una barra de pan. *There's not a single loaf of bread.*

Tampoco *not either* is the negative of **también** *also, too:*
Me gusta la cerveza también. *I also like beer.*
No me gusta tampoco la cerveza. *I don't like beer either.*

You don't use **no**:

- when a negative word/phrase is used on its own:

Who did you see?	**Nadie**. *Nobody.*
What did you do?	**Nada**. *Nothing.*
Will you go again?	**Nunca**. *Never.*
I didn't see it.	**Yo tampoco**. *Me neither.*

- when a negative word comes before the verb:
  ¿Nadie quiere ir? *Doesn't anybody want to go?*
  Nada pasó. *Nothing happened.*

It's possible to use several negatives together in one sentence:
Nunca quiere hacer nada. *He never wants to do anything.*
Nadie viene nunca a visitarme. *Nobody ever comes to visit me.*

sino (que)

The Spanish for *but* is usually **pero**, but after a negative statement you use **sino**. **Sino** can also mean *rather, but rather* or *instead*.
Podríamos ir en coche <u>pero</u> prefiero ir en tren. *We could go by car but I prefer to go by train.*
No viajamos en coche <u>sino</u> en tren. *We don't travel by car but by train.*
When two verbs are contrasted, you use **sino que**:
No llueve sino que nieva. *It's not raining, but rather snowing.*

Negative words feature in many useful phrases.
ahora no *not now*; **hoy no** *not today*; **todavía no** *not yet*
No importa. *It doesn't matter.* **Claro que no.** *Of course not.*
Creo que no. *I don't think so.* **Supongo que no.** *I suppose not.*
Esperas que no. *You hope not.*
yo no *not me*; **ya no** *not any more/no longer* (before the verb)
De nada. *It's nothing. Don't mention it.* **Nada más.** *Nothing more.*
nada malo *not bad*; **bueno para nada** *good for nothing*
¡De ninguna manera!/¡De ningún modo! *No way!*
casi nada *next to nothing*; **casi nadie** *next to nobody*
¡Ni hablar del peluquín! *It's out of the question!*
¡Ni pensarlo! *I wouldn't dream of it!*
¡Ni soñarlo! *Not on your life!*

---

asking questions

- To ask a closed question, expecting the answer *yes* or *no*, English brings in words like *do/does* or reverses the order of the subject and noun:
  Does your friend work here? Is she pregnant?
  In Spanish you simply reverse the order putting question marks at the start and end of the sentence (the first question mark is inverted):
  ¿Trabaja tu amiga aquí? ¿Está embarazada?

- In the perfect tense (page 154) the subject cannot go between the auxiliary verb *have* and the past participle as it can in English.
  ¿Han salido tus padres? *Have your parents gone out?*

- You can add **verdad** or **no** to your question, which correspond to all English question tags like *isn't it, is he, don't we, aren't you, did she, have you, won't they* … so they're really easy to use.
  The opening question mark goes before **verdad/no**, not at the beginning of the sentence.
  Trabajas aquí, ¿verdad?/¿no? *You work here, don't you?*
  No trabajas aquí, ¿verdad? *You don't work here, do you?*
  Está embarazada, ¿verdad?/¿no? *She's pregnant, isn't she?*

- Open-ended questions use question words such as **dónde** *where*, **por qué** *why*. These go at the beginning of the question. Unlike English, Spanish puts the verb straight after the question word and doesn't use extra words like *do/does*:
  ¿Cuándo se termina el concierto? *When does the concert finish?*
  Some question words can be preceded by a preposition:
  ¿Con quién vas al cine? *Who are you going to the cinema with?*
  ¿De dónde eres (tú)? *Where are you from?*

Question words have an accent to distinguish them from the same words used in statements. They retain the accent when used in indirect questions:
¿Dónde vive Marta? *Where does Marta live?*
Ésta es la casa donde vive Marta. *This is the house where Marta lives.*
Me pregunto dónde vive Marta. *I wonder where Marta lives.*

¿cuándo? ¿cómo? ¿dónde? ¿por qué?

Spanish question words fall into two groups: those that don't change and those that change to agree with the noun they're referring to. **¿Cuándo?**, **¿cómo?**, **¿dónde?** and **¿por qué?** never change.

- **¿Cuándo?** *when?*
  ¿Cuándo llegan? *When are they arriving?*
  ¿Cuándo abre el banco? *When does the bank open?*
  ¿Hasta cuándo estás aquí? *Until when are you here?*
  ¿Desde hace cuándo estás aquí? *Since when have you been here?*

- **¿Cómo?** *how?*
  ¿Cómo estás? *How are you?*
  ¿Cómo se dice ... en español? *How do you say ... in Spanish?*
  ¿Sabe usted cómo funciona? *Do you know how it works?*
  ¿Cómo te llamas? *What's your name?* lit. *How do you call yourself?*

> **¿Cómo?** can also be used to mean *Sorry, could you say that again?*

- **¿Dónde?** *where?*, which becomes **adónde** in *where ... to:*
  ¿Dónde está la parada de autobús? *Where's the bus stop?*
  ¿Dónde están las llaves? *Where are the keys?*
  ¿De dónde es usted? *Where are you from?*
  ¿Adónde vas? *Where are you going to?*

- **¿Por qué?** *why?*
  ¿Por qué llega tarde? *Why is she late?*
  ¿Por qué no nos vamos? ¿Por qué no? *Why don't we go? Why not?*
  ¿Por qué tanto interés? *Why so much interest?*

> Don't confuse **por qué** with **porque**, which means *because*.

¿qué? ¿cuál?

¿Qué? *which?, what?* doesn't change and is used in two ways:

- followed by a noun:

    ¿Qué trabajo haces? *What (work) do you do?*
    ¿Qué diferencia hay? *What difference is there?*
    ¿A qué hora? *(At) what time?*
    ¿Qué móvil te gusta más? *Which mobile do you like the most?*
    ¿Qué helado quiere? *Which ice cream would you like?*

- without a noun to ask for general information:

    ¿Qué es? *What is it?*
    ¿Qué puedo hacer? *What can I do?*
    ¿Qué sucede después? *What happens afterwards?*
    ¿Qué quieres comprar? *What do you want to buy?*
    ¿Qué diría Felipe? *What would Felipe say?*

¿Cuál? *which?, what?* is used:

- without a noun to ask for more specific information where there's a choice.
- as a pronoun meaning *which one(s)?*, becoming **cuáles** in the plural.

¿Cuál es el mejor? ¿Cuál? *Which is the best? Which one?*
¿Cuáles prefieres? ¿Cuáles? *Which do you prefer? Which ones?*
¿Cuál es la dirección? *What (lit. which one) is the address?*
¿Cuáles son los riesgos? *What (lit. which ones) are the risks?*
¿Cuál de los dos te gusta más? *Which of the two do you like more?*

The main difference between **qué** and **cuál** is that **qué** can be followed by a noun or a verb but **cuál** can only be followed by a verb (usually **ser** *to be* or **preferir** *to prefer*), or the preposition **de** *of* followed by a pronoun or a noun.

¿quién?

¿Quién? *who?, whom?* changes to **quiénes** in the plural.
¿Quién quiere ser millionario? *Who wants to be a millionaire?*
¿Sabes quién es? *Do you know who he is?*
¿Con quiénes trabajas? *Who (pl) do you work with?*
¿Según quién? *According to whom?*

¿De quién(es)? usually, but not always, means *whose?*:
¿De quién es esta chaqueta ? *Whose is this jacket?*
¿De quién es el coche rojo? *Whose is the red car?*
¿De quiénes son éstas? *Whose (pl) are these?*
¿De quién hablan? *Who are they talking about?*

> When **quién** acts as an object it takes the personal **a**:
> ¿A quién conoces en Madrid? *Who do you know in Madrid?*

¿cuánto?

¿Cuánto? *how?, how much?, how many?* can be used in three ways:
- with a verb, i.e. as an adverb. It doesn't change to agree with anything:
  ¿Cuánto cuesta? *How much does it cost?*
  ¿Cuánto es? *How much is it?*
  ¿Cuánto cuestan éstos? *How much do these cost?*

- with a noun, i.e. as an adjective, so it has to agree with the noun like any
  other adjective ending in **-o** (page 56):
  ¿Cuánto tiempo queda? *How much time is left?*
  ¿Cuánta agua hay? *How much water is there?*
  ¿Cuántos años tienes? *How old are you?*
  ¿Cuántas personas hay? *How many people are there?*

- instead of a noun, i.e. as a pronoun, so it has to agree with the noun
  it replaces:
  El vino: ¿cuánto quieres? *Wine: how much would you like?*
  La cerveza: ¿cuánta quieres? *Beer: how much would you like?*
  Helados: ¿cuántos quieres? *Ice creams: how many would you like?*
  Manzanas: ¿cuántas quieres? *Apples: how many would you like?*

checkpoint 13

1   Write the negative of these sentences.
    a **Trabajan con nosotros.**   b **Juan ha visto la película.**
    c **Me gusta el té.**   d **He estado en Perú.**
    e **Nosotros tenemos hijos.**   f **Yo sé donde viven.**

2   What do these words mean with **no**?
    nada, nadie, nunca, ninguno, ni ... ni, más.

3   **No hay** _____ **vino.**
    Is the missing word **ninguno, ningún,** or **ninguna?**

4   What's missing from this sentence: **No conozco** _____ **nadie?**

5   Rearrange these words to form two sentences.
    a **los ni me gustan ni no cebollas tomates las**
    b **el nunca María comido no avestruz ha**

6   Which two question words change to agree with a noun?

7   Which are the two words you can use for *what?*

8   Rearrange these words to form two questions.
    a **tren ? sale para Barcelona ¿ cúando el**
    b **hablar hermana ¿ quiere ? tu conmigo por qué**

9   What are the two Spanish words for *isn't it?*

10 Complete these questions with a word from the box.
    a ¿ _____ **habitaciones quiere usted?**
    b ¿ _____ **hacemos esta tarde?**
    c ¿De _____ **es usted?**
    d ¿De _____ **son estas revistas?**
    e ¿ _____ **quieres irte mañana?**
    f ¿ _____ **te gusta más?**

> quién
> por qué
> dónde
> cuántas
> qué
> cuál

Verbs: simple tenses

The following pages guide you through the simple tenses of Spanish verbs, showing you how to choose the one you need and which endings are involved.

You need to be familiar with the information on pages 109-117. Briefly:

- the balance of simple (one-word) and compound (two-word) tenses is different in English and Spanish, with the actual endings of Spanish verbs doing away with the need for support words like *am, is, are, will, was, would*.

- the verb endings carry precise information about a) how the verb is being used, b) when it's happening, and c) who/what is doing it. They fit onto the stem of the verb, which you find by removing **-ar**, **-er** or **-ir** from the end of the infinitive:
  trabajar *to work* → **trabaj-**
  vender *to sell* → **vend-**
  vivir *to live* → **viv-**

The replacement endings are very similar – but not identical – for the three groups of verbs. Irregular verbs deviate from the standard patterns in some way, but even most of these have endings that are similar to regular verb patterns.

On the whole it's easy to relate Spanish and English tenses, but you need to watch out for the same English translation being used for more than one Spanish tense. For example, English uses the word *would* in two senses: *We would buy it if we had the money,* which is the conditional, talking about a hypothetical situation, and *We would go back every year when we were little,* which is the imperfect tense, talking about the past.

present tense: regular verbs

	trabajar *to work*	vender *to sell*	vivir *to live*
yo	trabajo	vendo	vivo
tú	trabajas	vendes	vives
él/ella, usted	trabaja	vende	vive
nosotros/as	trabajamos	vendemos	vivimos
vosotros/as	trabajáis	vendéis	vivís
ellos/ellas, ustedes	trabajan	venden	viven

The **nosotros/as** and **vosotros/as** forms are the only ones to have the stress on the ending, like the infinitive. The others are stressed on the preceding syllable. You'll find that **nosotros/as** and **vosotros/as** are often the odd ones out in other ways too.

Most Spanish verbs are regular -ar verbs. The -er and -ir verbs are fewer and generally more irregular, with -ir verbs making up the smallest group.

Of the irregular verbs, there are different degrees of irregularity, but most still follow a recognisable pattern.

- Some verbs only change the letter immediately before certain regular ending to keep the sound the same as in the infinitive (page 133). For example, **dirigir** *to direct* becomes **dirijo** *I direct*.

- Some verbs change the vowel in the stem for all persons except **nosotros/as** and **vosotros/as** and are otherwise regular. These are called radical changing verbs (page 134): **querer** *to want* becomes **yo quiero** and **nosotros queremos**

- Some are very irregular. As in many languages, these are the most widely used verbs. For example, **voy** *I go* comes from **ir** *to go* and **doy** *I give* comes from **dar** *to give* (pages 135, 197-247).

stem spelling changes

Before certain endings, some verbs change the final letter of the stem in order to maintain the same overall sound as the infinitive. In the majority of cases, this involves the letters **c** and **g**, and Sounds and Spelling on page 17 explains how their sounds are affected by the letters that follow them.

In the **yo** form only:
- -ger/-gir → jo
  e.g. **coger** *to catch/grab*, **escoger** *to choose*, **proteger** *to protect*, **recoger** *to pick up*, **exigir** *to demand*, **fingir** *to pretend*
  cojo *I catch*, **finjo** *I pretend*

- -guir → go
  e.g. **distinguir** *to distinguish*, **extinguir** *to extinguish*
  distingo *I distinguish*, **extingo** *I extinguish*

- -cer/-cir → zo
  e.g. **convencer** *to convince*, **ejercer** *to practise* (a profession),
  convenzo *I convince*, **venzo** *I overcome*

- -ecer, -ocer, -ucir → zco
  e.g. **conocer** *to know*, **ofrecer** *to offer*, **reconocer** *to recognise*, **traducir** *to translate*, **conducir** *to drive*
  conozco *I know*, **conduzco** *I drive*

In all forms except **nosotros/as** and **vosotros/as**:
- many infinitives ending in -uir introduce **y**
  e.g. **construir** *to construct*, **contribuir** *to contribute*, **destruir** *to destroy*, **distribuir** *to distribute*, **excluir** *to exclude*, **influir** *to influence*, **incluir** *to include*
  influyo, influyes, influye, influimos, influís, influyen

- verbs with a weak -i or -u before the ending introduce an accent
  e.g. **criar** *to breed, bring up*, **continuar** *to continue*
  crío, crías, cría, criamos, criáis, crían

A few of the verbs that change their spelling are also radical changing (page 134) : **elegir** → **elijo** *I choose*; **cocer** → **cuezo** *I cook*, **seguir** → **sigo** *I follow*.

radical changing verbs

Radical changing verbs change the vowel **e** or **o** in their stem for all persons of the present tense except **nosotros/as** and **vosotros/as**. The endings are the same as for regular verbs.

The following are the most common radical changing verbs:

- **e → ie**
  e.g. **querer** *to want,* **cerrar** *to close,* **comenzar/empezar** *to start,* **pensar** *to think,* **entender** *to understand,* **perder** *to lose,* **preferir** *to prefer,* **sentir** *to feel*
  quiero, quieres, quiere, queremos, queréis, quieren

- **e → i in -ir verbs only**
  e.g. **pedir** *to ask for,* **seguir** *to follow,* **servir** *to serve*
  pido, pides, pide, pedimos, pedís, piden

- **o → ue**
  e.g. **volver** *to return,* **contar** *to count,* **costar** *to cost,* **encontrar** *to find,* **recordar** *to remember,* **doler** *to hurt,* **poder** *to be able,* **dormir** *to sleep,* **morir** *to die*
  vuelvo, vuelves, vuelve, volvemos, volvéis, vuelven

There are others with one-off changes:
jugar *to play* changes **u** to **ue**:
juego, juegas, juega, jugamos, jugáis, juegan
oler *to smell* changes **o** to **ue** and also adds **h** before all forms except **nosotros/as** and **vosotros/as**:
huele, hueles, huele, olemos, oléis, huelen

> The impersonal verbs (page 182) **llueve** *it's raining,* **nieva** *it's snowing* and **hiela** *it's freezing* are all examples of radical changing verbs. They come from **llover** *to rain,* **nevar** *to snow* and **helar** *to freeze.*

... and irregular verbs

Some of the most widely used Spanish verbs have substantial irregularities in the present tense.

	ser *to be*	haber *to have*	ir *to go*
yo	soy	he	voy
tú	eres	has	vas
él/ella, usted	es	ha	va
nosotros/as	somos	hemos	vamos
vosotros/as	sois	habéis	vais
ellos/ellas, ustedes	son	han	van

	tener *to have*	oír *to hear*	decir *to say*
yo	tengo	oigo	digo
tú	tienes	oyes	dices
él/ella, usted	tiene	oye	dice
nosotros/as	tenemos	oímos	decimos
vosotros/as	tenéis	oís	decís
ellos/ellas, ustedes	tienen	oyen	dicen

Several others are irregular in the **yo** form only:

● some end in –**y**:
   dar → **doy** *I give*
   estar → **estoy** *I am*

● some gain a **g**:
   hacer → **hago** *I make*   caer → **caigo** *I fall*
   poner → **pongo** *I put*   traer → **traigo** *I bring*
   salir → **salgo** *I leave*   valer → **valgo** *I'm worth*
   venir → **vengo** *I come*

● and some change completely:
   caber → **quepo** *I fit*
   saber → **sé** *I know*
   ver → **veo** *I see*

All these irregular verbs – and many more – are written out in full in all tenses in the verb tables (pages 194-247).

when to use the present tense

- Present tense endings replace the **-ar**, **-er**, **-ir** of the infinitive when in English you say *I do something* or *I'm doing something*.
  Trabajo en Londres. *I work in London.*
  Trabajamos hoy. *We're working today.*
  Trabajan mañana. *They're working tomorrow.*
  Ana entiende francés. *Ana understands French.*
  Vende helado. *He sells/He's selling ice cream.*
  Se van mañana. *They leave/They're leaving tomorrow.*
  Voy de vacaciones en agosto. *I'm going on holiday in August.*
  Mañana voy de compras. *Tomorrow I'm going shopping.*
  El vuelo sale el lunes. *The flight leaves on Monday.*

- For questions and negatives, you don't need extra words like *do*, *does*, *am*, *is*, *are*.
  ¿Trabajas? *Do you work?*
  ¿Trabajas mañana? *Are you working tomorrow?*
  No trabajo. *I'm not working. I don't work.*
  ¿Entiende Ana francés? *Does Ana understand French?*
  ¿Vende helado? *Is he selling ice cream?*
  No se van mañana. *They're not leaving/They don't leave tomorrow.*

- You use the present tense in questions like these, where English uses *shall*:
  ¿Te espero? *Shall I wait for you?*
  ¿Pago ahora? *Shall I pay now?*
  ¿Comemos? *Shall we eat?*

- You also use this tense with **desde** *since* and **desde hace** *for* to talk about something which started in the past and is still going on, where English uses *have/has been ...ing*.
  Trabajo aquí desde abril. *I've been working here since April.*
  Trabajo aquí desde hace tres años. *I've been working here for three years.*

present continuous

If you need to make the point that something's happening at this very minute, differentiating between e.g. *I'm learning Spanish* and *I'm learning about tenses (right now)*, you can use an alternative to the simple present tense called the present continuous.

This is made up of the present tense of **estar: estoy, estás, está, estamos, estáis, están** + the gerund of the main verb, formed by changing the infinitive endings as follows:

-ar → -ando	**trabajar** *to work*	**trabajando** *working*
-er → -iendo	**vender** *to sell*	**vendiendo** *selling*
-ir → -iendo	**vivir** *to live*	**viviendo** *living*

Some verbs have irregular gerunds (page 162).

¿Qué estás haciendo? *What are you doing right now?*
Estoy pensando en ti. *I'm thinking about you.*
Estamos comiendo. *We're just eating.*
Estoy viendo la tele. *I'm busy watching tv.*
Los tiempos están cambiando. *Times are changing.*

checkpoint 14

1   Write both the present simple and the present continuous of these verbs:

escoger (yo)	**venir (vosotros)**
pedir (nosotros)	**encontrar (usted)**
pensar (tú)	**construir (nosotros)**
decir (ustedes)	**leer (él)**
poder (ellas)	**oír (yo)**
dormir (ella)	**sentir (ellos)**

2   What's the Spanish for these?
   a *We start tomorrow.*   b *Does Paco speak English?*
   c *Shall we eat?*   d *I've been living here for twenty years.*

future tense

The future endings are the same for all three groups. Instead of **replacing** the infinitive ending as they do in other tenses, in the future they're **added** to the infinitive. This means that every single verb has an **-r** immediately before the ending in the future.

	trabajar *to work*	**vender** *to sell*	**vivir** *to live*
yo	trabajar**é**	vender**é**	vivir**é**
tú	trabajar**ás**	vender**ás**	vivir**ás**
él/ella, usted	trabajar**á**	vender**á**	vivir**á**
nosotros/as	trabajar**emos**	vender**emos**	vivir**emos**
vosotros/as	trabajar**éis**	vender**éis**	vivir**éis**
ellos/ellas, ustedes	trabajar**án**	vender**án**	vivir**án**

The **nosotros** ending is the only one that doesn't need an accent in the future.

when to use the future tense

- Future tense endings are added to the infinitive when in English you say *I will/shall do something*:
  Comenzaré mañana. *I'll start tomorrow.*
  Mi madre llegará el lunes. *My mother will arrive on Monday.*
  ¿Dónde dormirás? *Where will you sleep?*
  ¿Cuándo volverán? *When will they come back?*

- It's used in questions, to express speculation:
  ¿Qué fecha será? *I wonder what the date is?*
  ¿Nos visitarán? *I wonder if they'll visit us?*

- It's used to express probability or supposition, where English would also use *must*:
  Serán las siete de la mañana. *It will be/It's probably about seven o'clock in the morning.*
  Estaremos a una hora de la costa. *We must be an hour from the coast.*

irregular future tense forms

There are very few irregular verbs in the future tense. In the ones that are irregular, it's the stem that's different, not the endings.

- Some drop the -e from the infinitive ending:
  haber → **habré** *I will have* (in compound tenses); **poder** → **podré** *I will be able to*; **querer** → **querré** *I will want*; **saber** → **sabré** *I will know*

- Others drop the e or i of the infinitive ending and add **d**:
  poner → **pondré** *I will put*; **tener** → **tendré** *I will have*; **salir** → **saldré** *I will go out*; **venir** → **vendré** *I will come*

- A few have completely irregular stems:
  decir → **diré** *I will say*; **hacer** → **haré** *I will do/make*

---

other ways of talking about the future

As in English, there are two other ways of talking about the future without using the future tense.

- You can use the present tense in sentences like these:
  Regreso a Londres mañana. *I'm returning to London tomorrow.*
  El tren sale a las dieciocho horas. *The train leaves at six pm.*
  ¿Qué hacemos esta tarde? *What are we doing this afternoon?*
  No puedo venir el sábado. *I can't come on Saturday.*

- You can use **ir** *to go* to translate *going to do something*. It's followed by **a** and the infinitive of the main verb:
  Vamos a comprar un regalo. *We're going to buy a present.*
  ¿Vas a ver la película? *Are you going to see the film?*
  Voy a ir de vacaciones a España. *I'm going to go on holiday to Spain.*
  Van a salir esta noche. *They're going to go out tonight.*

the conditional

The conditional uses the same stem as the future tense (page 138) and, like the future, it uses the same set of endings for all three groups.

	trabajar *to work*	**vender** *to sell*	**vivir** *to live*
yo	trabajar**ía**	vender**ía**	vivir**ía**
tú	trabajar**ías**	vender**ías**	vivir**ías**
él/ella, usted	trabajar**ía**	vender**ía**	vivir**ía**
nosotros/as	trabajar**íamos**	vender**íamos**	vivir**íamos**
vosotros/as	trabajar**íais**	vender**íais**	vivir**íais**
ellos/ellas, ustedes	trabajar**ían**	vender**ían**	vivir**ían**

The conditional has other things in common with the future tense:

- Both have the distinctive **r** sound in all the endings.

- The same verbs are irregular in the future and the conditional, and they're irregular in a similar way, i.e. the regular endings are added to an irregular stem.

	future	conditional
poner *to put*	**pondré**	pondría
tener *to have*	**tendré**	tendría
salir *to go out*	**saldré**	saldría
venir *to come*	**vendré**	vendría
haber *to have*	**habré**	habría
poder *to be able to*	**podré**	podría
querer *to want to*	**querré**	querría
saber *to know*	**sabré**	sabría
decir *to say*	**diré**	diría
hacer *to do/make*	**haré**	haría

The conditional endings are exactly the same as the imperfect tense endings for **-er** and **-ir** verbs (page 142) – although they're on the same stem as the future tense.

when to use the conditional

Conditional endings are added to the infinitive when in English you say *would*.

Me gustaría mucho ... *I would really like to ...*
Saldría pero estoy muy ocupado. *I would go out but I'm busy.*
Nunca lo haría. *She would never do it.*
¿Preferirías quedarte aquí? *Would you prefer to stay here?*
¿Cuánto costarían? *How much would they cost?*
Si tuviera* suficiente dinero, pagaría con mucho gusto. *If I had enough money, I would willingly pay.*
* The verb with *if* is in the subjunctive (page 173).

You can use the conditional to:

- make a request sound more polite:
  ¿Podría ayudarme? *Could you help me?*
  ¿Me daría su dirección? *Would you give me your address?*
  ¿Querría venir? *Would you like to come?*
  Me gustaría un café. *I'd like a coffee.*

- express probability and supposition in the past:
  Sería medianoche cuando se fueron. *It would be/have been midnight when they left.*
  Estaríamos a media hora de las montañas. *We would have been about half an hour from the mountains.*

- make suggestions and give advice:
  Podríamos ir al gimnasio. *We could go to the gym.*
  No deberías beber demasiado café. *You shouldn't drink too much coffee.*

- report something that was originally in the future:
  Me dijo que vendría a verme. *He said he'd come to see me.*
  Dijeron que irían al teatro. *They said they'd go to the theatre.*

Would doesn't always indicate the need for the conditional in Spanish. It's also used in English to refer to something that used to happen regularly in the past, e.g. *When I was a child we would go to the beach every Sunday.* In sentences like these, you use the imperfect tense in Spanish (page 142).

the imperfect tense

	trabajar *to work*	**vender** *to sell*	**vivir** *to live*
yo	trabaj**aba**	vend**ía**	viv**ía**
tú	trabaj**abas**	vend**ías**	viv**ías**
él/ella, usted	trabaj**aba**	vend**ía**	viv**ía**
nosotros/as	trabaj**ábamos**	vend**íamos**	viv**íamos**
vosotros/as	trabaj**abais**	vend**íais**	viv**íais**
ellos/ellas, ustedes	trabaj**aban**	vend**ían**	viv**ían**

There are only three irregular verbs in the imperfect tense:
ir *to go* iba, ibas, iba, íbamos, ibais, iban
ser *to be* era, eras, era, éramos, erais, eran
ver *to see* veía, veías, veía, veíamos, veíais, veían

when to use the imperfect tense

You use the imperfect tense in Spanish to talk about an action in the past
which is either repeated or habitual. English has several ways of conveying
this: *was/were doing, used to do, would do, did*:
Visitaba a mi abuela a menudo. *I often used to visit/I often visited
my grandmother.*
Nadabas cada semana. *You would go/You used to go/You went
swimming every week.*
Vivíamos en Oviedo. *We were living in Oviedo.*
Cuando vivían en España, iban a la playa. *When they lived in Spain,
they used to go/they would go to the beach.*
Eran las dos de la tarde. *It was two o'clock in the afternoon.*
Cuando tenías dos años, eras un niño muy travieso. *When you were two,
you were/used to be a very naughty boy.*

Spanish also has a verb **soler** *to be accustomed to,* which in the
imperfect has a meaning of *used to do something*:
**Cuando estudiaba en España, solía ir a Madrid todos los
fines de semana.** *When I studied in Spain, I used to go to Madrid
every weekend.*

The imperfect is also used:

- to describe an emotional or a mental state in the past:
  Conchita se sentía triste. *Conchita felt sad.*
  Quería ir a la fiesta. *I wanted to go to the party.*

- with **mientras** *while* to talk about two things that were happening at the same time:
  Charlaban mientras estudiaban. *They were chatting whilst they were studying.*
  Ana veía la tele mientras cenaba. *Anne watched television whilst she ate supper.*

- to say what was going on when a separate one-off action happened (in the preterite):
  Llovía mucho cuando salimos de casa. *It was raining a lot when we left the house.*
  Cuando llegué a la fiesta, mis amigos bailaban. *When I arrived at the party, my friends were dancing.*
  In circumstances like these, if you want to emphasise the fact that something was happening right at that time, you could also use the imperfect of **estar** and a gerund:
  Estaban bailando cuando llegué. *They were dancing when I arrived.*

- with **desde** *since* and **desde hacía** *for* to say *had been doing*:
  Estaban casados desde 2006. *They'd been married since 2006.*
  Vivía en Madrid desde hacía un año. *He'd been living in Madrid for a year.*

For questions and negatives in Spanish, you don't need extra words like *did, were, would*:
¿Bailabas con Javier? *Were you dancing/Did you use to dance with Javier?*
No bailaba con Javier. *I wasn't dancing/didn't use to dance with Javier.*
¿Cantaban tus amigos? *Were your friends singing?*
No cantaban. *They weren't singing.*

the preterite tense

	trabajar *to work*	vender *to sell*	vivir *to live*
yo	trabaj**é**	vend**í**	viv**í**
tú	trabaj**aste**	vend**iste**	viv**iste**
él/ella, usted	trabaj**ó**	vend**ió**	viv**ió**
nosotros/as	trabaj**amos**	vend**imos**	viv**imos**
vosotros/as	trabaj**asteis**	vend**isteis**	viv**isteis**
ellos/ellas, ustedes	trabaj**aron**	vend**ieron**	viv**ieron**

The following spelling changes affect certain verbs in the preterite tense to maintain the pronunciation or comply with spelling rules:

- **-car** changes **c → qu** before **e**
  buscar → busqué / *looked for*; **explicar → expliqué** / *explained*; **practicar → practiqué** / *practised*; **sacar → saqué** / *took out*

- **-gar** changes **g → gu** before **e**
  llegar → llegué / *arrived*; **jugar → jugué** / *played*; **negar → negué** / *denied*; **pagar → pagué** / *paid*

- **-zar** changes **z → c** before **e**
  abrazar → abracé / *hugged*; **comenzar → comencé** / *started*; **cruzar → crucé** / *crossed*; **lanzar → lancé** / *threw*

- **-aer/-eer/-oír/-uir** changes **i → y** between two vowels
  caer(se) *to fall* **→ cayó, cayeron**; **creer** *to believe* **→ creyó, creyeron**; **desoír** *to ignore* **→ desoyó, desoyeron**; **construir** *to construct* **→ construyó, construyeron**; (**-aer/-eer/-oír** verbs also take an accent on all endings apart from **ellos/ustedes**: **leer** *to read* **→ leí, leíste, leyó, leímos, leísteis, leyeron**).

Some radical-changing **-ir** verbs change their stem in the **él/usted** and **ellos/ustedes** forms:

- **e → i**: **preferir** *to prefer*: **preferí, preferiste, prefirió, preferimos, preferisteis, prefirieron**

- **e → o**: **pedir** *to ask for*: **pedí, pediste, pidió, pedimos, pedisteis, pidieron**

- **o → u**: **dormir** *to sleep*: **dormí, dormiste, durmió, dormimos, dormisteis, durmieron**

irregular preterite tense forms

Most of the widely used verbs which are irregular in the present are irregular in the preterite too. **Ser** and **ir** are the same in this tense.

	ser/ir *to be/ to go*	hacer *to do, to make*	dar *to give*
yo	fui	hice	di
tú	fuiste	hiciste	diste
él/ella, usted	fue	hizo	dio
nosotros/as	fuimos	hicimos	dimos
vosotros/as	fuisteis	hicisteis	disteis
ellos/ellas, ustedes	fueron	hicieron	dieron

	estar *to be*	decir *to say*	ver *to see*
yo	estuve	dije	vi
tú	estuviste	dijiste	viste
él/ella, usted	estuvo	dijo	vio
nosotros/as	estuvimos	dijimos	vimos
vosotros/as	estuvisteis	dijisteis	visteis
ellos/ellas, ustedes	estuvieron	dijeron	vieron

Some verbs change their stem and add a different set of endings:
-e, -iste, -o, -imos, -isteis, -ieron.

They can:

- add **uv** like **estar**: **andar** *to walk* → **anduve**; **tener** *to have* → **tuve**

- change their vowel to **u**: **caber** *to fit* → **cupe**; **haber** *to have* → **hube**; **poder** *to be able* → **pude**; **poner** *to put* → **puse**; **saber** *to know* → **supe** or to **i** like **hacer**: **querer** *to want* → **quise**; **venir** *to come* → **vine**

- add **j** like **decir**: **atraer** *to attract* → **atraje**; **producir** *to produce* → **produje**; **traer** *to bring* → **traje**; **traducir** *to translate* → **traduje**

  All of these are written out in full in the verb tables (pages 197-247).

when to use the preterite tense

- You use the preterite tense when in English you say *did something* to describe a completed action in the past:
  Visité a mi abuela la semana pasada. *I visited my grandmother last week.*
  Nadaste en el mar ayer. *You swam in the sea yesterday.*
  Vivimos en Oviedo el año pasado. *We lived in Oviedo last year.*
  Bebieron un poco anoche. *They drank a little last night.*
  Fui al polideportivo el otro día. *I went to the sports centre the other day.*
  Hace un año compramos una casa. *We bought a house a year ago.*
  Estudiaron mucho en ese momento. *They studied a lot at that time.*

- It's used to describe completed actions or events which occurred once or several times in the past. If they happened regularly or over a period of time you use the imperfect tense (page 142).
  Compare: **Visité a mi madre tres veces el año pasado.**
  I visited my mother three times last year.
  with: **Visitaba a mi madre todos los días el año pasado.**
  I visited my mother every day last year

- The action may continue for a while, but the length of time is defined:
  Pasé tres meses en Madrid. *I spent three months in Madrid.*
  La película duró dos horas. *The film lasted two hours.*

- For questions and negatives, you don't need *did* and *didn't*:
  ¿Bailaste con Javier? *Did you dance with Javier?*
  No bailé con Javier. *I didn't dance with Javier.*
  ¿Cantaron tus amigos anoche? *Did your friends sing last night?*
  No cantaron anoche. *They didn't sing last night.*

Some verbs have a particular meaning when they're used in the preterite:

conocer *to know* (a person or thing) → *to meet*
saber *to know (a fact), to know how* → *to find out, discover*
poder *to be able to* → *to manage*
querer *to want to* → *to try*; **no querer** *to not want to* → *to refuse*
tener *to have* → *to receive, get*

Conocieron al primer ministro. *They met the Prime Minister.*
No pudisteis ir a la película. *You didn't manage to go the film.*
Quise acostarme temprano. *I tried to go to bed early.*
No quiso hacer sus deberes. *He refused to do his homework.*
Supiste el problema. *You found out the problem.*
Tuvimos una postal de Mallorca. *We got/received a postcard from Mallorca.*

checkpoint 15

1   Underline the expression of time that corresponds with the tense used (preterite or imperfect) and translate the sentences:

a **(El año pasado/a menudo) fuimos a Madrid.**

b **De joven, (siempre/una vez) hacía los deberes.**

c **Veía a mis amigos (ayer/con frecuencia).**

d **Lavó los platos (anteayer/cada día).**

e **(Finalmente/Generalmente) visitaron Sevilla.**

2   Preterite or imperfect? Fill in the gaps and translate the sentences:

a **Mientras Raúl** .... **(jugar) al fútbol,**
   .... **(empezar) a nevar.**

b **Carmen** .... **(ver) la tele, cuando**
   .... **(llegar) su novio.**

c **Cuando** .... **(ser) niña, Dolores**
   .... **(ir) a pie a la escuela.**

d **Mientras Paco** .... **(estudiar),**
   .... **(escuchar) música.**

word power

Most Spanish verbs are regular -**ar** verbs and convert easily from English to Spanish.

🇬🇧	🇪🇸	
-	-ar	**cancelar, confirmar, considerar, depositar, importar, insultar, inventar, presentar**
-e	-ar	**causar, combinar, comparar, conservar, continuar, examinar, notar, usar, votar**
-ate	-ar	**anticipar, calcular, celebrar, cultivar, educar, evaluar, fascinar, originar, separar**

The meaning of other verbs can be worked out by taking predictable letter changes into account (pages 22-23):
confesar *to confess*, **expresar** *to express*, **progresar** *to progress*, **pasar** *to pass*, **estudiar** *to study*, **fotocopiar** *to photocopy*, **fotografiar** *to photograph*, **aceptar** *to accept*, **afectar** *to affect*, **recomendar** *to recommend*

or by linking to related English words:
comenzar *to start (commence)*, **durar** *to last (duration)*, **felicitar** *to congratulate (felicitate)*, **lanzar** *to throw (lance)*, **odiar** *to hate (odious)*, **terminar** *to finish (terminate)*

Beware of false friends among -**ar** verbs, for example:

apuntar means *to write down*	*to appoint* is **nombrar**
decepcionar means *to disappoint*	*to deceive* is **engañar**
disgustar means *to upset*	*to disgust* is **repugnar**
recordar means *to remember*	*to record* is **grabar**
soportar means *to bear, to put up with someone*	*to support* is **apoyar**

Two of the most widely used verbs ending in -**ar** are **dar** *to give* (page 211) and **estar** *to be* (page 217). They are, however, completely irregular.

Some -**er** and -**ir** verbs also convert from English to Spanish:

🇬🇧	🇪🇸	
-	-er	absorber, aprehender, depender, extender, ofender, responder, suspender
-	-ir	admitir, convertir, insistir, permitir, preferir, consistir, existir, resistir
-e	-ir	describir, definir, servir, decidir, dividir, persuadir, asumir, disuadir de, seducir
-ish	-ir	abolir, disminuir, finir
-ute	-uir	contribuir, distribuir, atribuir, sustituir

The meaning of many others is easily worked out:
creer *to believe (credible)*, **perder** *to lose (perdition)*,
suspender *to hang something (suspend)* **dormir** *to sleep (dormant)*,
divertir *to amuse (divert)*, **escribir** *to write (scribe, inscribe)*,
nutrir *to nourish (nutrition)*, **sentir** *to feel (sentiment)*,
vestir *to dress (vestry/vestment/vest)*

Beware of false friends among -**er** and -**ir** verbs, for example:
atender means *to look after*   *to attend* is **asistir a**
pretender means *to claim*   *to pretend* is **fingir**
suceder means *to happen*   *to succeed* is **tener éxito**

Some irregular -**er** verbs behave in exactly the same way as other verbs which have the same root (see also page 135):

- **volver** *to return*, **devolver** *to return (something)*, **resolver** *to solve*, **revolver** *to stir*
- **tener** *to hold*, **contener** *to contain*, **detener** *to detain*, **mantener** *to maintain*, **obtener** *to obtain*, **retener** *to retain*, **sostener** *to sustain*

checkpoint 16

1   When you come across a new verb, you have to know its
    infinitive before you can look it up in a dictionary. Decide
    whether each of the following is in the present, future,
    conditional, imperfect or preterite, and what person it is,
    then work out what the infinitive is.
    E.g. **murió**: preterite, él/ella, usted → **morir** *to die*

llorabas	corrimos	sufriremos
cociné	ganarán	cerraban
descubren	parecía	enviaríais
abre	rompió	temíais
obtenemos	pagarás	recibirías
pintaron	explicarían	salíamos
aplaudíais	aprendería	prometerá

The meanings of the infinitives are given with the answers
(pages 260-261) for you to work out the translation of the
above words.

2   Replace the ending of these infinitives with the person and tense
    in brackets.

    llegar (yo, future)   organizar (nosotros/as, future)
    buscar (tú, conditional)   cenar (nosotros, present)
    crecer (ustedes, imperfect)   comprar (yo, future)
    abrir (yo, preterite)   creer (usted, imperfect)
    pensar (ustedes, imperfect)   escribir (vosotros, conditional)
    compartir (tú, future)   emigrar (usted, preterite)
    ofrecer (él/ella, imperfect)   bailar (ellos/ellas, present)

3   Pair these phrases to make four grammatically correct sentences.

    A   B
    Cuando tenía cinco años   pero no tengo dinero.
    Pagaría   escuchaba música.
    Me encantaría   fui a vivir a Madrid.
    Cuando cocinaba   ir a Madrid.

Verbs: compound tenses

Compound tenses are those which are made up of two parts:

- an auxiliary verb, e.g. *have*, *had* in English; the simple tenses of **haber** in Spanish
- the past participle of the main verb. Regular English past participles end in *-ed* while regular Spanish past participles end in **-ado** or **-ido**.

In Spanish the four main compound tenses are:

- **perfect**, which uses the present tense of **haber**:
  he trabajado / *have worked*
- **pluperfect**, which uses the imperfect tense of **haber**:
  había trabajado / *had worked*
- **future perfect**, which uses the future tense of **haber**:
  habré trabajado / *will have worked*
- **past conditional**, which uses the present conditional of **haber**:
  habría trabajado / *would have worked*

In all the compound tenses, the only thing that changes is the tense of **haber**; the past participle always remains the same. The two parts of the compound tense must always stay together. They can't be split up by an adverb or a negative as in English: *I have already done it, I haven't done it*.

the past participle

In English, the past participle is the form of a verb that comes after *has/have* in the perfect tense: *worked, slept, paid, played*.

To form a Spanish past participle, you change the infinitive like this:

	infinitive	past participle
-ar → -ado	**trabajar** *to eat*	**trabajado** *worked*
-er → -ido	**vender** *to sell*	**vendido** *sold*
-ir → -ido	**vivir** *to live*	**vivido** *lived*

Alongside regular past participles such as *lived, played, wanted, finished, decided*, there are many English verbs with irregular past participles: *given, thought, spent, eaten*. Spanish verbs too have irregular past participles – but the irregularities don't necessarily coincide in the two languages.

All **-ar** verbs have regular past participles, but the past participles of many common **-er** and **-ir** verbs are irregular:

abrir *to open*	→	**abierto** *opened*
cubrir *to cover*	→	**cubierto** *covered*
decir *to say*	→	**dicho** *said*
escribir *to write*	→	**escrito** *written*
freír *to fry*	→	**frito** *fried*
hacer *to do, to make*	→	**hecho** *done, made*
morir *to die*	→	**muerto** *died*
poner *to put*	→	**puesto** *put*
romper *to break*	→	**roto** *broken*
ver *to see*	→	**visto** *seen*
volver *to return*	→	**vuelto** *returned*

-er and **-ir** verbs with a stem ending in a vowel have participles ending in **-ído**:

caer *to fall*	→	**caído** *fallen*
traer *to bring*	→	**traído** *brought*
creer *to believe*	→	**creído** *believed*
leer *to read*	→	**leído** *read*
oír *to hear*	→	**oído** *heard*
reír *to laugh*	→	**reído** *laughed*

... and when it's used

- The main use of the past participle is after **haber** in compound tenses: perfect, pluperfect, future perfect, conditional perfect:
  Todavía no he comido. *I still haven't eaten.*
  Ya había vendido el coche. *I'd already sold the car.*
  El tren habrá salido. *The train will have left.*
  Habría preferido el otro. *I would have preferred the other one.*

- As in English, many past participles can be used as adjectives – agreeing with their noun like other adjectives ending in **-o**:
  Es mi vino preferido. *It's my favourite* (lit. *preferred*) *wine.*
  La carta está escrita en chino. *The letter is written in Chinese.*
  Los escritores son muy bien conocidos. *The writers are very well-known.*

- Using the past participle on its own is a simple and useful way of saying *having done something*:
  Vuelto a casa, encontré el mensaje. *When I got back home*
  (lit. *returned home*), *I found the message.*

- You can use a past participle after the infinitive **haber** to mean *to have done something*:
  Qué alivio de haber llegado. *What a relief to have arrived.*
  Es un placer haberlo conocido. *It's a pleasure to have met you* (**usted**).
  Putting **después** beforehand changes the meaning to *after having done something*, often translated in English as *after doing something*:
  Después de haberlo conocido … *After having met you/after meeting you …*

- Past participles can often be used as nouns; some of them masculine and others feminine:

batido *beaten*	→	**el batido** *milkshake*
helado *frozen*	→	**el helado** *ice cream*
entrado *entered*	→	**la entrada** *entrance*
salido *left*	→	**la salida** *exit,* **las salidas** *departures*
llegado *arrived*	→	**las llegadas** *arrivals*

- Past participles are also used with **ser** to express the passive (page 159).

the perfect tense

The perfect tense of Spanish verbs is made up of the present tense of **haber** *to have* plus the past participle of the main verb (page 152). The ending of the past participle never changes.

trabajar *to work*	yo	**he trabajado**
	tú	**has trabajado**
	él/ella, usted	**ha trabajado**
	nosotros/as	**hemos trabajado**
	vosotros/as	**habéis trabajado**
	ellos/ellas, ustedes	**han trabajado**
vender *to sell*	yo	**he vendido**
	tú	**has vendido**
	él/ella, usted	**ha vendido**
	nosotros/as	**hemos vendido**
	vosotros/as	**habéis vendido**
	ellos/ellas, ustedes	**han vendido**
vivir *to live*	yo	**he vivido**
	tú	**has vivido**
	él/ella, usted	**ha vivido**
	nosotros/as	**hemos vivido**
	vosotros/as	**habéis vivido**
	ellos/ellas, ustedes	**han vivido**

Haber and the past participle should never be separated:
Siempre hemos comido fruta. *We've always eaten fruit.*
No he bebido nada. *I haven't drunk anything.*
No hemos comido todavía. *We haven't yet eaten.*

Have is translated as **haber** only when forming the perfect tense. **Tener** is used for all other meanings of *to have*:
Tengo tres hijos. *I have three children.*

when to use the perfect tense

You use the Spanish perfect tense when in English you say *have/has ......ed*:

He comprado los billetes. *I have bought the tickets.*
Hemos comido mariscos. *We've eaten seafood.*
Felipe ha llegado. *Philip has arrived.*
Me he divertido mucho. *I (have) really enjoyed myself.*

It can also be used to translate the simple past when you're referring to the very recent past:

Felipe ha llegado hoy. *Philip arrived today.*
Se ha levantado a las ocho. *She got up at eight o'clock.*

- **No** goes before **haber**; other negative words go after the past participle (pages 122-123):
  Felipe no ha llegado. *Philip hasn't arrived/didn't arrive.*
  No he comprado los billetes. *I haven't bought the tickets.*
  No se ha levantado temprano. *She didn't get up early.*
  No hemos comido nada. *We haven't eaten anything.*

- Object pronouns (page 84), go before **haber**:
  Os han esperado. *They've waited for you.*
  Me lo has dicho ya. *You've already told me.*
  Te lo he dado. *I've given it to you.*
  ¿La has visto? *Have you seen her?*
  No, no la he visto nunca. *No, I've never seen her.*

... and when not to use it

- The present tense of **acabar de** followed by an infinitive is used to say *to have just done something*:
  Acabamos de desayunar. *We've just had breakfast.*
  Acaba de llegar. *He's just arrived.*

- The present tense of verbs is used with **desde hace** *for* and **desde** *since* to say *have been doing something since/for* – when that action is still going on:
  Están casados desde 2006. *They've been married since 2006.*
  Vive en Madrid desde hace un año. *He's been living in Madrid for a year.*

the pluperfect

The only difference in the formation of the pluperfect and the perfect is that the pluperfect uses the imperfect of **haber** instead of the present. Pronouns and negative words go in the same place. The **yo** and the **él/ella** forms are the same in the pluperfect, and all the imperfect forms of **haber** have an accent on the **í**.

trabajar *to work*	yo	**había trabajado**
	tú	**habías trabajado**
	él/ella, usted	**había trabajado**
	nosotros/as	**habíamos trabajado**
	vosotros/as	**habíais trabajado**
	ellos/ellas, ustedes	**habían trabajado**
vender *to sell*	yo	**había vendido**
	tú	**habías vendido**
	él/ella, usted	**había vendido**
	nosotros/as	**habíamos vendido**
	vosotros/as	**habíais vendido**
	ellos/ellas, ustedes	**habían vendido**
vivir *to live*	yo	**había vivido**
	tú	**habías vivido**
	él/ella, usted	**había vivido**
	nosotros/as	**habíamos vivido**
	vosotros/as	**habíais vivido**
	ellos/ellas, ustedes	**habían vivido**

You use the pluperfect when in English you say *had done something*:
Había terminado. *I had finished.*
¿Habían comido ya? *Had they already eaten?*
¿No habías visto aquella película? *Had you not seen that film?*
Habíamos regresado a la casa cuando empezó a llover. *We had got back to the house when it started to rain.*
Se había levantado todavía cuando me llegué. *She had already got up when I arrived.*

the future perfect

The future of **haber** + past participle give you the future perfect. Pronouns and negative words go in the same place as for the perfect (page 155). All the future forms of **haber** have an accent on the last syllable, apart from the **nosotros** form.

trabajar *to work*	yo	**habré trabajado**
	tú	**habrás trabajado**
	él/ella, usted	**habrá trabajado**
	nosotros/as	**habremos trabajado**
	vosotros/as	**habréis trabajado**
	ellos/ellas, ustedes	**habrán trabajado**
vender *to sell*	yo	**habré vendido**
	tú	**habrás vendido**
	él/ella, usted	**habrá vendido**
	nosotros/as	**habremos vendido**
	vosotros/as	**habréis vendido**
	ellos/ellas, ustedes	**habrán vendido**
vivir *to live*	yo	**habré vivido**
	tú	**habrás vivido**
	él/ella, usted	**habrá vivido**
	nosotros/as	**habremos vivido**
	vosotros/as	**habréis vivido**
	ellos/ellas, ustedes	**habrán vivido**

You use the future perfect when in English you say *will have done something*:
Habrán visto todo. *They will have seen everything.*
No habremos visto nada. *We won't have seen anything.*
Habrá llegado para las cinco. *He will have arrived by five o'clock.*

You can also use it to express probability in the past:
Ya habrá terminado. *He must have finished already.*

the past conditional

The conditional of **haber** + past participle give you the past conditional. Pronouns and negative words go in the same place as for the perfect tense. The **yo** and **él/ella** forms are the same, and all the conditional forms of **haber** have an accent on the í.

trabajar *to work*	**yo**	**habría trabajado**
	tú	**habrías trabajado**
	él/ella, usted	**habría trabajado**
	nosotros/as	**habríamos trabajado**
	vosotros/as	**habríais trabajado**
	ellos/ellas, ustedes	**habrían trabajado**

vender *to sell*	**yo**	**habría vendido**
	tú	**habrías vendido**
	él/ella, usted	**habría vendido**
	nosotros/as	**habríamos vendido**
	vosotros/as	**habríais vendido**
	ellos/ellas, ustedes	**habrían vendido**

vivir *to live*	**yo**	**habría vivido**
	tú	**habrías vivido**
	él/ella, usted	**habría vivido**
	nosotros/as	**habríamos vivido**
	vosotros/as	**habríais vivido**
	ellos/ellas, ustedes	**habrían vivido**

You use the past conditional when in English you say *would have done something*:
Habría pagado. *I would have paid.*
Habría ido pero no podía. *He would have gone but he couldn't.*
When it's followed by **si** *if*, the verb after *if* has to be in the pluperfect subjunctive (page 171):
Habría ido si hubiera sabido. *I would have gone if I'd known.*
Unlike English, the past conditional is needed after phrases like *he said (that), he thought (that), he hoped (that)*:
María dijo que habría ido. *Maria said she would go/have gone.*
Pensé que habrías esperado. *I thought you would wait/would have waited.*

the passive

In both Spanish and English, a past participle can be used with **ser** *to be* to form the passive. This is when something is done **to** the subject rather than **by** it: e.g. *the room was booked by Ana* rather than *Ana booked the room*.

In Spanish the past participle agrees with the subject:
El vino blanco es servido fresco. *White wine is served chilled.*
Los coches fueron fabricados el año pasado. *The cars were manufactured last year.*

The passive often includes **por** *by*:
La cena será preparada por mi marido. *The dinner will be prepared by my husband.*
Los pasteles fueron hechos por mi abuela. *The cakes were made by my grandmother.*

The passive is used far less often in Spanish than in English because Spanish prefers to use these other ways of expressing it:

- Using **se** in front of the verb to make it reflexive; the verb is singular or plural depending on whether the subject is singular or plural:
  El vino blanco se sirve fresco. *White wine is served chilled.* lit. *The white wine serves itself chilled.*
  Los coches se fabricaron el año pasado. *The cars were manufactured last year.* lit. *The cars manufactured themselves last year.*

- Using the **ellos** form of the verb, i.e. *they*:
  Sirven fresco el vino blanco. *They serve white wine chilled.*
  Fabricaron los coches el año pasado. *They manufactured the cars last year.*

- Using the impersonal **se** (page 83), particularly in expressions like **se cree** *it is believed*, **se dice** *it is said*, **se permite** *it is allowed*, **se prohíbe** *it is forbidden*.
  Se nos dice que llueve mucho en Inglaterra. *We are told that it rains a lot in England.*
  Aquí se habla inglés. *English is spoken here.*

checkpoint 17

1   What are the past participles of these verbs?
    (11 of them are irregular)

    comprar   vender   escribir   romper
    comenzar   morir   trabajar   construir
    querer   hacer   abrir   freír
    cubrir   venir   tener   decir
    comer   ver   vestir   decidir
    beber   poner   volver   andar

2   Fill the gaps to create the perfect tense.
    a ustedes _____ dormido   b nosotros _____ llegado
    c tú _____ aprendido   d ellos no _____ usado
    e usted _____ escogido   f vosotros _____ seguido
    g yo me _____ divertido   h él no _____ organizado nada

3   Change these from the present to the tense indicated and
    translate them:
    a No entiendo nada. _____ pluperfect
    b Vamos al parque. _____ past conditional
    c Raúl llega tarde. _____ perfect
    d ¿Cuándo coméis? _____ future perfect
    e No se levanta temprano. _____ pluperfect
    f ¿Qué haces en el colegio? _____ perfect
    g Organizáis una cena. _____ past conditional
    h Invitan a todos sus amigos. _____ future perfect
    i ¿Terminas el libro? _____ perfect
    j Se visten con prisa (they get dressed in a hurry) _____
      pluperfect

Gerund, imperative, subjunctive

Spanish verb endings not only provide information about tense, i.e. whether things are happening in the past, present or future, they indicate other functions of the verb too.

In this unit, the focus is on:

- the **gerund**, the equivalent of the *-ing* ending in English, although in Spanish it's used less and not always in the same way.

- The **imperative**, used to tell somebody what to do. In English there's only one version but there are four in Spanish because of the four different words for *you*: **tú**, **vosotros/as**, **usted**, **ustedes**. There's also a **nosotros** imperative, used to make suggestions, as in *Let's* ....

- The **subjunctive**, no longer used much in English but used extensively in Spanish. A verb in the subjunctive doesn't convey hard fact but is usually the second verb of a sentence, following another verb which expresses someone's attitude or opinion, doubt or uncertainty.
  The sort of phrase that triggers a subjunctive includes words like *hope*, *wish*, *doubt*, *suppose*, *fear*, *advise*, *suggest* followed by **que** *that*.

the gerund

The gerund is the equivalent of the English *-ing* ending, formed by changing the infinitive ending to **-ando** or **-iendo**. This ending never changes:

	infinitive	gerund
-ar → -ando	**trabajar** *to eat*	**trabajando** *working*
-er → -iendo	**vender** *to sell*	**vendiendo** *selling*
-ir → -iendo	**vivir** *to live*	**viviendo** *living*

There are a few irregular gerunds in Spanish:

- -er/-ir verbs with a stem ending in a vowel take **-yendo**:
  caer → cayendo *falling*; **creer → creyendo** *believing*; **leer → leyendo** *reading*; **traer → trayendo** *bringing*; **construir → construyendo** *building*; **oír → oyendo** *hearing*; and **ir → yendo** *going*

- -ir radical-changing verbs:
  e → i: **decir → diciendo** *saying*; **freír → friendo** *frying*; **pedir → pidiendo** *asking*; **reír → riendo** *laughing*; **sentir → sintiendo** *feeling*; **venir → viniendo** *coming*
  o → u: **dormir → durmiendo** *sleeping*; **morir → muriendo** *dying*; **poder → pudiendo** *being able to*

...and when to use it

- Probably the most common use of the gerund is with the present tense of **estar** *to be* to emphasise that something is happening at this very minute:
  ¿Qué estás buscando? *What are you looking for?*
  Está cantando fuerte. *He's singing loudly.*
  ...or with the imperfect of **estar** to say what was going on at the moment something else happened:
  Estaba leyendo cuando vino. *I was reading when he came.*
  Estaba esperando a Olga cuando llamaron a la puerta. *She was waiting for Olga when there was a knock on the door.*

> Pronouns can either come before **estar** or attach themselves to the end of the gerund. When they're attached, an accent is added to keep the stress in the same place as when there's no pronoun:
> **La estaba esperando cuando...** *I was waiting for <u>her</u> when...*
> **Estaba esperándola cuando...**
> **Nuestra madre nos está llamando.** *Our mother's calling <u>us</u>.*
> **Nuestra madre está llamándonos.**

- A gerund can be used on its own to mean *while/on doing something*:
  Considerando el pasado, entiendo. *Looking back, I understand.*
  Siguiendo tu ejemplo, me fui. *Following your example, I left.*
  In sentences like these, pronouns are always attached to the gerund:
  Siguiéndote, se fue. *Following you, he left.*

  The gerund can also be used after several verbs other than **estar**, with very different meanings in English.

- After **seguir** and **continuar**, it means *to go on doing something/ to continue doing something*:
  Sigue/continúa llorando. *She goes on/continues crying.*
  Siguieron/continuaron hablando. *They went on/continued talking.*

- After **llevar** and a period of time, it means *to have been doing something for…*:
  Llevo una hora buscando mis llaves. *I've been looking for my keys for an hour.*
  Lleva cinco años tocando el piano. *She's been playing the piano for five years.*

- After **pasar** and a period of time, it means *to spend …… doing something*:
  Pasan much tiempo escuchando música. *They spend a lot of time listening to music.*
  Pasas horas viendo la tele. *You spend hours watching television.*

- After **entrar** *to come in/go in*, **salir** *to come out/to go out* and **irse** *to leave*, a gerund such as **corriendo** *running* can be used to translate *to run in* or *out*:
  Salieron/Se fueron corriendo de la casa. *They ran out of the house.* lit. *They went running out of the house.*
  Entraron corriendo a la casa. *They ran into the house.*

when not to use the gerund

You use the infinitive, not the gerund:

- after most other verbs (page 114):
  Me gusta cantar. *I like singing.*
  Prefiero quedarme aquí. *I prefer staying here.*

- where the English *-ing* form of a verb is used as a noun:
  Hacer ejercicio es bueno para la salud. *Exercising is good for the health.*
  Ver para creer. *Seeing is believing.*

- after prepositions:
  Se fueron … *They left …*
  … antes de pagar. *… before paying.*
  … después de comer. *… after eating.*
  … en vez de quedarse. *… instead of staying.*
  … sin hablar. *… without speaking.*

Nor is the gerund used when the English *-ing* form is an adjective or a noun, as seen opposite.

checkpoint 18

1   Write the gerund of the following verbs – keeping an eye open for verbs similar to the above – and work out what they all mean.

a **distribuir**	b **contravenir**
c **maldecir**	d **perseguir**
e **releer**	f **contradecir**
g **sonreír**	h **contribuir**
i **intervenir**	j **distraer**

2   Gerund or infinitive?
    a [buscar] **Estaba** _____ **un sito web.**
    b [pagar] **Se fue sin** _____ .
    c [nadar] **No me gusta** _____ .
    d [tocar] **Siguió** _____ **la guitarra.**
    e [hacer] **¿Qué estás** _____ ?
    f [continuar] **Preferiría volver a casa en vez de** _____ .

word **power**

As well as the gerund (pages 162-163), Spanish has another verb form that corresponds to the English *-ing* ending. It's formed by replacing the infinitive ending as follows:

-ar → -ante
-er → -ente
-ir → -iente or **-ente**

These forms are used as adjectives, some of which have a direct English equivalent ending in *-ing*:

platillos volantes *flying saucers*
datos fascinantes *fascinating facts*
vendedores ambulantes *travelling salesmen*
isla flotante *floating island* (dessert)
circunstancias agravantes *aggravating circumstances*
la semana precedente *the preceding week*
la semana siguiente *the following week*
agua corriente *running water*
los muertos vivientes *the living dead*
la Bella durmiente *Sleeping Beauty*

… and some of which no longer have English translations ending in *-ing*:

brillante *brilliant* lit. *shining*
ignorante *ignorant* lit. *not knowing*
benevolente *benevolent* lit. *well-wishing*
malevolente *malevolent* lit. *evil-wishing*

Some also become nouns. For example **un participante** *a participant* literally means *one participating*, from **participar** *to participate*.

asistir *to assist*	**un asistente** *an assistant*
cantar *to sing*	**un cantante** *a singer*
emigrar *to emigrate*	**un emigrante** *an emigrant*
residir *to reside*	**un residente** *a resident*
presidir *to preside*	**un presidente** *a president*

the imperative

You use the imperative to tell people what to do or not to do, to give advice and instructions. Because there are four words for *you*, there are four *you* imperatives. There's also a **nosotros/as** imperative, used to make suggestions starting with *Let's*.

- Most **tú** imperatives are identical to the **él/ella/usted** form of the present indicative.

- **Vosotros** imperatives replace the final -r of the infinitive with -**d**.

- **Usted**, **ustedes** and **nosotros/as** imperatives are identical to the equivalent forms in the present subjunctive (pages 168-169).

	-ar	**-er**	**-ir**
	trabajar *to work*	**vender** *to sell*	**vivir** *to live*
tú	trabaj**a**	vend**e**	viv**e**
usted	trabaj**e**	vend**a**	viv**a**
nosotros/as	trabaj**emos**	vend**amos**	viv**amos**
vosotros/as	trabaj**ad**	vend**ed**	viv**id**
ustedes	trabaj**en**	vend**an**	viv**an**

tú	**Espera aquí.** *Wait here.*
usted	**Siga todo recto.** *Carry straight on.*
vosotros/as	**¡Mirad la cuenta!** *Look at the bill!*
ustedes	**Giren a la derecha.** *Turn right.*
nosotros/as	**Comamos.** *Let's eat.*

The following verbs have irregular **tú** imperatives:

decir *to say* → **di**   **hacer** *to do, to make* → **haz**   **ir** *to go* → **ve**
poner *to put* → **pon**   **salir** *to leave, to go out* → **sal**   **ser** *to be* → **sé**
tener *to have* → **ten**   **venir** *to come* → **ven**

Ven conmigo. *Come with me.*
Sé bueno. *Be good.*
Ten cuidado. *Take care.*
Hazlo tú mismo. *Do it yourself.*

In positive imperatives, i.e. when telling someone to do something, object pronouns are attached to the end of the verb. An accent is added to keep the stress in the same place as it would be without the pronoun:

Háblame. *Speak to me.*   **Escríbenos.** *Write to us.*

When **nos** is attached to the **nosotros** form, you drop the final **-s**:
Levantémonos. *Let's stand up.*
And when **os** is attached to the **vosotros** form, you drop the final **-d**. You also add an accent for **-ir** verbs:
Sentaos. *Sit down.*   **Arrepentíos.** *Repent.*

To tell someone ***not*** to do something, you put **no** in front of the relevant form of the present subjunctive (pages 168-169):

tú	**No abras la puerta.** *Don't open the door.*
usted	**No espere.** *Don't wait.*
nosotros/as	**No bebamos aquí.** *Let's not drink here.*
vosotros/as	**No digáis eso.** *Don't say that.*
ustedes	**¡No olviden!** *Don't forget!*

Object pronouns come ***before*** the verb in negative imperatives:
No me hables. *Don't speak to me.*
No nos escribas. *Don't write to us.*

Many everyday expressions are imperatives:
¿Diga?/¿Dígame? *Hello. (on the phone)* lit. *Speak./Speak to me.*
¡No me digas! *You don't say!*
Oiga. *Excuse me.* lit. *Hear.*
Póngame un kilo de patatas. *Give me (lit. put me) a kilo of potatoes.*
¡Vaya! *Well!*
¡Vaya coche! *What a car!* **¡Vaya hombre!** *What a man!*

In written instructions, such as signs or recipes, the infinitive is often used instead of an imperative:
Llevar puesto el cinturón de seguridad. *Wear your seatbelt.*
No aparcar. *No parking.*
Añadir la harina y mezclar. *Add the flour and mix in.*

the present subjunctive

	-ar	-er	-ir
	trabajar to work	**vender** to sell	**vivir** to live
yo	trabaj**e**	vend**a**	viv**a**
tú	trabaj**es**	vend**as**	viv**as**
él/ella, usted	trabaj**e**	vend**a**	viv**a**
nosotros/as	trabaj**emos**	vend**amos**	viv**amos**
vosotros/as	trabaj**éis**	vend**áis**	viv**áis**
ellos/ellas, ustedes	trabaj**en**	vend**an**	viv**an**

To form the present subjunctive, simply take the **yo** form of the present tense, i.e. the present indicative (page 132), remove the -o ending and add the subjunctive endings. This works for most verbs, including those with stem or spelling changes in the present tense (page 133) and verbs which are irregular in the **yo** form of the present tense (page 134).

	present tense	present subjunctive
caber to fit	quepo	quepa
caer to fall	caigo	caiga
cerrar to close	cierro	cierre
coger to catch	cojo	coja
contar to count	cuento	cuente
convencer to convince	convenzo	convenza
distinguir to distinguish	distingo	distinga
elegir to choose	elijo	elija
entender to understand	entiendo	entienda
hablar to speak	hablo	hable
hacer to make/do	hago	haga
parecer to look like	parezco	parezca
poner to put	pongo	ponga
salir to go out	salgo	salga
traer to bring	traigo	traiga
valer to be worth	valgo	valga
ver to see	veo	vea
volver to return	vuelvo	vuelva

There are six main verbs which don't follow the above rule for forming the present subjunctive:

dar	estar	haber	ir	saber	ser
to give	*to be*	*to have*	*to go*	*to know*	*to be*
dé	esté	haya	vaya	sepa	sea
des	estés	hayas	vayas	sepas	seas
dé	esté	haya	vaya	sepa	sea
demos	estemos	hayamos	vayamos	sepamos	seamos
deis	estéis	hayáis	vayáis	sepáis	seáis
den	estén	hayan	vayan	sepan	sean

- In contrast to the present tense, some radical-changing -ir verbs have a different stem change in the **nosotros** and **vosotros** forms of the present subjunctive.
  -**e** to -**ie** verbs, such as **sentir** *to feel*:
  sienta, sientas, sienta, sintamos, sintáis, sientan
  -**o** to -**ue** verbs, such as **dormir** *to sleep*:
  duerma, duermas, duerma, durmamos, durmáis, duerman

- Verbs which end in -**uir** have **y** in all forms of the present subjunctive.
  construir *to construct, to build*
  construya, construyas, construya, construyamos, construyáis, construyan

- Some verbs which end in -**iar** and -**uar** have an accent on the **í** or **ú** in the present subjunctive apart from the **nosotros** and **vosotros** forms.
  vaciar *to empty*
  vacíe, vacíes, vacíe, vaciemos, vaciéis, vacíen
  actuar *to act*
  actúe, actúes, actúe, actuemos, actuéis, actúen

the imperfect subjunctive

The imperfect subjunctive is unique in that it has two different sets of endings. They are interchangeable, although the -ara/-iera endings are more common than the -ase/-iese. The stem for them is found by removing -aron/-ieron from the **ellos** form of the preterite tense (page 144).

trabajar *to work*			
	yo	trabaj**ara**	trabaj**ase**
	tú	trabaj**aras**	trabaj**ases**
	él/ella, usted	trabaj**ara**	trabaj**ase**
	nosotros/as	trabaj**áramos**	trabaj**ásemos**
	vosotros/as	trabaj**arais**	trabaj**aseis**
	ellos/ellas, ustedes	trabaj**aran**	trabaj**asen**
vender *to sell*			
	yo	vend**iera**	vend**iese**
	tú	vend**ieras**	vend**ieses**
	él/ella, usted	vend**iera**	vend**iese**
	nosotros/as	vend**iéramos**	vend**iésemos**
	vosotros/as	vend**ierais**	vend**ieseis**
	ellos/ellas, ustedes	vend**ieran**	vend**iesen**
vivir *to live*			
	yo	viv**iera**	viv**iese**
	tú	viv**ieras**	viv**ieses**
	él/ella, usted	viv**iera**	viv**iese**
	nosotros/as	viv**iéramos**	viv**iésemos**
	vosotros/as	viv**ierais**	viv**ieseis**
	ellos/ellas, ustedes	viv**ieran**	viv**iesen**

Verbs which are irregular or have spelling/stem changes in the preterite have the same changes in the imperfect subjunctive:

poseer *to possess* **poseyeron** → **poseyera/poseyese**
mentir *to lie* **mintieron** → **mintiera/mintiese**
seguir *to follow* **siguieron** → **siguiera/siguiese**
morir *to die* **murieron** → **muriera/muriese**
saber *to know* **supieron** → **supiera/supiese**
dar *to give* **dieron** → **diera/diese**
ir/ser *to go/to be* **fueron** → **fuera/fuese**
ver *to see* **vieron** → **viera/viese**

the perfect/pluperfect subjunctive

The perfect subjunctive of all verbs is formed from the present subjunctive of **haber** (page 169) and the past participle:

yo haya trabajado
tú hayas trabajado
él/ella, usted haya trabajado
nosotros hayamos trabajado
vosotros hayáis trabajado
ellos/ellas, ustedes hayan trabajado

The pluperfect subjunctive is formed from the imperfect subjunctive of **haber** and the past participle.

yo hubiera/hubiese trabajado
tú hubieras/hubiese trabajado
él/ella, usted hubiera/hubiese trabajado
nosotros hubiéramos/hubiésemos trabajado
vosotros hubierais/hubieseis trabajado
ellos/ellas, ustedes hubieran/hubiesen trabajado

which tense to choose?

- When the subjunctive is introduced by **que**
  If the verb before **que** is in the present tense you use the present or the perfect subjunctive.
  If the verb before **que** is in a past tense you use the imperfect or the pluperfect subjunctive.

- When the subjunctive is introduced by **si**
  If the verb before **si** is in the present conditional you use the imperfect subjunctive.
  If the verb before **si** is in the past conditional you use the pluperfect subjunctive.

when to use the subjunctive

In English, the subjunctive is no longer widely used, and appears most often in expressions like these: *if only it were true; be that as it may; until death do us part; perish the thought.*

In Spanish it's used much more widely; it's needed whenever opinions and attitudes are involved, whenever you're talking about things that aren't actually fact.

The subjunctive is generally the second verb in a sentence, introduced by **que** and it's used after verbs that express:

- influence, for example wishes or advice:
  Quiero que lo hagas. *I'd like you to do it.*
  Te aconsejo que estudies más. *I advise you to study more.*
  ¡Que lo pases bien! *Have a good time!*
  Prefiero que no vayas. *I'd prefer you not to go.*
  Habría preferido que hubieras salido. *I would have preferred you to go out/to have gone out.*

  WIth verbs such as **preferir** and **querer** if the subject of the two verbs is the same, the second verb is in the infinitive:
  Quiero hacerlo. *I'd like to do it*
  Habría preferido salir. *I would have preferred to go out.*

- emotions, such as hope, doubt, fear, regret:
  Espero que no haya tráfico. *I hope there's no traffic.*
  Dudo que vengan. *I doubt they'll come.*
  Siento que no podamos hacerlo. *I'm sorry we can't do it.*
  Temía que terminara mal. *He was afraid it might end badly.*
  Era una vergüenza que no tuviera dinero. *It was a disgrace that he didn't have any money.*

- opinion in the negative:
  No creo que sea importante. *I don't believe it's important.*
  No creo que Paco se vaya. *I don't believe Paco's leaving.*
  No digo que lo lea. *I'm not saying I'll read it.*
  No pienso que entiendan. *I don't think they understand.*
  No pienso que hayan entendido. *I don't think they've understood.*
  No pensaba que entendieran. *I didn't think they understood*
  No pensaba que hubieran entendido. *I didn't think they had understood.*

The subjunctive is also used:

- in impersonal expressions:
  Es probable que llueva. *It's likely it'll rain.*
  Es posible que vengan. *It's possible they'll come.*
  Es posible que ya se haya ido. *He might already have left.*
  Es necesario que vengáis hoy. *It's necessary for you to come today.*
  Era probable que Paco ya se hubiera ido. *Paco had probably left already.*
  Es posible que vengan. *It's possible they'll come.*
  …unless they express certainty:
  Es cierto que vienen. *It's certain they're coming.*

- with commands and orders:
  Dile que nos llame. *Tell him to call us.*
  Les mandó que se fueran. *He ordered them to leave.*
  Le pedí que lo comprara. *I asked him to buy it.*

- in set expressions with **lo que**:
  pase lo que pase *come what may*; **sea lo que sea** *be it as it may*
  digan lo que digan *whatever they say*

- after **aunque** *although,* **para que** *in order to,* **a condición de que** *on condition that,* **antes de que** *before,* **con tal (de) que** *provided that,* **sin que** *without,* **de manera que/de modo que** *so that,* **excepto que/salvo que/a no ser que** *unless,* **a menos que** *unless*:
  aunque no me guste mucho *even though I don't like it much*
  para que puedas ir mañana *so that you can go tomorrow*
  antes de que sea demasiado tarde *before it's too late*
  a menos que hiele *unless it freezes.*

- after **si** *if,* except for conditions that are 'open' (i.e. they might or might not be true):
  Lo compraría si costara menos. *I'd buy it if it cost less.*
  Lo habría comprado si hubiera costado menos. *I would have bought it if it had cost less.*
  Si llueve no vamos a salir. *If it rains we won't go out.*

- after **cuando** *when,* **mientras** *while,* **en cuanto** *as soon as* and **hasta que** *until,* if the action hasn't yet happened:
  Te llamaré cuando llegue. *I'll call you when I arrive.*
  Saldré en cuanto venga mi novia. *I'll go out as soon as my girlfriend comes.*

1 Identify the imperatives in this set of directions.

"Bueno … no tome la primera a la izquierda, sino que siga todo recto hasta los semáforos. Gire a la izquierda, cruce la plaza y luego tome la segunda a la derecha. No se preocupe – no está lejos."

2 If you followed the directions on this map, would you end up at A, B, C or D?

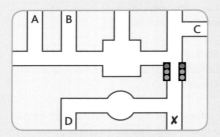

3 Is the person giving the directions using **tú** or **usted**? How would s/he give them using the other one?

4 Find the correct ending from list B for the phrases in list A.

A	B
Compraría una casa grande si	esté contento.
Creo que usted	termine sus deberes.
No puede salir a menos que	fuera rica.
No creo que usted	vengan a la fiesta.
Habría comprado el coche si	está triste.
Espero que ustedes	hubiera tenido el dinero.

Key verbs

In Spanish, as in most languages, some verbs are used more frequently than others. These include verbs like **ir** *to go*, **dar** *to give*, **decir** *to say*, **comer** *to eat* and **pensar** *to think*, which relate to basic human activity.

Liking falls into the category of basic human activity, but Spanish expresses likes and dislikes very differently from English, using **gustar** *to be pleasing*.

Some verbs are used very frequently because their grammatical uses extend beyond their fundamental meaning:

- **deber** *to have to*, **poder** *to be able to*, **querer** *to want to* and **saber** *to know how to*, known as modal verbs, are used with the infinitive of a second verb;
- **estar** *to be* can be used with the gerund (page 162) and can also be followed by **para** + infinitive to mean *to be about to*;
- **ser** *to be* can be used in a passive construction (page 159) and can also be used impersonally to mean *it's*;
- **haber** *to have* is used with a past participle to form past tenses (pages 154-158); it also features in many expressions that don't use the word *have* in English;
- **hacer** *to do/make* is used in a whole range of situations when it's not translated as *do* or *make*.
  Apart from **deber**, these are all irregular and are written out in full in the verb tables (pages 197-247).

Some common Spanish verbs don't have a direct equivalent in English. Both **saber** and **conocer** translate *to know*, but they're not at all interchangeable. **Saber** means to know information and facts, and to know how to do something, whereas you use **conocer** when you're talking about knowing or being acquainted with a person or a place.

ser or estar?

In Spanish, there are two verbs which mean *to be*: **ser** and **estar**, both of which are irregular. It's important to learn the different ways in which each is used.

	ser	estar
yo	soy	estoy
tú	eres	estás
él/ella, usted	es	está
nosotros/as	somos	estamos
vosotros/as	sois	estáis
ellos/ellas, ustedes	son	están

ser

You use **ser**:

- before adjectives to describe characteristics or permanent qualities such as colour, nationality, religion:
  Los gatos son inteligentes. *Cats are intelligent.*
  La manzana es verde. *The apple is green.*
  Es musulmán. *He's Muslim.*
  Sois franceses. *You're French.*

- before a noun or pronoun in definitions:
  Es un libro de gramática. *It's a grammar book.*
  Son dentistas. *They're dentists.*
  Era mi vecina. *She was my neighbour.*
  ¿Eres tú? *Is it you?*
  Sí, soy yo. *Yes, it's me.*

- for origin:
  Paco es de Valencia. *Paco's from Valencia.*
  Estas naranjas son de Sevilla. *These oranges are from Seville.*

- for possession:
  Es de Ana. *It's Anna's.*
  ¿Son vuestros? *Are they yours?*

- for *made of*:
  Es de seda. *It's made of silk.*
  Los pendientes son de plata. *The earrings are made of silver.*

- for the time, the day, the date and calculations:
  Era la una y media. *It was half past one.*
  Es lunes. *It's Monday.*
  Es el primero de enero. *It's January 1st.*
  Son cien euros. *It's 100 euros.*

- in impersonal constructions (page 179):
  Es muy importante. *It's very important.*
  No fue posible. *It wasn't possible.*

- in set expressions:
  es igual/es lo mismo *it's the same*; **es para él** *it's for him*
  sea … sea … *either … or …;* **sea como sea** *be that as it may*
  o sea *that is to say;* **a no ser por** *but for*

estar

You use **estar**:
- before adjectives to describe a temporary state or condition, such as health and emotions:
  La manzana está verde. *The apple is unripe.*
  Tu coche está bastante sucio. *Your car's quite dirty.*
  El agua está demasiado caliente. *The water is too hot.*
  ¿Estás enfermo? *Are you unwell?*
  No estamos contentos. *We're not happy.*

- to talk about location:
  Estamos en el centro de la ciudad. *We're in the city centre.*
  Londres está en el sur de Inglaterra. *London is in the south of England.*
  Estamos en el cine. *We're at the cinema.*

- to talk about marital status:
  Estoy casada. *I'm married.*
  Están divorciados. *They're divorced.*
  Javier está soltero. *Javier is single.*

- before the gerund (page 162) to form the continuous tenses:
  Estamos cantando. *We're singing.*
  Estaban comiendo. *They were eating.*

- in expressions followed by the infinitive:
  estar a punto de *to be about to*; **estar para** *to be about to*;
  estar por *to be in favour of*

- in many set expressions:
  estar a sus anchas *to be comfortable*; **estar al corriente** *to be up-to-date*;
  estar de luto *to be in mourning*; **estar de moda** *to be in fashion*
  estar de paso *to be passing through*; **estar de pie** *to be standing*
  estar de rodillas *to be kneeling*; **estar de vacaciones** *to be on holiday*
  estar de viaje *to be on a trip*; **estar de vuelta** *to be back*
  estar de acuerdo *to agree*; **estar de buen/mal humor** *to be in a good/bad mood*

The past participle is used:
- as an adjective with **estar** to describe how something is:
  La puerta está abierta. *The door is open.*
- in a passive construction (page 159) with **ser** to describe an action:
  La puerta fue abierta a las nueve. *The door was opened at nine o'clock.*

Certain adjectives have a different English translation depending on whether they're used with **ser** or **estar**:
La película es bastante aburrida. *The film's quite boring.*
Estamos aburridos. *We are bored.*
Mis estudiantes son listos. *My students are clever.*
¿Estás listo para salir? *Are you ready to go out?*
Es muy cansada. *She is very tiring.*
No estoy cansada. *I'm not tired.*

ser

- As in English, **ser** *to be* can be used impersonally, i.e. to talk about *it* when *it* doesn't refer to anything in particular:
  Es importante beber agua. *It's important to drink water.*
  Fue imposible salir ayer. *It was impossible to go out yesterday.*
  Será necesario terminarlo. *It will be necessary to finish it.*

- If a Spanish impersonal expression followed by **que** expresses certainty, it's followed by the indicative:
  Es obvio que te gusta la fruta. *It's obvious you like fruit.*
  Es verdad que llueve. *It's true it's raining.*
  Es evidente que tienen mucho trabajo. *It's true that they have a lot of work.*

  Otherwise it's followed by the subjunctive (page 173):
  Es importante que vengas mañana. *It's important for you to come tomorrow.*
  Es imposible que lo hagamos ahora. *It's impossible for us to do it now.*
  Es necesario que lo visite. *It's necessary for me to visit him.*

- **Ser** is also used in time expressions:
  es temprano *it's early*
  es tarde *it's late*

When actually telling the time (page 29), remember to use **son** with times except *one o'clock*, *midday* and *midnight*:
Es la una. *It's one o'clock.*
Es la una y cinco. *It's five past one.*
Es mediodía *it's midday*
Es medianoche *it's midnight*
Son las dos/tres/cuatro. *It's two/three/four o'clock.*
Son las nueve y cuarenta y cinco. *It's 9.45.*

gustar

In English to *like* is a regular verb which takes a direct object:
I like walking.   *I like cheese.*   *I like mushrooms.*

To say what you like and don't like in Spanish you use the verb **gustar**,
which literally means *to be pleasing to*. So to translate the above examples,
what you literally say is:
Walking is pleasing to me = **Me gusta andar.**
Cheese is pleasing to me = **Me gusta el queso.**
Mushrooms are pleasing to me = **Me gustan los champiñones.**

So, when talking about liking one thing, you use the singular **gusta**, and
when you're talking about more than one thing, you use the plural **gustan**.

If you're talking about what somebody else likes, you simply replace **me**
with the relevant indirect object pronoun:
Le gusta el queso. *He likes cheese.*
Les gusta el queso. *They like cheese.*
Nos gusta el queso. *We like cheese.*
Te gustan los champiñones. *You like mushrooms.*

When you're specifying a person, the order is:
personal **a** + the person + indirect object pronoun + **gustar**:
A Ana le gustan los champiñones. *Anna likes mushrooms.*
A mi hijo no le gusta caminar. *My son doesn't like walking.*

Spanish often uses this same pattern with two pronouns:
A ella le gustan los champiñones. *She likes mushrooms.*
A él no le gusta caminar. *He doesn't like walking.*

To talk about liking something in the past, you use the imperfect, perfect or
preterite tense of **gustar**:
Me gustaba la casa donde vivíamos. *I liked the house where we lived/used
to live.*
A mi hija no le gustaba estudiar. *My daughter didn't (use to) like studying.*
Me ha gustado mucho la comida. *I really liked the food/the meal.*
¿No te gustaron las fotos? *Didn't you like the photos?*
A ella le gustó la película. *She liked the film.*

verbs used like gustar

There are other verbs which are used in the same way as **gustar**:

- **doler** *to hurt*
  Me duele la mano. *My hand hurts.* lit. *My hand is hurting me.*
  Te duelen los hombros. *Your shoulders hurt.* lit. *Your shoulders are hurting you.*

- **faltar** *to be short of, to lack*
  Me falta el libro de matemáticas. *I don't have my maths book.* lit. *My maths book is lacking to me.*
  No le había faltado nunca nada. *He had never gone short of anything.*

- **importar** *to matter*
  No me importa tu opinión. *Your opinion doesn't matter (to me).*
  ¿A quien le importa? *Who cares?*

- **parecer** *to think (of)*
  ¿Qué te parece si vamos a España de vacaciones? *How about going on holiday to Spain?* lit. *How does it seem to you if we go on holiday to Spain?*

- **quedar** *to have left*
  Le quedan dos años para terminar sus estudios. *She has two years left before finishing her studies.*
  ¿Cuántos euros te quedan? *How many euros have you got left?*

  and:
  apasionar *to love passionately*
  apetecer *to feel like*
  disgustar *to dislike, to hate*
  encantar *to love*
  enloquecer *to drive mad*
  fascinar *to fascinate*
  hacer falta *to need*
  interesar *to interest*
  molestar *to bother*
  sobrar *to have more than enough/some left over*
  tocarle a alguien *to be one's turn*

impersonal verbs

Impersonal verbs don't refer to anything specific so are used in the *it* form. Some verbs, such as **llover** *to rain* and **nevar** *to snow*, are always impersonal. Other common verbs such as **hacer**, **haber** and **ser** (page 179) are only sometimes used as impersonal verbs.

llover and nevar

Although these verbs are always impersonal, they can be used in the full range of tenses.

Llueve mucho. *It rains/it's raining a lot.*
Nieva un poco. *It snows a little/it's snowing a little.*
Va a llover pasado mañana. *It's going to rain the day after tomorrow.*
No va a nevar este fin de semana. *It's not going to snow this weekend.*
Estaba lloviendo en España. *It was raining in Spain.*
¿Estaba nevando en las montañas? *Was it snowing in the mountains?*

hacer

Hacer means *to do, to make* but is also used:

● in weather phrases:
Hoy hace calor, pero no hace viento. *Today's it's hot, but not windy.*
No hacía sol de vacaciones. *It wasn't sunny on holiday.*
Va a hacer frío mañana. *It will be cold tomorrow.*

● in the expression **hace falta** *it is necessary*:
Hace falta trabajar. *It's necessary to work.*
No hace falta decirle. *It's not necessary to tell him.*
¿Hace falta hacerlo hoy? *Does it need to be done today?*
No nos hace falta nada. *We don't need anything.*
Nos hacía falta otra solución. *We needed another solution.*

- in time expressions to mean *for*, where the verb is in the present tense rather than the perfect tense as in English (page 136):
Hace un año **que** Raúl trabaja en un bar.
Raúl trabaja en un bar **desde hace** un año.
Raul's been working in a bar for a year.
Hace tres meses **que** no voy a una fiesta.
No voy a una fiesta desde hace tres meses.
I haven't been to a party for three months.

and *ago*:
Hace un año fui a Granada. *I went to Granada a year ago.*
Hace una semana montaron a caballo. *A week ago they went horse riding.*

hay

- **Hay** *there is*, *there are*, comes from **haber**, which is also the verb used for compound (two-word) tenses such as the perfect and the pluperfect (pages 151-158).
Hay un sillón en el salón. *There's an armchair in the lounge.*
Hay dos sillones en el salón. *There are two armchairs in the lounge.*
Había cuatro sillas de madera. *There were four wooden chairs.*
No hubo mucho ruido. *There wasn't much noise.*
¿Habrá una fiesta? *Will there be a party?*

- **Hay** is also used to talk about the weather:
hay nubes *it's cloudy*; **hay tempestad** *it's stormy*
hay neblina *it's misty*; **hay niebla** *it's foggy*
hay lluvia *it's raining*; **hay nieve** *it's snowing*

- **Hay que** followed by an infinitive expresses necessity:
Hay que llenar el formulario. *You need/We need/One needs to fill in the form.*
¿Cuánto hay que pagar? *How much do we need to pay?*
Habrá que terminarlo. *You'll need to finish it.*

modal verbs

Modal verbs are used to express opinion and intention – *should*, *can*, *must*. The main modal verbs in Spanish are **deber** *to have to*, **poder** *to be able to*, **querer** *to want to* and **saber** *to know how to*.

Poder, **querer** and **saber** are irregular (pages 230, 233, 236) and in certain tenses they can have particular meanings.

- Verbs which follow a modal verb are always in the infinitive:
  Puedes escoger. *You can choose.*
  No saben jugar al tenis. *They don't know how to play tennis.*
  ¿Me debo cambiar de ropa? *Do I have to change?*
  Queremos sentarnos. *We want to sit down.*

- There are two possible positions for pronouns with modal verbs – they can either go before the modal verb or after the infinitive:
  La debo llamar./Debo llamarla. *I should phone her.*
  No lo sabía tocar./No sabía tocarlo. *I didn't know how to play it.*
  (musical instrument)
  ¿Cómo te lo puedo explicar?/¿Cómo puedo explicártelo?
  How can I explain it to you?
  Se los querían mandar./Querían mandárselos. *They wanted to send them to him.*

This also applies when **deber**, **poder**, **querer** and **saber** are used with reflexive verbs (page 116):
Debo levantarme./Me debo levantar. *I ought to get up.*
No te quieres sentar?/No quieres sentarte? *Don't you want to sit down?*

deber

Deber *to have to, must* can also mean *to owe*: **¿Cuánto te debo?** *How much do I owe you?* This is quite separate from its use as a modal verb, when it has a range of English translations:

- *have to, must* – present tense:
  Debo volver a casa. *I have to go back home.*
  ¿A qué hora debes irte? *What time do you have to leave?*
  No debemos olvidar. *We must not forget.*

  You can add **de** when making assumptions:
  Las llaves deben (de) estar en la habitación. *The keys must be in the room.*
  Debe de ser complicado. *It must be complicated.*

- *had to* – perfect, preterite, imperfect and imperfect subjunctive, all with slight differences in meaning:
  Debía trabajar tanto. *I had to (used to have to) work so much.*
  ¿Por qué debiste salir? *Why did you have to go out?*
  Ha debido irse a mediodía. *He had to leave at midday.*
  Si debiera escoger … *If he had to choose …*

- *ought to, should* – conditional
  Debería reducir el precio. *He ought to reduce the price.*
  No debería quejarme. *I ought not to/shouldn't complain.*
  Debería ir a ver Madrid. *You should go to see Madrid.*

- *should have, was/were supposed to* – past conditional
  Habría debido ir a la oficina. *I should have gone to the office.*
  Habrías debido llamar el banco. *You were supposed to ring the bank.*

Necessity can be expressed more strongly by **tener que** *to have to* and the impersonal **hay que** *it is necessary to* (page 183):
Tenemos que irnos ahora mismo. *We have to leave right now.*
¿Dónde tengo que bajar? *Where do I have to get off?*
¿Hay que pagar la cuenta en seguida? *Is it necessary to pay the bill straightaway?*

poder, saber

Poder

Poder *to be able to*, is a modal verb with a range of English translations:

- *can, may, be able to* – present tense:
  ¿Puedes explicarlo? *Can you explain?*
  No podemos venir hoy. *We can't come today.*
  ¿Podemos pagar con tarjeta de crédito? *May we pay by credit card?*

- *could* – preterite, imperfect, perfect, conditional and subjunctive:
  Pude ayudar. *I could help (managed to help).*
  Podía ayudar. *I could help (was able to help).*
  He podido ayudar. *I have helped (been able to help).*
  Podría ayudar. *I could help (would be able to help).*
  ¿Podría ayudarme? *Could you (would you be able to) help me?*
  Si pudiera ayudar, ayudaría. *If I could (were able to) help, I would help.*

- *could have, might have* – past conditional:
  Habría podido ayudarte. *I could have helped you.*
  Habría podido ser estupendo. *It could have been superb.*
  Por lo menos habría podido preguntarle. *You might at least have asked him.*

Saber

When *can* means *know how to*, you use **saber** not **poder**.
¿Sabes nadar? *Can you swim?*
No sé cocinar. *I can't cook.*

Used in the preterite, **saber** has the specific meaning of *realised* or *found out*:
Supieron el problema. *They found out/realised the problem.*

Se puede is very often used instead of **puedo** or **podemos** to ask if you can do something or if something can be done:
¿Se puede reservar una habitación? *Can we/one book a room?*
¿Se puede comprar un billete aquí? *Can we/one buy a ticket here?*

querer

Querer *to want* can be used with a noun or pronoun:

Te quiero. *I love you.*

Quisiera un café, por favor. *I'd like a coffee, please.*

Quería una habitación más grande. *I wanted a bigger room.*

When it's followed by another verb. i.e. when it's used as a modal, **querer** has a range of English translations:

- *want*, *would like*, *will* (polite request) – present:

  No quiero quedarme aquí. *I don't want to stay here.*

  Queremos ver el museo. *We want to see the museum.*

  ¿Qué quiere? *What would you like?*

  ¿Quiere firmar aquí? *Will you sign here?*

- *wanted* – imperfect and preterite, with slightly different implications:

  Quería salir. *I wanted to go out (and this might or might not have happened).*

  Quise salir. *I wanted to go out (and this is what happened).*

  In the preterite there are different meanings in the positive and the negative:

  Quise ayudarte. *I tried to help you.*

  No quisieron ir. *They refused to go.*

- *would like* – imperfect subjunctive and conditional– express *want* more politely:

  Quisiera aparcar aquí. *I'd like to park here.*

  Querría ver la habitación. *I'd like to see the room.*

- *would have liked* - past conditional:

  Habría querido ver la habitación. *I would have liked to see the room.*

Querer is used in these phrases:

Quieras o no, tendrás que hacerlo. *Whether you want to or not, you'll have to do it.*

¿Qué quiere decir? *What does it mean?*

Lo hizo sin querer. *He did it accidentally.*

checkpoint 20

1   **Ser** or **estar**? Complete with the appropriate form.

   a **La cocina** .... **moderna.** *The kitchen is modern.*

   b **La casas** .... **muy limpias.** *The houses are very clean.*

   c **La silla** .... **de plástico.** *The chair is made of plastic.*

   d .... **contables.** *They're accountants.*

   e **Pedro** .... **de Bilbao.** *Pedro's from Bilbao.*

   f .... **en el campo.** *I'm in the country.*

   g **Lima** .... **la capital de Perú.** *Lima is the capital of Peru.*

   h **¿** .... **(tú form) triste?** *Are you sad?*

   i **Las casas** .... **grandes.** *The houses are big.*

   j **¿Dónde** .... **la piscina?** *Where's the swimming pool?*

2   Fill the gaps in the weather expressions with either **hace** or **hay**:

a .... **nubes**		b .... **niebla**	
c .... **sol**		d .... **nieve**	
e .... **calor**		f .... **neblina**	
g .... **viento**		h .... **frío**	
i .... **lluvia**		j .... **tempestad**	

3   Choose the correct ending and translate the sentences:

A	B
A Enrique no le gustan	el pescado cuando eras joven.
No te gustaba	esquiar.
A mis amigos les gusta	las cerezas que compré.
Os gustaron	los mariscos.
Nos gustaban	la película que vi anoche.
Me gustó mucho	los caramelos cuando éramos jóvenes.

Verbs followed by prepositions

Spanish verbs are linked to other words in a sentence in various ways.

They can be:

- followed directly by another verb. This second verb is always in the infinitive in Spanish, even though in English it can be an infinitive, e.g. *to think*, *to work* or a gerund, e.g. *thinking*, *working*:
  Quiero dormir. *I want to sleep.*
  Me gusta estudiar. *I like studying.*

- followed by **a**, **de**, **con**, **en** or **por** before the second verb. More often than not, the preposition has no equivalent in English:
  terminar de hablar *to finish talking*; **quedar en ir** *to agree to go*

- followed by **a** + person + **a** + verb. Again they may have no English translation:
  invitar a alguien a cenar *to invite somebody to have dinner*

- followed by **a**, **de**, **con**, **en** or **por** before a noun:
  decir algo a alguien *to say something to somebody*
  enfadarse con alguien *to get annoyed with somebody*
  entrar en una casa *to enter (into) a house*

  It's not always this straightforward because the preposition often has no equivalent in English or has an unexpected translation:
  jugar al fútbol *to play football*; **llenar de agua** *to fill with water*

Lists of common verbs needing a preposition have been included here because the English translation provides no clue as to why, for example **a** is needed in **accedo a pagar** *I agree to pay*, **de** in **me olvidé de pagar** *I forgot to pay*, and no preposition in **quiero pagar** *I want to pay*. All you can do at first is remember which preposition is needed – but after a while you'll start to get a feel for which one actually **sounds** right.

verbs followed by a

Some Spanish verbs are always linked to the rest of the sentence by **a**.
The most common are listed opposite and include verbs of movement such as **ir** *to go* and **venir** *to come*.

- When these verbs are followed by another verb, this is always in the infinitive in Spanish, even though in English it can be an infinitive or a gerund. There is no English equivalent for **a** with most verbs:
  ¿Aprendes a conducir? *Are you learning to drive?*
  El niño empieza a andar. *The toddler's starting to walk.*
  Os acostumbráis a levantaros temprano. *You're getting used to getting up early.*
  ¿Cuándo vienes a verme? *When are you coming to see me?*
  Volví a leer el libro. *I read the book again.*

- When these verbs are followed by a noun, **a** often has no equivalent in English or has an unexpected translation:
  When **a** is followed by **el**, they combine to become **al**:
  ¿Quieres jugar al tenis? *Do you want to play tennis?*
  Se parece tanto a su abuelo. *He looks so much like his grandfather.*
  Llegamos tarde a la fiesta. *We arrived late at the party.*
  Subimos al autobús. *We got on the bus.*

- **a** can be used with an indirect object after certain verbs (page 85):
  dar algo a alguien *to give something to someone*
  decir algo a alguien *to say something to someone*
  Di un regalo a mi amiga. *I gave my friend a present.* lit. *I gave a present to my friend.*
  Siempre decimos la verdad a nuestros hijos. *We always tell the truth to our children. We always tell our children the truth.*

  To replace **a** + person with a pronoun, you use an indirect object pronoun (page 84):
  Le di un regalo. *I gave her a present.*
  Siempre les decimos la verdad. *We always tell them the truth.*

As in English, some of these verbs, like **llegar a** *to manage to*, can only be followed by another verb; others, such as **jugar a** *to play*, are followed by a noun. But many verbs, like **acostumbrarse a** *to get used to* or **dedicarse a** *to devote oneself to*, **resignarse a** *to resign oneself to*, can be followed by either a verb or a noun.

acceder a *to agree to*
acertar a *to manage to*
acostumbrarse a *to get used to*
aficionarse a *to grow fond of*
alcanzar a *to manage to*
aprender a *to learn to*
apresurarse a *to hurry to*
aspirar a *to aspire to*
atreverse a *to dare to*
comenzar a *to start to*
comprometerse a *to undertake to*
conducir a *to lead to*
contribuir a *to contribute to*
decidirse a *to decide to*
dedicarse a *to devote oneself to*
disponerse a *to get ready to*
echarse a *to begin to*
empezar a *to begin to*
esperar a *to wait until*
inclinarse a (also **por**) *to be inclined to*
ir a *to be going to*
jugar a *to play a game, gamble*

llegar a *to manage to*
llevar a *to lead to*
meterse a *to get down to, get on with*
negarse a *to refuse to*
oler a algo *to smell of something*
oponerse a *to be opposed to*
parecerse a algo/alguien *to look like something/someone*
pasar a *to go on to*
ponerse a *to begin to*
precipitarse a *to rush to*
prepararse a *to get ready to*
regresar a *to go back to*
resignarse a *to resign oneself to*
resistirse a *to resist*
romper a *to start (suddenly) to*
salir a *to go out to*
subir a *to get on (bus/train)*
tender a *to tend to*
venir a *to come to*
volver a *to do (something) again*

verb + a + person + a + infinitive

Whereas in English you help someone to do something, in Spanish you help to them **to** do something:

ayudar a alguien a hacer algo

There are several other verbs which behave in the same way:

> **animar a algn* a** *to encourage s.o. to*
> **convidar a algn a** *to invite s.o. to*
> **desafiar a algn a** *to challenge s.o. to*
> **enseñar a algn a** *to teach s.o. to*
> **forzar a algn a** *to force s.o. to*
> **impulsar a algn a** *to urge s.o. to*
> **incitar a algn a** *to incite s.o. to*
> **inspirar a algn a** *to inspire s.o. to*
> **invitar a algn a** *to invite s.o. to*
> **obligar a algn a** *to oblige s.o. to*
>
> *****alguien** *someone*

El gerente obligó a los empleados a trabajar más tarde. *The manager obliged the employees to work later.*
Invité a mi amiga a ir de compras. *I invited my friend to go shopping.*
Inspiras a tus estudiantes a tener éxito. *You inspire your students to succeed.*
Enseñaba a su hija a tocar la guitarra. *He used to teach his daughter to play the guitar.*

To replace **a** + person with a pronoun, you use an indirect object pronoun (page 84):
El gerente les obligó a trabajar más tarde. *The manager obliged them to work later.*
La invité a ir de compras. *I invited her to go shopping.*
Les inspiras a tener éxito. *You inspire them to succeed.*
La enseñaba a tocar la guitarra. *He used to teach her to play the guitar.*

verbs followed by de

Some Spanish verbs are always linked to the rest of the sentence by **de**. The most common are listed below.

- When they're followed by another verb, it's in the infinitive in Spanish, even though in English it may be an infinitive or a gerund.

  Trato de beber más agua. *I try to drink more water.*

  Se aburrieron de hacer la misma cosa. *They got bored with doing the same thing.*

  Acaba de limpiar el coche. *He's just finished cleaning the car.*

  ¡Nunca cesáis de hablar! *You never stop talking!*

  ¿A qué hora terminas de pasear al perro? *At what time do you finish walking the dog?*

- When they're followed by a noun, **de** is often not translated. When **de** is followed by **el**, the two combine to become **del**:

  Tengo miedo de los ratones. *I'm frightened of mice.*

  No se queja del ruido. *He's not complaining about the noise.*

  Les acusaron del robo. *They accused them of the robbery.*

  ¿Te ocupas de tu madre? *Do you look after your mother?*

---

aburrirse de *to get bored with*
acabar de *to have just*
acordarse de *to remember*
acusar de *to accuse of*
alegrarse de *to be pleased about*
alejarse de *to move away from*
asombrarse de *to be surprised at*
asustarse de *to be frightened at*
avergonzarse de *to be ashamed of*
bajarse de *to get off* (bus, train)
burlarse de *to make fun of*
cansarse de *to tire of*
cesar de *to stop*
cuidar de *to look after*
darse cuenta de *to realise*
dejar de *to stop*
depender de *to depend on*
despedirse de *to say goodbye to*
disuadir de *to dissuade from*
encargarse de *to take charge of*

guardarse de *to take care not to*
haber de *to have to*
hartarse de *to be fed up with*
ocuparse de *to take care of*
olvidarse de *to forget to*
parar de *to stop*
pensar de *to think of*
preocuparse de (also **por**) *to worry about*
quejarse de *to complain about*
reírse de *to laugh at*
salir de *to go out of*
tener ganas de *to feel like*
tener intención de *to intend to*
tener miedo de (also **a**) *to be afraid of*
tener necesidad de *to need to*
terminar de *to stop*
tratar de *to try to*
tratarse de *to be a question of*

verbs + con, en, por

A few verbs are followed by **con**, **en** or **por**.

- Some can be followed by a verb in the infinitive or by a noun:

> **amenazar con** *to threaten to*
> **soñar con** *to dream about*
> **consentir en** *to agree to*
> **consisitir en** *to consist of*
> **insistir en** *to insist*
> **interesarse en** *to be interested in*
> **pensar en** *to think about*
> **perseverar en** *to persevere in*
> **persistir en** *to persist*
> **quedar en** *to agree to*
> **empezar por** *to begin by/with*
> **luchar por** *to struggle, fight to*

¿En qué piensas? *What are you thinking about?*
Pienso en volver a Madrid. *I'm thinking about going back to Madrid.*
Soñé contigo anoche. *I dreamed about you last night.*
Sueñan con ganar la lotería. *They dream about winning the lottery.*
Me mostró la casa, empezando por la cocina. *He showed me the house, starting with the kitchen.*
Empiezo por tomar un café. *In the morning I begin by having a coffee.*

- Others can only be followed by a noun:

> **casarse con** *to get married to*
> **comparar con** *to compare with*
> **contar con** *to rely on*
> **encontrarse con** *to meet* (by chance)
> **enfadarse con** *to get annoyed with*
> **estar de acuerdo con** *to agree with*
> **hablar con** *to talk to*
> **entrar en** *to enter*
> **interesarse por** *to ask about, to be interested in*
> **preocuparse por** (also **de**) *to worry about*

Me enfadé con el funcionario. *I got annoyed with the official.*
Entramos en la Catedral. *We entered the Cathedral.*
Se preocupa por sus exámenes. *She's worrying about her exams.*

verbs with no preposition in Spanish

Although these verbs have a preposition when they're used before a noun in English, they don't need one in Spanish because it's built into the word. This means that their object is a direct object.

> **apagar** *to turn off (a light)*
> **bajar** *to go down*
> **borrar** *to rub out*
> **buscar** *to look for*
> **caerse** *to fall down*
> **colgar** *to hang up*
> **encender** *to light up*
> **escuchar** *to listen to*
> **esperar** *to wait for*
> **lograr** *to succeed in*
> **mirar** *to look at*
> **pagar** *to pay for*
> **pedir** *to ask for*
> **poner** *to turn on (radio, TV)*
> **quitar** *to take off*
> **sacar** *to take out*
> **salir** *to go out*
> **subir** *to go up*

He pedido una cerveza. *I've asked for a beer.*
Pagaré el vino. *I'll pay for the wine.*
Busca su pasaporte. *He's looking for his passport.*
Esperan el autobús. *They're waiting for the bus.*

When the direct object is a specific person, you use the personal **a** (page 99):
Busco a Dolores. *I'm looking for Dolores.*
Espero a uno de mis amigos. *I'm waiting for one of my friends.*

checkpoint 21

1 Does **a** or **de** belong in the gap?
   a He dejado .... comer patatas fritas. *I've stopped eating chips.*
   b ¿Puedes ayudar a Paco .... llevarlos? *Can you help Paco to carry them?*
   c Os aburríais .... estudiar. *You used to get bored with studying.*
   d Invitó a sus amigos .... ir de copas. *He invited his friends to go for a drink.*
   e Me gustaría aprender .... esquiar. *I'd like to learn to ski.*
   f Nos alegramos .... verte. *We're pleased to see you.*
   g ¿Tienes miedo .... salir? *Are you afraid of going out?*
   h Comenzó .... llover. *It started to rain.*

2 Fill these gaps with a preposition + *the*. Use **al** or **del** where appropriate.
   a Se encargó .... situación. *He took charge of the situation.*
   b No quisieron entrar .... casa. *They refused to enter the house.*
   c Te preocupas .... perro. *You're worrying about the dog.*
   d Nos enfadamos .... dependienta. *We got annoyed with the shop assistant.*
   e Me quejé .... precio. *I complained about the price.*
   f ¿Quieres venir .... concierto? *Do you want to come to the concert?*
   g Me he acostumbrado .... frío. *I've got used to the cold.*

3 Translate these into Spanish.
   a *They're waiting for the train.*
   b *I like playing golf.*
   c *We always listen to music.*
   d *You're (vosotros) trying not to smoke.*
   e *I intend to visit you.*
   f *Do they want to eat now?*
   g *We enter the stadium.*
   h *Are you (tú) looking after the neighbour's dog?*

Verb tables

The following pages present 50 key verbs, which are listed on page 248 for easy reference:

- **hablar** *to speak*, **comer** *to eat* and **vivir** *to live* which provide the regular patterns for **-ar** verbs, **-er** verbs and **-ir** verbs.

- **lavarse** *to wash oneself*, to show how a regular reflexive verb behaves.

- radical-changing verbs such as **encontrar** *to meet*, **cerrar** *to close* and **pedir** *to ask (for)*, which have regular endings but which change their stems in some tenses.

- verbs such as **conducir** *to drive*, **pagar** *to pay* and **cruzar** *to cross* which illustrate the common spelling changes that some verbs undergo in some tenses.

- key irregular verbs such as **ser** *to be*, **tener** *to have*, **ir** *to go* and the modal verbs **poder** *to be able to*, **querer** *to want to* and **saber** *to know how to*.

- other irregular verbs such as **decir** *to say* and **poner** *to put*, which provide the pattern for verbs that behave in the same way. These are listed underneath.

All 50 verbs are written out in all persons in the present, future, conditional, imperfect, preterite, perfect, present subjunctive and imperfect subjunctive.

The imperfect subjunctive has two forms. The more commonly-used version is listed first.

1 andar *to walk*

	present	future	conditional
yo	ando	andaré	andaría
tú	andas	andarás	andarías
él/ella,usted	anda	andará	andaría
nosotros/as	andamos	andaremos	andaríamos
vosotros/as	andáis	andaréis	andaríais
ellos/ellas, ustedes	andan	andarán	andarían

	imperfect	preterite	perfect
yo	andaba	anduve	he andado
tú	andabas	anduviste	has andado
él/ella,usted	andaba	anduvo	ha andado
nosotros/as	andábamos	anduvimos	hemos andado
vosotros/as	andabais	anduvisteis	habéis andado
ellos/ellas, ustedes	andaban	anduvieron	han andado

	present subjunctive	imperfect subjunctive
yo	ande	anduviera/anduviese
tú	andes	anduvieras/anduvieses
él/ella,usted	ande	anduviera/anduviese
nosotros/as	andemos	anduviéramos/anduviésemos
vosotros/as	andéis	anduvierais/anduvieseis
ellos/ellas, ustedes	anden	anduvieran/anduviesen

past participle **andado**

gerund **andando**

imperative **(tú) anda, (vosotros) andad**

2 buscar *to look for*

	present	future	conditional
yo	busco	buscaré	buscaría
tú	buscas	buscarás	buscarías
él/ella,usted	busca	buscará	buscaría
nosotros/as	buscamos	buscaremos	buscaríamos
vosotros/as	buscáis	buscaréis	buscaríais
ellos/ellas, ustedes	buscan	buscarán	buscarían

	imperfect	preterite	perfect
yo	buscaba	busqué	he buscado
tú	buscabas	buscaste	has buscado
él/ella,usted	buscaba	buscó	ha buscado
nosotros/as	buscábamos	buscamos	hemos buscado
vosotros/as	buscabais	buscasteis	habéis buscado
ellos/ellas, ustedes	buscaban	buscaron	han buscado

	present subjunctive	imperfect subjunctive
yo	busque	buscara/buscase
tú	busques	buscaras/buscases
él/ella,usted	busque	buscara/buscase
nosotros/as	busquemos	buscáramos/buscásemos
vosotros/as	busquéis	buscarais/buscaseis
ellos/ellas, ustedes	busquen	buscaran/buscasen

past participle **buscado**

gerund **buscando**

imperative **(tú) busca**, **(vosotros) buscad**

3   caber *to fit*

	present	future	conditional
yo	quepo	cabré	cabría
tú	cabes	cabrás	cabrías
él/ella,usted	cabe	cabrá	cabría
nosotros/as	cabemos	cabremos	cabríamos
vosotros/as	cabéis	cabréis	cabríais
ellos/ellas, ustedes	caben	cabrán	cabrían

	imperfect	preterite	perfect
yo	cabía	cupe	he cabido
tú	cabías	cupiste	has cabido
él/ella,usted	cabía	cupo	ha cabido
nosotros/as	cabíamos	cupimos	hemos cabido
vosotros/as	cabíais	cupisteis	habéis cabido
ellos/ellas, ustedes	cabían	cupieron	han cabido

	present subjunctive	imperfect subjunctive
yo	quepa	cupiera/cupiese
tú	quepas	cupieras/cupieses
él/ella,usted	quepa	cupiera/cupiese
nosotros/as	quepamos	cupiéramos/cupiésemos
vosotros/as	quepáis	cupierais/cupieseis
ellos/ellas, ustedes	quepan	cupieran/cupiesen

past participle **cabido**

gerund **cabiendo**

imperative (**tú**) **cabe**, (**vosotros**) **cabed**

4 caer *to fall*

	present	future	conditional
yo	caigo	caeré	caería
tú	caes	caerás	caerías
él/ella, usted	cae	caerá	caería
nosotros/as	caemos	caeremos	caeríamos
vosotros/as	caéis	caeréis	caeríais
ellos/ellas, ustedes	caen	caerán	caerían

	imperfect	preterite	perfect
yo	caía	caí	he caído
tú	caías	caíste	has caído
él/ella, usted	caía	cayó	ha caído
nosotros/as	caíamos	caímos	hemos caído
vosotros/as	caíais	caísteis	habéis caído
ellos/ellas, ustedes	caían	cayeron	han caído

	present subjunctive	imperfect subjunctive
yo	caiga	cayera/cayese
tú	caigas	cayeras/cayeses
él/ella, usted	caiga	cayera/cayese
nosotros/as	caigamos	cayéramos/cayésemos
vosotros/as	caigáis	cayerais/cayeseis
ellos/ellas, ustedes	caigan	cayeran/cayesen

past participle **caído**

gerund **cayendo**

imperative (tú) **cae**, (vosotros) **caed**

Verbs that follow the same pattern as **caer** include **decaer** *to decline* and **recaer** *to relapse*.

5   cerrar *to close*

	present	future	conditional
yo	cierro	cerraré	cerraría
tú	cierras	cerrarás	cerrarías
él/ella, usted	cierra	cerrará	cerraría
nosotros/as	cerramos	cerraremos	cerraríamos
vosotros/as	cerráis	cerraréis	cerraríais
ellos/ellas, ustedes	cierran	cerrarán	cerrarían

	imperfect	preterite	perfect
yo	cerraba	cerré	he cerrado
tú	cerrabas	cerraste	has cerrado
él/ella, usted	cerraba	cerró	ha cerrado
nosotros/as	cerrábamos	cerramos	hemos cerrado
vosotros/as	cerrabais	cerrasteis	habéis cerrado
ellos/ellas, ustedes	cerraban	cerraron	han cerrado

	present subjunctive	imperfect subjunctive
yo	cierre	cerrara/cerrase
tú	cierres	cerraras/cerrases
él/ella, usted	cierre	cerrara/cerrase
nosotros/as	cerremos	cerráramos/cerrásemos
vosotros/as	cerréis	cerrarais/cerraseis
ellos/ellas, ustedes	cierren	cerraran/cerrasen

past participle **cerrado**

gerund **cerrando**

imperative **(tú) cierra**, **(vosotros) cerrad**

Verbs that follow the same pattern as **cerrar** include **atravesar** *to cross*, **despertar** *to wake up*, **pensar** *to think*, **sentarse** *to sit*.

6 coger *to catch*

	present	future	conditional
yo	cojo	cogeré	cogería
tú	coges	cogerás	cogerías
él/ella,usted	coge	cogerá	cogería
nosotros/as	cogemos	cogeremos	cogeríamos
vosotros/as	cogéis	cogeréis	cogeríais
ellos/ellas, ustedes	cogen	cogerán	cogerían

	imperfect	preterite	perfect
yo	cogía	cogí	he cogido
tú	cogías	cogiste	has cogido
él/ella,usted	cogía	cogió	ha cogido
nosotros/as	cogíamos	cogimos	hemos cogido
vosotros/as	cogíais	cogisteis	habéis cogido
ellos/ellas, ustedes	cogían	cogieron	han cogido

	present subjunctive	imperfect subjunctive
yo	coja	cogiera/cogiese
tú	cojas	cogieras/cogieses
él/ella,usted	coja	cogiera/cogiese
nosotros/as	cojamos	cogiéramos/cogiésemos
vosotros/as	cojáis	cogierais/cogieseis
ellos/ellas, ustedes	cojan	cogieran/cogiesen

past participle **cogido**

gerund **cogiendo**

imperative **(tú) coge**, **(vosotros) coged**

7 comenzar *to begin*

	present	future	conditional
yo	comienzo	comenzaré	comenzaría
tú	comienzas	comenzarás	comenzarías
él/ella,usted	comienza	comenzará	comenzaría
nosotros/as	comenzamos	comenzaremos	comenzaríamos
vosotros/as	comenzáis	comenzaréis	comenzaríais
ellos/ellas, ustedes	comienzan	comenzarán	comenzarían

	imperfect	preterite	perfect
yo	comenzaba	comencé	he comenzado
tú	comenzabas	comenzaste	has comenzado
él/ella,usted	comenzaba	comenzó	ha comenzado
nosotros/as	comenzábamos	comenzamos	hemos comenzado
vosotros/as	comenzabais	comenzasteis	habéis comenzado
ellos/ellas, ustedes	comenzaban	comenzaron	han comenzado

	present subjunctive	imperfect subjunctive
yo	comience	comenzara/comenzase
tú	comiences	comenzaras/comenzases
él/ella,usted	comience	comenzara/comenzase
nosotros/as	comencemos	comenzáramos/comenzásemos
vosotros/as	comencéis	comenzarais/comenzaseis
ellos/ellas, ustedes	comiencen	comenzaran/comenzasen

past participle **comenzado**

gerund **comenzando**

imperative **(tú) comienza**, **(vosotros) comenzad**

Verbs that follow the same pattern as **comenzar** include **empezar** *to begin* and **tropezar** *to stumble*.

8 comer *to eat*

	present	future	conditional
yo	como	comeré	comería
tú	comes	comerás	comerías
él/ella,usted	come	comerá	comería
nosotros/as	comemos	comeremos	comeríamos
vosotros/as	coméis	comeréis	comeríais
ellos/ellas, ustedes	comen	comerán	comerían

	imperfect	preterite	perfect
yo	comía	comí	he comido
tú	comías	comiste	has comido
él/ella,usted	comía	comió	ha comido
nosotros/as	comíamos	comimos	hemos comido
vosotros/as	comíais	comisteis	habéis comido
ellos/ellas, ustedes	comían	comieron	han comido

	present subjunctive	imperfect subjunctive
yo	coma	comiera/comiese
tú	comas	comieras/comieses
él/ella,usted	coma	comiera/comiese
nosotros/as	comamos	comiéramos/comiésemos
vosotros/as	comáis	comierais/comieseis
ellos/ellas, ustedes	coman	comieran/comiesen

past participle **comido**

gerund **comiendo**

imperative (**tú**) **come**, (**vosotros**) **comed**

9   conducir *to drive*

	present	future	conditional
yo	conduzco	conduciré	conduciría
tú	conduces	conducirás	conducirías
él/ella, usted	conduce	conducirá	conduciría
nosotros/as	conducimos	conduciremos	conduciríamos
vosotros/as	conducís	conduciréis	conduciríais
ellos/ellas, ustedes	conducen	conducirán	conducirían

	imperfect	preterite	perfect
yo	conducía	conduje	he conducido
tú	conducías	condujiste	has conducido
él/ella, usted	conducía	condujo	ha conducido
nosotros/as	conducíamos	condujimos	hemos conducido
vosotros/as	conducíais	condujisteis	habéis conducido
ellos/ellas, ustedes	conducían	condujeron	han conducido

	present subjunctive	imperfect subjunctive
yo	conduzca	condujera/condujese
tú	conduzcas	condujeras/condujeses
él/ella, usted	conduzca	condujera/condujese
nosotros/as	conduzcamos	condujéramos/condujésemos
vosotros/as	conduzcáis	condujerais/condujeseis
ellos/ellas, ustedes	conduzcan	condujeran/condujesen

past participle **conducido**

gerund **conduciendo**

imperative **(tú) conduce, (vosotros) conducid**

Verbs that follow the same pattern as **conducir** include **deducir** *to deduce*, **producir** *to produce*, **reducir** *to reduce*, **traducir** *to translate*.

10 conocer *to know*

	present	future	conditional
yo	conozco	conoceré	conocería
tú	conoces	conocerás	conocerías
él/ella,usted	conoce	conocerá	conocería
nosotros/as	conocemos	conoceremos	conoceríamos
vosotros/as	conocéis	conoceréis	conoceríais
ellos/ellas, ustedes	conocen	conocerán	conocerían

	imperfect	preterite	perfect
yo	conocía	conocí	he conocido
tú	conocías	conociste	has conocido
él/ella,usted	conocía	conoció	ha conocido
nosotros/as	conocíamos	conocimos	hemos conocido
vosotros/as	conocíais	conocisteis	habéis conocido
ellos/ellas, ustedes	conocían	conocieron	han conocido

	present subjunctive	imperfect subjunctive
yo	conozca	conociera/conociese
tú	conozcas	conocieras/conocieses
él/ella,usted	conozca	conociera/conociese
nosotros/as	conozcamos	conociéramos/conociésemos
vosotros/as	conozcáis	conocierais/conocieseis
ellos/ellas, ustedes	conozcan	conocieran/conociesen

past participle **conocido**

gerund **conociendo**

imperative **(tú) conoce, (vosotros) conoced**

11   construir *to build*

	present	future	conditional
yo	construyo	construiré	construiría
tú	construyes	construirás	construirías
él/ella, usted	construye	construirá	construiría
nosotros/as	construimos	construiremos	construiríamos
vosotros/as	construís	construiréis	construiríais
ellos/ellas, ustedes	construyen	construirán	construirían

	imperfect	preterite	perfect
yo	construía	construí	he construido
tú	construías	construiste	has construido
él/ella, usted	construía	construyó	ha construido
nosotros/as	construíamos	construimos	hemos construido
vosotros/as	construíais	construisteis	habéis construido
ellos/ellas, ustedes	construían	construyeron	han construido

	present subjunctive	imperfect subjunctive
yo	construya	construyera/construyese
tú	construyas	construyeras/construyeses
él/ella, usted	construya	construyera/construyese
nosotros/as	construyamos	construyéramos/construyésemos
vosotros/as	construyáis	construyerais/construyeseis
ellos/ellas, ustedes	construyan	construyeran/construyesen

past participle **construido**

gerund **construyendo**

imperative **(tú) construye**, **(vosotros) construid**

Verbs that follow the same pattern as **construir** include **concluir** *to conclude*, **destruir** *to destroy*, **incluir** *to include*, **influir** *to influence*.

12   creer *to believe*

	present	future	conditional
yo	creo	creeré	creería
tú	crees	creerás	creerías
él/ella,usted	cree	creerá	creería
nosotros/as	creemos	creeremos	creeríamos
vosotros/as	creéis	creeréis	creeríais
ellos/ellas, ustedes	creen	creerán	creerían

	imperfect	preterite	perfect
yo	creía	creí	he creído
tú	creías	creíste	has creído
él/ella,usted	creía	creyó	ha creído
nosotros/as	creíamos	creímos	hemos creído
vosotros/as	creíais	creísteis	habéis creído
ellos/ellas, ustedes	creían	creyeron	han creído

	present subjunctive	imperfect subjunctive
yo	crea	creyera/creyese
tú	creas	creyeras/creyeses
él/ella,usted	crea	creyera/creyese
nosotros/as	creamos	creyéramos/creyésemos
vosotros/as	creáis	creyerais/creyeseis
ellos/ellas, ustedes	crean	creyeran/creyesen

past participle **creído**

gerund **creyendo**

imperative **(tú) cree, (vosotros) creed**

Verbs that follow the same pattern as **creer** include **leer** *to read*, **poseer** *to possess*, **releer** *to re-read*.

13 cruzar *to cross*

	present	future	conditional
yo	cruzo	cruzaré	cruzaría
tú	cruzas	cruzarás	cruzarías
él/ella, usted	cruza	cruzará	cruzaría
nosotros/as	cruzamos	cruzaremos	cruzaríamos
vosotros/as	cruzáis	cruzaréis	cruzaríais
ellos/ellas, ustedes	cruzan	cruzarán	cruzarían

	imperfect	preterite	perfect
yo	cruzaba	crucé	he cruzado
tú	cruzabas	cruzaste	has cruzado
él/ella, usted	cruzaba	cruzó	ha cruzado
nosotros/as	cruzábamos	cruzamos	hemos cruzado
vosotros/as	cruzabais	cruzasteis	habéis cruzado
ellos/ellas, ustedes	cruzaban	cruzaron	han cruzado

	present subjunctive	imperfect subjunctive
yo	cruce	cruzara/cruzase
tú	cruces	cruzaras/cruzases
él/ella, usted	cruce	cruzara/cruzase
nosotros/as	crucemos	cruzáramos/cruzásemos
vosotros/as	crucéis	cruzarais/cruzaseis
ellos/ellas, ustedes	crucen	cruzaran/cruzasen

past participle **cruzado**

gerund **cruzando**

imperative **(tú) cruza, (vosotros) cruzad**

14 dar *to give*

	present	future	conditional
yo	doy	daré	daría
tú	das	darás	darías
él/ella,usted	da	dará	daría
nosotros/as	damos	daremos	daríamos
vosotros/as	dais	daréis	daríais
ellos/ellas, ustedes	dan	darán	darían

	imperfect	preterite	perfect
yo	daba	di	he dado
tú	dabas	diste	has dado
él/ella,usted	daba	dio	ha dado
nosotros/as	dábamos	dimos	hemos dado
vosotros/as	dabais	disteis	habéis dado
ellos/ellas, ustedes	daban	dieron	han dado

	present subjunctive	imperfect subjunctive
yo	dé	diera/diese
tú	des	dieras/dieses
él/ella,usted	dé	diera/diese
nosotros/as	demos	diéramos/diésemos
vosotros/as	deis	dierais/dieseis
ellos/ellas, ustedes	den	dieran/diesen

past participle **dado**

gerund **dando**

imperative **(tú) da**, **(vosotros) dad**

15 decir *to say*

	present	future	conditional
yo	digo	diré	diría
tú	dices	dirás	dirías
él/ella,usted	dice	dirá	diría
nosotros/as	decimos	diremos	diríamos
vosotros/as	decís	diréis	diríais
ellos/ellas, ustedes	dicen	dirán	dirían

	imperfect	preterite	perfect
yo	decía	dije	he dicho
tú	decías	dijiste	has dicho
él/ella,usted	decía	dijo	ha dicho
nosotros/as	decíamos	dijimos	hemos dicho
vosotros/as	decíais	dijisteis	habéis dicho
ellos/ellas, ustedes	decían	dijeron	han dicho

	present subjunctive	imperfect subjunctive
yo	diga	dijera/dijese
tú	digas	dijeras/dijeses
él/ella,usted	diga	dijera/dijese
nosotros/as	digamos	dijéramos/dijésemos
vosotros/as	digáis	dijerais/dijeseis
ellos/ellas, ustedes	digan	dijeran/dijesen

past participle **dicho**

gerund **diciendo**

imperative (**tú**) **di**, (**vosotros**) **decid**

Verbs that follow the same pattern as **decir** include **contradecir** *to contradict*, **bendecir** *to bless* and **predicir** *to predict*.

16 dormir *to sleep*

	present	future	conditional
yo	duermo	dormiré	dormiría
tú	duermes	dormirás	dormirías
él/ella,usted	duerme	dormirá	dormiría
nosotros/as	dormimos	dormiremos	dormiríamos
vosotros/as	dormís	dormiréis	dormiríais
ellos/ellas, ustedes	duermen	dormirán	dormirían

	imperfect	preterite	perfect
yo	dormía	dormí	he dormido
tú	dormías	dormiste	has dormido
él/ella,usted	dormía	durmió	ha dormido
nosotros/as	dormíamos	dormimos	hemos dormido
vosotros/as	dormíais	dormisteis	habéis dormido
ellos/ellas, ustedes	dormían	durmieron	han dormido

	present subjunctive	imperfect subjunctive
yo	duerma	durmiera/durmiese
tú	duermas	durmieras/durmieses
él/ella,usted	duerma	durmiera/durmiese
nosotros/as	durmamos	durmiéramos/durmiésemos
vosotros/as	durmáis	durmierais/durmieseis
ellos/ellas, ustedes	duerman	durmieran/durmiesen

past participle **dormido**

gerund **durmiendo**

imperative **(tú) duerme, (vosotros) dormid**

Verbs that follow the same pattern as **dormir** include **morir** *to die*. **Morir** has an irregular past participle, **muerto**.

17 elegir *to choose*

	present	future	conditional
yo	elijo	elegiré	elegiría
tú	eliges	elegirás	elegirías
él/ella, usted	elige	elegirá	elegiría
nosotros/as	elegimos	elegiremos	elegiríamos
vosotros/as	elegís	elegiréis	elegiríais
ellos/ellas, ustedes	eligen	elegirán	elegirían

	imperfect	preterite	perfect
yo	elegía	elegí	he elegido
tú	elegías	elegiste	has elegido
él/ella, usted	elegía	eligió	ha elegido
nosotros/as	elegíamos	elegimos	hemos elegido
vosotros/as	elegíais	elegisteis	habéis elegido
ellos/ellas, ustedes	elegían	eligieron	han elegido

	present subjunctive	imperfect subjunctive
yo	elija	eligiera/eligiese
tú	elijas	eligieras/eligieses
él/ella, usted	elija	eligiera/eligiese
nosotros/as	elijamos	eligiéramos/eligiésemos
vosotros/as	elijáis	eligierais/eligieseis
ellos/ellas, ustedes	elijan	eligieran/eligiesen

past participle **elegido**

gerund **eligiendo**

imperative **(tú) elige, (vosotros) elegid**

Verbs that follow the same pattern as **elegir** include **corregir** *to correct*, **reelegir** *to re-elect*, **regir** *to govern*.

18 encontrar *to find*

	present	future	conditional
yo	encuentro	encontraré	encontraría
tú	encuentras	encontrarás	encontrarías
él/ella, usted	encuentra	encontrará	encontraría
nosotros/as	encontramos	encontraremos	encontraríamos
vosotros/as	encontráis	encontraréis	encontraríais
ellos/ellas, ustedes	encuentran	encontrarán	encontrarían

	imperfect	preterite	perfect
yo	encontraba	encontré	he encontrado
tú	encontrabas	encontraste	has encontrado
él/ella, usted	encontraba	encontró	ha encontrado
nosotros/as	encontrábamos	encontramos	hemos encontrado
vosotros/as	encontrabais	encontrasteis	habéis encontrado
ellos/ellas, ustedes	encontraban	encontraron	han encontrado

	present subjunctive	imperfect subjunctive
yo	encuentre	encontrara/encontrase
tú	encuentres	encontraras/encontrases
él/ella, usted	encuentre	encontrara/encontrase
nosotros/as	encontremos	encontráramos/encontrásemos
vosotros/as	encontréis	encontrarais/encontraseis
ellos/ellas, ustedes	encuentren	encontraran/encontrasen

past participle **encontrado**

gerund **encontrando**

imperative **(tú) encuentra, (vosotros) encontrad**

Verbs that follow the same pattern as **encontrar** include **acostarse** *to go to bed*, **contar** *to count*, **costar** *to cost*, **mostrar** *to show*.

19 enviar *to send*

	present	future	conditional
yo	envío	enviaré	enviaría
tú	envías	enviarás	enviarías
él/ella,usted	envía	enviará	enviaría
nosotros/as	enviamos	enviaremos	enviaríamos
vosotros/as	enviáis	enviaréis	enviaríais
ellos/ellas, ustedes	envían	enviarán	enviarían

	imperfect	preterite	perfect
yo	enviaba	envié	he enviado
tú	enviabas	enviaste	has enviado
él/ella,usted	enviaba	envió	ha enviado
nosotros/as	enviábamos	enviamos	hemos enviado
vosotros/as	enviabais	enviasteis	habéis enviado
ellos/ellas, ustedes	enviaban	enviaron	han enviado

	present subjunctive	imperfect subjunctive
yo	envíe	enviara/enviase
tú	envíes	enviaras/enviases
él/ella,usted	envíe	enviara/enviase
nosotros/as	enviemos	enviáramos/enviásemos
vosotros/as	enviéis	enviarais/enviaseis
ellos/ellas, ustedes	envíen	enviaran/enviasen

past participle **enviado**

gerund **enviando**

imperative (**tú**) **envía**, (**vosotros**) **enviad**

Verbs that follow the same pattern as **enviar** include **criar** *to breed*, **fotografiar** *to photograph*, **guiar** *to guide*, **variar** *to vary*.

20 estar *to be*

	present	future	conditional
yo	estoy	estaré	estaría
tú	estás	estarás	estarías
él/ella,usted	está	estará	estaría
nosotros/as	estamos	estaremos	estaríamos
vosotros/as	estáis	estaréis	estaríais
ellos/ellas, ustedes	están	estarán	estarían

	imperfect	preterite	perfect
yo	estaba	estuve	he estado
tú	estabas	estuviste	has estado
él/ella,usted	estaba	estuvo	ha estado
nosotros/as	estábamos	estuvimos	hemos estado
vosotros/as	estabais	estuvisteis	habéis estado
ellos/ellas, ustedes	estaban	estuvieron	han estado

	present subjunctive	imperfect subjunctive
yo	esté	estuviera/estuviese
tú	estés	estuvieras/estuvieses
él/ella,usted	esté	estuviera/estuviese
nosotros/as	estemos	estuviéramos/estuviésemos
vosotros/as	estéis	estuvierais/estuvieseis
ellos/ellas, ustedes	estén	estuvieran/estuviesen

past participle **estado**

gerund **estando**

imperative (**tú**) **está**, (**vosotros**) **estad**

21 haber *to have*

	present	future	conditional
yo	he	habré	habría
tú	has	habrás	habrías
él/ella,usted	ha*	habrá	habría
nosotros/as	hemos	habremos	habríamos
vosotros/as	habéis	habréis	habríais
ellos/ellas, ustedes	han	habrán	habrían

	imperfect	preterite	perfect
yo	había	hube	he habido
tú	habías	hubiste	has habido
él/ella,usted	había	hubo	ha habido
nosotros/as	habíamos	hubimos	hemos habido
vosotros/as	habíais	hubisteis	habéis habido
ellos/ellas, ustedes	habían	hubieron	han habido

	present subjunctive	imperfect subjunctive
yo	haya	hubiera/hubiese
tú	hayas	hubieras/hubieses
él/ella,usted	haya	hubiera/hubiese
nosotros/as	hayamos	hubiéramos/hubiésemos
vosotros/as	hayáis	hubierais/hubieseis
ellos/ellas, ustedes	hayan	hubieran/hubiesen

past participle **habido**

gerund **habiendo**

imperative not used

*__hay__ is used impersonally - see page 183

22 hablar *to speak*

	present	future	conditional
yo	hablo	hablaré	hablaría
tú	hablas	hablarás	hablarías
él/ella,usted	habla	hablará	hablaría
nosotros/as	hablamos	hablaremos	hablaríamos
vosotros/as	habláis	hablaréis	hablaríais
ellos/ellas, ustedes	hablan	hablarán	hablarían

	imperfect	preterite	perfect
yo	hablaba	hablé	he hablado
tú	hablabas	hablaste	has hablado
él/ella,usted	hablaba	habló	ha hablado
nosotros/as	hablábamos	hablamos	hemos hablado
vosotros/as	hablabais	hablasteis	habéis hablado
ellos/ellas, ustedes	hablaban	hablaron	han hablado

	present subjunctive	imperfect subjunctive
yo	hable	hablara/hablase
tú	hables	hablaras/hablases
él/ella,usted	hable	hablara/hablase
nosotros/as	hablemos	habláramos/hablásemos
vosotros/as	habléis	hablareis/hablaseis
ellos/ellas, ustedes	hablen	hablaran/hablasen

past participle **hablado**

gerund **hablando**

imperative **(tú) habla, (vosotros) hablad**

23 hacer *to do, to make*

	present	future	conditional
yo	hago	haré	haría
tú	haces	harás	harías
él/ella,usted	hace	hará	haría
nosotros/as	hacemos	haremos	haríamos
vosotros/as	hacéis	haréis	haríais
ellos/ellas, ustedes	hacen	harán	harían

	imperfect	preterite	perfect
yo	hacía	hice	he hecho
tú	hacías	hiciste	has hecho
él/ella,usted	hacía	hizo	ha hecho
nosotros/as	hacíamos	hicimos	hemos hecho
vosotros/as	hacíais	hicisteis	habéis hecho
ellos/ellas, ustedes	hacían	hicieron	han hecho

	present subjunctive	imperfect subjunctive
yo	haga	hiciera/hiciese
tú	hagas	hicieras/hicieses
él/ella,usted	haga	hiciera/hiciese
nosotros/as	hagamos	hiciéramos/hiciésemos
vosotros/as	hagáis	hicierais/hicieseis
ellos/ellas, ustedes	hagan	hicieran/hiciesen

past participle **hecho**

gerund **haciendo**

imperative **(tú) haz, (vosotros) haced**

Verbs that follow the same pattern as **hacer** include **deshacer** *to undo* and **rehacer** *to re-do*.

24 ir *to go*

	present	future	conditional
yo	voy	iré	iría
tú	vas	irás	irías
él/ella,usted	va	irá	iría
nosotros/as	vamos	iremos	iríamos
vosotros/as	vais	iréis	iríais
ellos/ellas, ustedes	van	irán	irían

	imperfect	preterite	perfect
yo	iba	fui	he ido
tú	ibas	fuiste	has ido
él/ella,usted	iba	fue	ha ido
nosotros/as	íbamos	fuimos	hemos ido
vosotros/as	ibais	fuisteis	habéis ido
ellos/ellas, ustedes	iban	fueron	han ido

	present subjunctive	imperfect subjunctive
yo	vaya	fuera/fuese
tú	vayas	fueras/fueses
él/ella,usted	vaya	fuera/fuese
nosotros/as	vayamos	fuéramos/fuésemos
vosotros/as	vayáis	fuerais/fueseis
ellos/ellas, ustedes	vayan	fueran/fuesen

past participle **ido**

gerund **yendo**

imperative (**tú**) **ve**, (**vosotros**) **id**

25 jugar *to play*

	present	future	conditional
yo	juego	jugaré	jugaría
tú	juegas	jugarás	jugarías
él/ella,usted	juega	jugará	jugaría
nosotros/as	jugamos	jugaremos	jugaríamos
vosotros/as	jugáis	jugaréis	jugaríais
ellos/ellas, ustedes	juegan	jugarán	jugarían

	imperfect	preterite	perfect
yo	jugaba	jugué	he jugado
tú	jugabas	jugaste	has jugado
él/ella,usted	jugaba	jugó	ha jugado
nosotros/as	jugábamos	jugamos	hemos jugado
vosotros/as	jugabais	jugasteis	habéis jugado
ellos/ellas, ustedes	jugaban	jugaron	han jugado

	present subjunctive	imperfect subjunctive
yo	juegue	jugara/jugase
tú	juegues	jugaras/jugases
él/ella,usted	juegue	jugara/jugase
nosotros/as	juguemos	jugáramos/jugásemos
vosotros/as	juguéis	jugarais/jugaseis
ellos/ellas, ustedes	jueguen	jugaran/jugasen

past participle **jugado**

gerund **jugando**

imperative **(tú) juega, (vosotros) jugad**

26 lavarse *to wash oneself*

	present	future	conditional
yo	me lavo	me lavaré	me lavaría
tú	te lavas	te lavarás	te lavarías
él/ella,usted	se lava	se lavará	se lavaría
nosotros/as	nos lavamos	nos lavaremos	nos lavaríamos
vosotros/as	os laváis	os lavaréis	os lavaríais
ellos/ellas, ustedes	se lavan	se lavarán	se lavarían

	imperfect	preterite	perfect
yo	me lavaba	me lavé	me he lavado
tú	te lavabas	te lavaste	te has lavado
él/ella,usted	se lavaba	se lavó	se ha lavado
nosotros/as	nos lavábamos	nos lavamos	nos hemos lavado
vosotros/as	os lavabais	os lavasteis	os habéis lavado
ellos/ellas, ustedes	se lavaban	se lavaron	se han lavado

	present subjunctive	imperfect subjunctive
yo	me lave	me lavara/lavase
tú	te laves	te lavaras/lavases
él/ella,usted	se lave	se lavara/lavase
nosotros/as	nos lavemos	nos laváramos/lavásemos
vosotros/as	os lavéis	os lavarais/lavaseis
ellos/ellas, ustedes	se laven	se lavaran/lavasen

past participle **lavado**

gerund **lavándose**

imperative **(tú) lávate, (vosotros) lavaos**

27 mover *to move*

	present	future	conditional
yo	muevo	moveré	movería
tú	mueves	moverás	moverías
él/ella,usted	mueve	moverá	movería
nosotros/as	movemos	moveremos	moveríamos
vosotros/as	movéis	moveréis	moveríais
ellos/ellas, ustedes	mueven	moverán	moverían

	imperfect	preterite	perfect
yo	movía	moví	he movido
tú	movías	moviste	has movido
él/ella,usted	movía	movió	ha movido
nosotros/as	movíamos	movimos	hemos movido
vosotros/as	movíais	movisteis	habéis movido
ellos/ellas, ustedes	movían	movieron	han movido

	present subjunctive	imperfect subjunctive
yo	mueva	moviera/moviese
tú	muevas	movieras/movieses
él/ella,usted	mueva	moviera/moviese
nosotros/as	movamos	moviéramos/moviésemos
vosotros/as	mováis	movierais/movieseis
ellos/ellas, ustedes	muevan	movieran/moviesen

past participle **movido**

gerund **moviendo**

imperative(**tú**) **mueve**, (**vosotros**) **moved**

Verbs that follow the same pattern include **conmover** *to shake, to move,* **conmoverse** *to be shaken, to be moved,* **doler** *to hurt,* **llover** *to rain.*

28 oír *to hear*

	present	future	conditional
yo	oigo	oiré	oiría
tú	oyes	oirás	oirías
él/ella,usted	oye	oirá	oiría
nosotros/as	oímos	oiremos	oiríamos
vosotros/as	oís	oiréis	oiríais
ellos/ellas, ustedes	oyen	oirán	oirían

	imperfect	preterite	perfect
yo	oía	oí	he oído
tú	oías	oíste	has oído
él/ella,usted	oía	oyó	ha oído
nosotros/as	oíamos	oímos	hemos oído
vosotros/as	oíais	oísteis	habéis oído
ellos/ellas, ustedes	oían	oyeron	han oído

	present subjunctive	imperfect subjunctive
yo	oiga	oyera/oyese
tú	oigas	oyeras/oyeses
él/ella,usted	oiga	oyera/oyese
nosotros/as	oigamos	oyéramos/oyésemos
vosotros/as	oigáis	oyerais/oyeseis
ellos/ellas, ustedes	oigan	oyeran/oyesen

past participle **oído**

gerund **oyendo**

imperative (tú) **oye**, (vosotros) **oíd**

29 oler *to smell*

	present	future	conditional
yo	huelo	oleré	olería
tú	hueles	olerás	olerías
él/ella,usted	huele	olerá	olería
nosotros/as	olemos	oleremos	oleríamos
vosotros/as	oléis	oleréis	oleríais
ellos/ellas, ustedes	huelen	olerán	olerían

	imperfect	preterite	perfect
yo	olía	olí	he olido
tú	olías	oliste	has olido
él/ella,usted	olía	olió	ha olido
nosotros/as	olíamos	olimos	hemos olido
vosotros/as	olíais	olisteis	habéis olido
ellos/ellas, ustedes	olían	olieron	han olido

	present subjunctive	imperfect subjunctive
yo	huela	oliera/oliese
tú	huelas	olieras/olieses
él/ella,usted	huela	oliera/oliese
nosotros/as	olamos	oliéramos/oliésemos
vosotros/as	oláis	olierais/olieseis
ellos/ellas, ustedes	huelan	olieran/oliesen

past participle **olido**

gerund **oliendo**

imperative (tú) **huele**, (vosotros) **oled**

30 pagar *to pay*

	present	future	conditional
yo	pago	pagaré	pagaría
tú	pagas	pagarás	pagarías
él/ella,usted	paga	pagará	pagaría
nosotros/as	pagamos	pagaremos	pagaríamos
vosotros/as	pagáis	pagaréis	pagaríais
ellos/ellas, ustedes	pagan	pagarán	pagarían

	imperfect	preterite	perfect
yo	pagaba	pagué	he pagado
tú	pagabas	pagaste	has pagado
él/ella,usted	pagaba	pagó	ha pagado
nosotros/as	pagábamos	pagamos	hemos pagado
vosotros/as	pagabais	pagasteis	habéis pagado
ellos/ellas, ustedes	pagaban	pagaron	han pagado

	present subjunctive	imperfect subjunctive
yo	pague	pagara/ pagase
tú	pagues	pagaras/pagases
él/ella,usted	pague	pagara/pagase
nosotros/as	paguemos	pagáramos/pagásemos
vosotros/as	paguéis	pagarais/pagaseis
ellos/ellas, ustedes	paguen	pagaran/pagasen

past participle **pagado**

gerund **pagando**

imperative **(tú) paga, (vosotros) pagad**

31 pedir *to ask for*

	present	future	conditional
yo	pido	pediré	pediría
tú	pides	pedirás	pedirías
él/ella,usted	pide	pedirá	pediría
nosotros/as	pedimos	pediremos	pediríamos
vosotros/as	pedís	pediréis	pediríais
ellos/ellas, ustedes	piden	pedirán	pedirían

	imperfect	preterite	perfect
yo	pedía	pedí	he pedido
tú	pedías	pediste	has pedido
él/ella,usted	pedía	pidió	ha pedido
nosotros/as	pedíamos	pedimos	hemos pedido
vosotros/as	pedíais	pedisteis	habéis pedido
ellos/ellas, ustedes	pedían	pidieron	han pedido

	present subjunctive	imperfect subjunctive
yo	pida	pidiera/pidiese
tú	pidas	pidieras/pidieses
él/ella,usted	pida	pidiera/pidiese
nosotros/as	pidamos	pidiéramos/pidiésemos
vosotros/as	pidáis	pidierais/pidieseis
ellos/ellas, ustedes	pidan	pidieran/pidiesen

past participle **pedido**

gerund **pidiendo**

imperative (tú) **pide**, (vosotros) **pedid**

Verbs that follow the same pattern as **pedir** include **despedirse** *to say goodbye*, **repetir** *to repeat*, **servir** *to serve*, **vestirse** *to get dressed*.

32 perder *to lose*

	present	future	conditional
yo	pierdo	perderé	perdería
tú	pierdes	perderás	perderías
él/ella,usted	pierde	perderá	perdería
nosotros/as	perdemos	perderemos	perderíamos
vosotros/as	perdéis	perderéis	perderíais
ellos/ellas, ustedes	pierden	perderán	perderían

	imperfect	preterite	perfect
yo	perdía	perdí	he perdido
tú	perdías	perdiste	has perdido
él/ella,usted	perdía	perdió	ha perdido
nosotros/as	perdíamos	perdimos	hemos perdido
vosotros/as	perdíais	perdisteis	habéis perdido
ellos/ellas, ustedes	perdían	perdieron	han perdido

	present subjunctive	imperfect subjunctive
yo	pierda	perdiera/perdiese
tú	pierdas	perdieras/perdieses
él/ella,usted	pierda	perdiera/perdiese
nosotros/as	perdamos	perdiéramos/perdiésemos
vosotros/as	perdáis	perdierais/perdieseis
ellos/ellas, ustedes	pierdan	perdieran/perdiesen

past participle **perdido**

gerund **perdiendo**

imperative (tú) **pierde**, (vosotros) **perded**

Verbs that follow the same pattern as **perder** include **defender** *to defend*, **encender** *to light*, **entender** *to understand*.

33 poder *to be able to*

	present	future	conditional
yo	puedo	podré	podría
tú	puedes	podrás	podrías
él/ella,usted	puede	podrá	podría
nosotros/as	podemos	podremos	podríamos
vosotros/as	podéis	podréis	podríais
ellos/ellas, ustedes	pueden	podrán	podrían

	imperfect	preterite	perfect
yo	podía	pude	he podido
tú	podías	pudiste	has podido
él/ella,usted	podía	pudo	ha podido
nosotros/as	podíamos	pudimos	hemos podido
vosotros/as	podíais	pudisteis	habéis podido
ellos/ellas, ustedes	podían	pudieron	han podido

	present subjunctive	imperfect subjunctive
yo	pueda	pudiera/pudiese
tú	puedas	pudieras/pudieses
él/ella,usted	pueda	pudiera/pudiese
nosotros/as	podamos	pudiéramos/pudiésemos
vosotros/as	podáis	pudierais/pudieseis
ellos/ellas, ustedes	puedan	pudieran/pudiesen

past participle **podido**

gerund **pudiendo**

imperative (tú) **puede**, (vosotros) **poded**

34 poner *to put*

	present	future	conditional
yo	pongo	pondré	pondría
tú	pones	pondrás	pondrías
él/ella, usted	pone	pondrá	pondría
nosotros/as	ponemos	pondremos	pondríamos
vosotros/as	ponéis	pondréis	pondríais
ellos/ellas, ustedes	ponen	pondrán	pondrían

	imperfect	preterite	perfect
yo	ponía	puse	he puesto
tú	ponías	pusiste	has puesto
él/ella, usted	ponía	puso	ha puesto
nosotros/as	poníamos	pusimos	hemos puesto
vosotros/as	poníais	pusisteis	habéis puesto
ellos/ellas, ustedes	ponían	pusieron	han puesto

	present subjunctive	imperfect subjunctive
yo	ponga	pusiera/pusiese
tú	pongas	pusieras/pusieses
él/ella, usted	ponga	pusiera/pusiese
nosotros/as	pongamos	pusiéramos/pusiésemos
vosotros/as	pongáis	pusierais/pusieseis
ellos/ellas, ustedes	pongan	pusieran/pusiesen

past participle **puesto**

gerund **poniendo**

imperative (tú) **pon**, (vosotros) **poned**

Verbs that follow the same pattern as **poner** include **exponer** *to expose*, **oponerse a** *to oppose*, **proponer** *to propose*, **suponer** *to suppose*.

35 preferir *to prefer*

	present	future	conditional
yo	prefiero	preferiré	preferiría
tú	prefieres	preferirás	preferirías
él/ella, usted	prefiere	preferirá	preferiría
nosotros/as	preferimos	preferiremos	preferiríamos
vosotros/as	preferís	preferiréis	preferiríais
ellos/ellas, ustedes	prefieren	preferirán	preferirían

	imperfect	preterite	perfect
yo	prefería	preferí	he preferido
tú	preferías	preferiste	has preferido
él/ella, usted	prefería	prefirió	ha preferido
nosotros/as	preferíamos	preferimos	hemos preferido
vosotros/as	preferíais	preferisteis	habéis preferido
ellos/ellas, ustedes	preferían	prefirieron	han preferido

	present subjunctive	imperfect subjunctive
yo	prefiera	prefiriera/prefiriese
tú	prefieras	prefirieras/prefirieses
él/ella, usted	prefiera	prefiriera/prefiriese
nosotros/as	prefieramos	prefiriéramos/prefiriésemos
vosotros/as	prefieráis	prefirierais/prefirieseis
ellos/ellas, ustedes	prefieran	prefirieran/prefiriesen

past participle **preferido**

gerund **prefiriendo**

imperative **(tú) prefiere, (vosotros) preferid**

Verbs that follow the same pattern as **preferir** include **consentir** *to consent*, **mentir** *to lie*, **sentir** *to feel*, **sugerir** *to suggest*.

36 querer *to want to*

	present	future	conditional
yo	quiero	querré	querría
tú	quieres	querrás	querrías
él/ella,usted	quiere	querrá	querría
nosotros/as	queremos	querremos	querríamos
vosotros/as	queréis	querréis	querríais
ellos/ellas, ustedes	quieren	querrán	querrían

	imperfect	preterite	perfect
yo	quería	quise	he querido
tú	querías	quisiste	has querido
él/ella,usted	quería	quiso	ha querido
nosotros/as	queríamos	quisimos	hemos querido
vosotros/as	queríais	quisisteis	habéis querido
ellos/ellas, ustedes	querían	quisieron	han querido

	present subjunctive	imperfect subjunctive
yo	quiera	quisiera/quisiese
tú	quieras	quisieras/quisieses
él/ella,usted	quiera	quisiera/quisiese
nosotros/as	queramos	quisiéramos/quisiésemos
vosotros/as	queráis	quisierais/quisieseis
ellos/ellas, ustedes	quieran	quisieran/quisiesen

past participle **querido**

gerund **queriendo**

imperative (tú) **quiere**, (vosotros) **quered**

37 reír *to laugh*

	present	future	conditional
yo	río	reiré	reiría
tú	ríes	reirás	reirías
él/ella, usted	ríe	reirá	reiría
nosotros/as	reímos	reiremos	reiríamos
vosotros/as	reís	reiréis	reiríais
ellos/ellas, ustedes	ríen	reirán	reirían

	imperfect	preterite	perfect
yo	reía	reí	he reído
tú	reías	reíste	has reído
él/ella, usted	reía	rió	ha reído
nosotros/as	reíamos	reímos	hemos reído
vosotros/as	reíais	reísteis	habéis reído
ellos/ellas, ustedes	reían	rieron	han reído

	present subjunctive	imperfect subjunctive
yo	ría	riera/riese
tú	rías	rieras/rieses
él/ella, usted	ría	riera/riese
nosotros/as	riamos	riéramos/riésemos
vosotros/as	riais	rierais/rieseis
ellos/ellas, ustedes	rían	rieran/riesen

past participle reído

gerund riendo

imperative (tú) ríe, (vosotros) reíd

Verbs that follow the same pattern as reír include desleír *to dissolve something*, freír *to fry* (past participle frito), sonreír *to smile*.

	present	future	conditional
yo	riño	reñiré	reñiría
tú	riñes	reñirás	reñirías
él/ella,usted	riñe	reñirá	reñiría
nosotros/as	reñimos	reñiremos	reñiríamos
vosotros/as	reñís	reñiréis	reñiríais
ellos/ellas, ustedes	riñen	reñirán	reñirían

	imperfect	preterite	perfect
yo	reñía	reñí	he reñido
tú	reñías	reñiste	has reñido
él/ella,usted	reñía	riñó	ha reñido
nosotros/as	reñíamos	reñimos	hemos reñido
vosotros/as	reñíais	reñisteis	habéis reñido
ellos/ellas, ustedes	reñían	riñeron	han reñido

	present subjunctive	imperfect subjunctive
yo	riña	riñera/riñese
tú	riñas	riñeras/riñeses
él/ella,usted	riña	riñera/riñese
nosotros/as	riñamos	riñéramos/riñésemos
vosotros/as	riñáis	riñerais/riñeseis
ellos/ellas, ustedes	riñan	riñeran/riñesen

past participle **reñido**

gerund **riñendo**

imperative (tú) **riñe**, (vosotros) **reñid**

Verbs that follow the same pattern as **reñir** include **ceñir** *to surround*, **desteñir** *to fade*, **teñir** *to dye*.

39 saber *to know*

	present	future	conditional
yo	sé	sabré	sabría
tú	sabes	sabrás	sabrías
él/ella, usted	sabe	sabrá	sabría
nosotros/as	sabemos	sabremos	sabríamos
vosotros/as	sabéis	sabréis	sabríais
ellos/ellas, ustedes	saben	sabrán	sabrían

	imperfect	preterite	perfect
yo	sabía	supe	he sabido
tú	sabías	supiste	has sabido
él/ella, usted	sabía	supo	ha sabido
nosotros/as	sabíamos	supimos	hemos sabido
vosotros/as	sabíais	supisteis	habéis sabido
ellos/ellas, ustedes	sabían	supieron	han sabido

	present subjunctive	imperfect subjunctive
yo	sepa	supiera/supiese
tú	sepas	supieras/supieses
él/ella, usted	sepa	supiera/supiese
nosotros/as	sepamos	supiéramos/supiésemos
vosotros/as	sepáis	supierais/supieseis
ellos/ellas, ustedes	sepan	supieran/supiesen

past participle **sabido**

gerund **sabiendo**

imperative (tú) **sabe**, (vosotros) **sabed**

40 salir *to go out*

	present	future	conditional
yo	salgo	saldré	saldría
tú	sales	saldrás	saldrías
él/ella,usted	sale	saldrá	saldría
nosotros/as	salimos	saldremos	saldríamos
vosotros/as	salís	saldréis	saldríais
ellos/ellas, ustedes	salen	saldrán	saldrían

	imperfect	preterite	perfect
yo	salía	salí	he salido
tú	salías	saliste	has salido
él/ella,usted	salía	salió	ha salido
nosotros/as	salíamos	salimos	hemos salido
vosotros/as	salíais	salisteis	habéis salido
ellos/ellas, ustedes	salían	salieron	han salido

	present subjunctive	imperfect subjunctive
yo	salga	saliera/saliese
tú	salgas	salieras/salieses
él/ella,usted	salga	saliera/saliese
nosotros/as	salgamos	saliéramos/saliésemos
vosotros/as	salgáis	salierais/salieseis
ellos/ellas, ustedes	salgan	salieran/saliesen

past participle **salido**

gerund **saliendo**

imperative **(tú) sal**, **(vosotros) salid**

41 seguir *to follow*

	present	future	conditional
yo	sigo	seguiré	seguiría
tú	sigues	seguirás	seguirías
él/ella,usted	sigue	seguirá	seguiría
nosotros/as	seguimos	seguiremos	seguiríamos
vosotros/as	seguís	seguiréis	seguiríais
ellos/ellas, ustedes	siguen	seguirán	seguirían

	imperfect	preterite	perfect
yo	seguía	seguí	he seguido
tú	seguías	seguiste	has seguido
él/ella,usted	seguía	siguió	ha seguido
nosotros/as	seguíamos	seguimos	hemos seguido
vosotros/as	seguíais	seguisteis	habéis seguido
ellos/ellas, ustedes	seguían	siguieron	han seguido

	present subjunctive	imperfect subjunctive
yo	siga	siguiera/siguiese
tú	sigas	siguieras/siguieses
él/ella,usted	siga	siguiera/siguiese
nosotros/as	sigamos	siguiéramos/siguiésemos
vosotros/as	sigáis	siguierais/siguieseis
ellos/ellas, ustedes	sigan	siguieran/siguiesen

past participle **seguido**

gerund **siguiendo**

imperative **(tú) sigue, (vosotros) seguid**

Verbs that follow the same pattern as **seguir** include **conseguir** *to obtain*, **perseguir** *to persecute*, **proseguir** *to proceed with*.

42 ser *to be*

	present	future	conditional
yo	soy	seré	sería
tú	eres	serás	serías
él/ella,usted	es	será	sería
nosotros/as	somos	seremos	seríamos
vosotros/as	sois	seréis	seríais
ellos/ellas, ustedes	son	serán	serían

	imperfect	preterite	perfect
yo	era	fui	he sido
tú	eras	fuiste	has sido
él/ella,usted	era	fue	ha sido
nosotros/as	éramos	fuimos	hemos sido
vosotros/as	erais	fuisteis	habéis sido
ellos/ellas, ustedes	eran	fueron	han sido

	present subjunctive	imperfect subjunctive
yo	sea	fuera/fuese
tú	seas	fueras/fueses
él/ella,usted	sea	fuera/fuese
nosotros/as	seamos	fuéramos/fuésemos
vosotros/as	seáis	fuerais/fueseis
ellos/ellas, ustedes	sean	fueran/fuesen

past participle **sido**

gerund **siendo**

imperative (tú) **sé**, (vosotros) **sed**

43 tener *to have*

	present	future	conditional
yo	tengo	tendré	tendría
tú	tienes	tendrás	tendrías
él/ella, usted	tiene	tendrá	tendría
nosotros/as	tenemos	tendremos	tendríamos
vosotros/as	tenéis	tendréis	tendríais
ellos/ellas, ustedes	tienen	tendrán	tendrían

	imperfect	preterite	perfect
yo	tenía	tuve	he tenido
tú	tenías	tuviste	has tenido
él/ella, usted	tenía	tuvo	ha tenido
nosotros/as	teníamos	tuvimos	hemos tenido
vosotros/as	teníais	tuvisteis	habéis tenido
ellos/ellas, ustedes	tenían	tuvieron	han tenido

	present subjunctive	imperfect subjunctive
yo	tenga	tuviera/tuviese
tú	tengas	tuvieras/tuvieses
él/ella, usted	tenga	tuviera/tuviese
nosotros/as	tengamos	tuviéramos/tuviésemos
vosotros/as	tengáis	tuvierais/tuvieseis
ellos/ellas, ustedes	tengan	tuvieran/tuviesen

past participle **tenido**

gerund **teniendo**

imperative (**tú**) **ten**, (**vosotros**) **tened**

Contener *to contain*, **mantener** *to maintain*, **obtener** *to obtain*, **retener** *to retain* and **sostener** *to sustain* follow the same pattern.

	present	future	conditional
yo	tuerzo	torceré	torcería
tú	tuerces	torcerás	torcerías
él/ella,usted	tuerce	torcerá	torcería
nosotros/as	torcemos	torceremos	torceríamos
vosotros/as	torcéis	torceréis	torceríais
ellos/ellas, ustedes	tuercen	torcerán	torcerían

	imperfect	preterite	perfect
yo	torcía	torcí	he torcido
tú	torcías	torciste	has torcido
él/ella,usted	torcía	torció	ha torcido
nosotros/as	torcíamos	torcimos	hemos torcido
vosotros/as	torcíais	torcisteis	habéis torcido
ellos/ellas, ustedes	torcían	torcieron	han torcido

	present subjunctive	imperfect subjunctive
yo	tuerza	torciera/torciese
tú	tuerzas	torcieras/torcieses
él/ella,usted	tuerza	torciera/torciese
nosotros/as	torzamos	torciéramos/torciésemos
vosotros/as	torzáis	torcierais/torcieseis
ellos/ellas, ustedes	tuerzan	torcieran/torciesen

past participle **torcido**

gerund **torciendo**

imperative **(tú) tuerce, (vosotros) torced**

Verbs that follow the same pattern as **torcer** include **cocer** *to cook, boil,* **retorcerse** *to writhe.*

45 traer *to bring*

	present	future	conditional
yo	traigo	traeré	traería
tú	traes	traerás	traerías
él/ella, usted	trae	traerá	traería
nosotros/as	traemos	traeremos	traeríamos
vosotros/as	traéis	traeréis	traeríais
ellos/ellas, ustedes	traen	traerán	traerían

	imperfect	preterite	perfect
yo	traía	traje	he traído
tú	traías	trajiste	has traído
él/ella, usted	traía	trajo	ha traído
nosotros/as	traíamos	trajimos	hemos traído
vosotros/as	traíais	trajisteis	habéis traído
ellos/ellas, ustedes	traían	trajeron	han traído

	present subjunctive	imperfect subjunctive
yo	traiga	trajera/trajese
tú	traigas	trajeras/trajeses
él/ella, usted	traiga	trajera/trajese
nosotros/as	traigamos	trajéramos/trajésemos
vosotros/as	traigáis	trajerais/trajeseis
ellos/ellas, ustedes	traigan	trajeran/trajesen

past participle **traído**

gerund **trayendo**

imperative **(tú) trae, (vosotros) traed**

Verbs that follow the same pattern as **traer** include **atraer** *to attract*, **contraer** *to contract*, **distraer** *to entertain, to distract*.

46 vencer *to defeat*

	present	future	conditional
yo	venzo	venceré	vencería
tú	vences	vencerás	vencerías
él/ella,usted	vence	vencerá	vencería
nosotros/as	vencemos	venceremos	venceríamos
vosotros/as	vencéis	venceréis	venceríais
ellos/ellas, ustedes	vencen	vencerán	vencerían

	imperfect	preterite	perfect
yo	vencía	vencí	he vencido
tú	vencías	venciste	has vencido
él/ella,usted	vencía	venció	ha vencido
nosotros/as	vencíamos	vencimos	hemos vencido
vosotros/as	vencíais	vencisteis	habéis vencido
ellos/ellas, ustedes	vencían	vencieron	han vencido

	present subjunctive	imperfect subjunctive
yo	venza	venciera/venciese
tú	venzas	vencieras/vencieses
él/ella,usted	venza	venciera/venciese
nosotros/as	venzamos	venciéramos/venciésemos
vosotros/as	venzáis	vencierais/vencieseis
ellos/ellas, ustedes	venzan	vencieran/venciesen

past participle **vencido**

gerund **venciendo**

imperative **(tú) vence, (vosotros) venced**

Verbs that follow the same pattern as **vencer** include **convencer** *to convince* and **ejercer** *to practise a profession*.

47 venir *to come*

	present	future	conditional
yo	vengo	vendré	vendría
tú	vienes	vendrás	vendrías
él/ella,usted	viene	vendrá	vendría
nosotros/as	venimos	vendremos	vendríamos
vosotros/as	venís	vendréis	vendríais
ellos/ellas, ustedes	vienen	vendrán	vendrían

	imperfect	preterite	perfect
yo	venía	vine	he venido
tú	venías	viniste	has venido
él/ella,usted	venía	vino	ha venido
nosotros/as	veníamos	vinimos	hemos venido
vosotros/as	veníais	vinisteis	habéis venido
ellos/ellas, ustedes	venían	vinieron	han venido

	present subjunctive	imperfect subjunctive
yo	venga	viniera/viniese
tú	vengas	vinieras/vinieses
él/ella,usted	venga	viniera/viniese
nosotros/as	vengamos	viniéramos/viniésemos
vosotros/as	vengáis	vinierais/vinieseis
ellos/ellas, ustedes	vengan	vinieran/viniesen

past participle **venido**

gerund **viniendo**

imperative **(tú) ven, (vosotros) venid**

Contravenir *to contravene*, **convenir** *to agree on*, **intervenir en** *to take part in* and **prevenir** *to prevent* follow the same pattern.

48 **ver** *to see*

	present	future	conditional
yo	veo	veré	vería
tú	ves	verás	verías
él/ella, usted	ve	verá	vería
nosotros/as	vemos	veremos	veríamos
vosotros/as	veis	veréis	veríais
ellos/ellas, ustedes	ven	verán	verían

	imperfect	preterite	perfect
yo	veía	vi	he visto
tú	veías	viste	has visto
él/ella, usted	veía	vio	ha visto
nosotros/as	veíamos	vimos	hemos visto
vosotros/as	veíais	visteis	habéis visto
ellos/ellas, ustedes	veían	vieron	han visto

	present subjunctive	imperfect subjunctive
yo	vea	viera/viese
tú	veas	vieras/vieses
él/ella, usted	vea	viera/viese
nosotros/as	veamos	viéramos/viésemos
vosotros/as	veáis	vierais/vieseis
ellos/ellas, ustedes	vean	vieran/viesen

past participle **visto**

gerund **viendo**

imperative **(tú) ve, (vosotros) ved**

Verbs that follow the same pattern as **ver** include **entrever** *to glimpse* and **prever** *to foresee*.

49 vivir *to live*

	present	future	conditional
yo	vivo	viviré	viviría
tú	vives	vivirás	vivirías
él/ella,usted	vive	vivirá	viviría
nosotros/as	vivimos	viviremos	viviríamos
vosotros/as	vivís	viviréis	viviríais
ellos/ellas, ustedes	viven	vivirán	vivirían

	imperfect	preterite	perfect
yo	vivía	viví	he vivido
tú	vivías	viviste	has vivido
él/ella,usted	vivía	vivió	ha vivido
nosotros/as	vivíamos	vivimos	hemos vivido
vosotros/as	vivíais	vivisteis	habéis vivido
ellos/ellas, ustedes	vivían	vivieron	han vivido

	present subjunctive	imperfect subjunctive
yo	viva	viviera/viviese
tú	vivas	vivieras/vivieses
él/ella,usted	viva	viviera/viviese
nosotros/as	vivamos	viviéramos/viviésemos
vosotros/as	viváis	vivierais/vivieseis
ellos/ellas, ustedes	vivan	vivieran/viviesen

past participle **vivido**

gerund **viviendo**

imperative **(tú) vive, (vosotros) vivid**

50 volver *to return*

	present	future	conditional
yo	vuelvo	volveré	volvería
tú	vuelves	volverás	volverías
él/ella,usted	vuelve	volverá	volvería
nosotros/as	volvemos	volveremos	volveríamos
vosotros/as	volvéis	volveréis	volveríais
ellos/ellas, ustedes	vuelven	volverán	volverían

	imperfect	preterite	perfect
yo	volvía	volví	he vuelto
tú	volvías	volviste	has vuelto
él/ella,usted	volvía	volvió	ha vuelto
nosotros/as	volvíamos	volvimos	hemos vuelto
vosotros/as	volvíais	volvisteis	habéis vuelto
ellos/ellas, ustedes	volvían	volvieron	han vuelto

	present subjunctive	imperfect subjunctive
yo	vuelva	volviera/volviese
tú	vuelvas	volvieras/volvieses
él/ella,usted	vuelva	volviera/volviese
nosotros/as	volvamos	volviéramos/volviésemos
vosotros/as	volváis	volvierais/volvieseis
ellos/ellas, ustedes	vuelvan	volvieran/volviesen

past participle **vuelto**

gerund **volviendo**

imperative **(tú) vuelve**, **(vosotros) volved**

Absolver *to absolve*, **disolver** *to dissolve*, **envolver** *to wrap up*, **resolver** *to resolve*, **revolver** *to stir up* and **volverse** *to become, to turn round* follow the same pattern.

Verb index

Pages 197-247

Grammar terms

Abstract nouns are the words for intangible things like *liberty*, *silence*, *poverty*, *fear*, *happiness*. They're the opposite of **concrete nouns** such as *table*, *dog*, *water*.

Adjectives are words that describe or add information to nouns and pronouns: ***small*** *car*, *It was* ***superb***, ***Spanish*** *wine*, ***first*** *class*, ***my*** *name*, ***Which*** *hotel?*, ***those*** *people*.

Adverbs add information to adjectives, verbs and other adverbs: ***very*** *small car*, *She speaks* ***clearly***, *She speaks* ***really*** *clearly*.

Agreement Unlike English, adjectives and articles in Spanish change according to the noun/pronoun they relate to, needing to agree, i.e. match, in terms of gender (masculine/feminine) and number (singular/plural).

Articles are **the** (definite article), **a/an** (indefinite article) and **some** (partitive article). Spanish has more than English.

Auxiliary verbs are verbs that support the main verb: *We* ***have*** *eaten,* ***Has*** *she gone?* In English, but not Spanish, *do/does* is used as an auxiliary verb in questions like *Do you understand?*

Cardinal numbers are *one, two, three, four,* etc.

Comparatives are used when making comparisons. English has two ways of comparing with adjectives: adding -er as in *bigger*, *cheaper*, and using the word *more* as in *more expensive*. Spanish always uses the second alternative, with **más** *more* or **menos** *less*.

Compound tenses are two-word tenses. Most English tenses are compound whereas most Spanish tenses are simple one-word tenses, except for past tenses, e.g. the **perfect** *I have waited*, the **pluperfect** *I had waited*.

The **conditional** is a verb form used to say what would or could happen: *I would like to go, Would/Could you help me?* The **past conditional** translates *would have: I would have liked to go*.

Conjunctions are linking words like *and, but, while, because*.

Consonants and **vowels** make up the alphabet. The vowels are **a**, **e**, **i**, **o**, **u**; the rest: **b**, **c**, **d**, **f**, etc. are the consonants.

Continuous tenses are used to say *I **am/was doing** something*. Spanish uses **estar** where English uses *to be*.

The **definite article** is the word *the*, which has several Spanish translations.

Demonstrative words are used to point things out. *This, these, that, those* are demonstrative adjectives; *this one, that one, these (ones), those (ones)* are demonstrative pronouns.

A **direct object** is directly at the receiving end of a verb. In the sentence *We saw John, we* is the subject, *saw* is the verb and *John* is the direct object. Compare with **indirect object**.

Direct object pronouns are *me, us, you, him, her, it, them*.

Feminine See **gender**.

Formal is used to describe **usted**, the word for *you* when talking to someone you don't know well. The informal word for *you* is **tú**.

The **future perfect** translates *will have: She will have gone to work*.

The **future tense** of a verb translates the English *will: We will be there, I'll go later, She'll be at work*.

Gender Every Spanish noun is either masculine or feminine, as are any articles and adjectives that relate to that noun.

A **gerund** in English ends in *-ing: working, living*. In Spanish it ends in **-ando** or **-iendo**: **trabajando, viviendo**.

Imperative is the verb form used to give instructions or commands: ***Wait** for me, **Don't do** that, **Turn** the top clockwise*.

The **imperfect tense** of a verb is used to describe how things were and to talk about things that happened over a period of time or repeatedly: *she **was** furious, We **were watching** the match, We **used to go** there often*.

An **impersonal verb** is a verb form that doesn't relate to people or things and generally starts with *it: It's raining, It's possible*.

The **indefinite article** is **a/an** in English; **un/una** in Spanish.

The **indicative mood** is used for factual statements: *He **goes** to school.* See also **mood**.

An **indirect object** is usually separated from its verb by *to* or *for*. In the sentence *We talked to John, we* is the subject, *talked* is the verb and *John* is the indirect object. Compare with **direct object**.

Indirect object pronouns usually have *to* or *for* in front of **direct object pronouns**, e.g. *to/for me, to/for them* in English. In Spanish they're a single word.

Infinitive Spanish verbs are listed in a dictionary in the infinitive form, ending in **-ar**, **-er** or **-ir**. The English equivalent uses *to:* **ayudar** *to help*, **aprender** *to learn*, **abrir** *to open*.

Informal is used to describe **tú**, the word for *you* when talking to someone you call by their first name. The formal word for *you* is **usted**.

Interrogative words are used in questions, e.g. *who, what, when, where, how, why, how much/many.*

Intransitive verbs need only a subject to make sense: *go, laugh;* unlike **transitive verbs** which need a subject and a direct object.

Invariable words don't change to agree with/match anything else.

Irregular nouns, verbs or adjectives don't behave in a predictable way like regular ones, and have to be learnt separately.

Masculine See **gender**.

Modal verbs are verbs like *want, be able to, must,* which are followed by other verbs: *I **want** to stay here, I **can** swim, You **ought** to leave.*

The **mood** of a verb defines how it's used, e.g. **the indicative mood** is used for factual statements: *He **goes** to school;* while the **subjunctive mood** indicates that hard facts are not involved: *If he **were** to **go** to school …*

Negatives are words like *not, never, nothing, nobody;* and *not … ever, not … anybody, not … anything.*

Nouns are the words for living beings, things, places and concepts: *son, doctor, dog, table, house, Scotland, time, freedom.* See also **proper nouns**.

Number refers to the difference between singular (one) and plural (more than one).

Numbers See **cardinal numbers** and **ordinal numbers**.

The **object** of a sentence is at the receiving end of the verb. It can be direct: *They have **two children***; or indirect: *Anna talks **to the children***.

Object pronoun. See **direct object pronouns, indirect object pronouns**.

Ordinal numbers are *first, second, third, fourth*, etc.

Parts of speech are the grammatical building blocks of a sentence: *adjective, article, noun, pronoun, verb*, etc.

The **passive** describes something done ***to*** the subject rather than ***by*** it: *The meat is cooked in the oven, The room was booked by my friend*.

The **past participle** of a verb is used with *have* when talking about the past: *I have **finished**, He has **eaten**, They had **gone***. Some past participles can also be used as adjectives: *the **finished** product*.

The **perfect tense** of a verb is used in Spanish to talk about actions which have happened in the past; equivalent to the English *I have worked*.

The **person** of a verb indicates who or what is doing something:

first person = the speaker: *I* (singular), *we* (plural)

second person = the person(s) being addressed: *you*

third person = who/what is being talked about: *he/she/it/they*

Personal pronouns are words like *I, you, we, she, her, them*.

The **pluperfect tense** translates *had* done something: *She had worked hard all day*.

Plural means more than one.

Possessive relates to ownership: the **possessive adjectives** are *my, our, your, his/her/its, their*; the **possessive pronouns** are *mine, ours, yours, his/ hers, theirs*.

Prepositions are words like *by, in, on, with, for, through, next to*. They relate a noun/pronoun to another part of the sentence by e.g. place, time, purpose: *It's **on** the back seat, We're here **until** Friday, I've got a letter **for** Tom.*

The **present tense** of a verb is used to talk about things being done now: *I work, I'm working.*

The **preterite** tense of a verb is used to describe a completed action in the past: *I worked, we ate, they spoke.*

Pronouns replace nouns to avoid the need to repeat them. They can be personal: *we, she, us*; demonstrative: *this one, those*; possessive: *mine, theirs*. They can also involve *one/ones: the big one, the red ones.*

Proper nouns are the names of specific people, places or organisations. They're written with a capital letter: *Sally, Cambridge, European Union.*

Reflexive pronouns are **me, te, se, nos, os**, used as an integral part of reflexive verbs in Spanish.

Reflexive verbs have **-se** at the end of the infinitive in Spanish. There's no consistent English equivalent, although many reflexive verbs include *get* or *oneself* in the translation: **casarse** *to get married*, **divertirse** *to enjoy oneself*.

Regular nouns, adjectives, verbs etc. behave in a predictable way, conforming to the pattern for that particular part of speech.

Relative pronouns are words like *which, who, that,* used to join together parts of a sentence without repeating the noun.

Simple tenses are one-word tenses like *I play, I played.* Spanish has more simple tenses than English.

Singular means one.

The **stem** of a Spanish verb is what's left when you remove the **-ar**, **-er** or **-ir** ending of the infinitive. You can then add other endings to this stem.

Stressed pronouns are the pronouns used in Spanish after prepositions: **mí, ti, él, ella, usted, nosotros/as, vosotros/as, ellos/ellas, ustedes.**

The **subject** of a sentence is whoever or whatever is carrying out the verb: ***They** have two children, **Anna** reads the paper, **This house** cost a lot of money, **Peace** is possible.*

Subject pronouns are *I, we, you, he, she, it, they.*

Subjunctive is a form of a verb that's much more widely used in Spanish than English. It equates to the English *may* or *were*: **May** *all your dreams come true, if I* **were** *rich,* but it's also used in a range of well-defined grammatical circumstances. See also **mood**.

Superlative is the *most/least* … when comparing several things. In English you can add *-est* to many adjectives: *biggest, cheapest,* or you can use *most: most expensive.* There's no Spanish equivalent of *-est.*

A **syllable** is a unit that contains a vowel and consists of a single sound: *can* has one syllable, *can-ter* has two, while *Can-ter-bu-ry* has four.

The **tense** of a verb indicates when something is done:

in the past	perfect tense: *I have worked*
	imperfect tense: *I was working, I used to work*
now	present tense: *I work, I'm working*
in the future	future tense: *I will work*

Transitive verbs need both a **subject** and a **direct object**: *use, give, throw,* unlike **intransitive verbs** which need only a subject: *sleep*, *sit*, *sneeze*. Some verbs can be used both transitively and intransitively: *The pilot flew the plane* (transitive), *I flew at eight o'clock this morning* (intransitive).

Verbs are words like *to go, to sleep, to eat, to like, to have, to be, to think;* they refer to doing and being.

Vowels and **consonants** make up the alphabet. Vowels are the sounds made by the letters **a**, **e**, **i**, **o**, **u**; the rest: **b**, **c**, **d**, **f**, etc. are the consonants.

Answers

Getting started
Page 9
1 *a* Ana N; glossy ADJ; magazine N; organises V; interviews N; hires V; professional ADJ; models N; photographers N; travels V; world N; boyfriend N; well-known ADJ; actor N; *b* my ADJ; father N; comes V; Salamanca N; lives V; Madrid N; works V; central ADJ; office N; large ADJ; company N; *c* prepared V; fantastic ADJ; meal N; ate V; grilled ADJ; fish N; fresh ADJ; asparagus N; new ADJ; potatoes N; drank V; superb ADJ; Spanish ADJ; white ADJ; wine N; dessert N; incredible ADJ

2 *a* very ADV; reasonable ADJ; rather ADV; dilapidated ADJ; really ADV; small ADJ; overgrown ADJ; *b* superbly ADV; terribly ADV; uneven ADJ; deliberately ADV; unfair ADJ

Sounds and spelling
Page 17
almer**ee**a; hheehh**on**; le**on**; sebeelya; tarrag**on**a; balyathol**eeth**; armath**ee**lyo; cheew**a**wa; hhagw**ar**; lyama; mosk**ee**to; chok**o**late; flan; pa**e**lya; p**ee**nya kol**a**tha; s**a**lsa; tort**ee**lya

Checkpoint 1
Page 24
1 Men: C**a**rlos – Charles; Felipe – Philip; Franc**i**sco – Francis; Guill**e**rmo – William; Ju**a**n – John; P**e**dro – Peter
   Women: Alej**a**ndra – Alexandra; Beatr**i**z – Beatrice; El**e**na – Helen; Crist**i**na – Christina; Ju**a**na – Joan/Jean/Jane; S**a**ra – Sarah
   Countries: Argent**i**na – Argentina; Bel**i**ce – Belize; Filip**i**nas – Philippines; Gr**e**cia – Greece; Per**ú** – Peru; Turqu**í**a – Turkey

2 kwest**yon**, question; meesyon**e**ro, missionary; atrakt**ee**bo, attractive; tiyland**es**, Thai; hheograf**ee**a, geography; teor**ee**a, theory; pas**ee**bo, passive; kaneebal**ee**smo, cannibalism

3 Barcelona and Valencia

4 peengw**ee**no; hhener**al**; hheemn**a**syo; g**ee**a; g**e**rra

5 arroba

6 Tanzania

7 the acute accent

8 Papa

9 you – tú; yes – sí

10 Check on page 21.

Checkpoint 2
Page 32
1 *a* cero; *b* 0,5 (cero coma cinco)

2 greater

3 seis; dieciséis; veintiséis; sesenta y seis

4 2.400.000 or 2 400 000

5 *a* It's five o'clock; *b* at seven in the evening; *c* after midnight; *d* at nine o'clock last night; *e* at half past three; *f* twice a day; *g* it's quarter past one; *h* at eleven o'clock at night; *i* on Saturday at three o'clock on the

dot; *j* on Monday at 18.20

6 *a* Son las once; *b* a las diez de la mañana; *c* a mediodía; *d* antes de las diecinueve horas; *e* a eso de las nueve horas; *f* mañana a las diez; *g* a las diez horas ayer; *h* el domingo a las dieciséis horas; *i* a las siete y pico; *j* antes de las tres de la tarde

7 treinta (thirty)

8 en los años setenta

9 el primero de enero; el veinticinco de diciembre; el treinta y uno de diciembre

10 Monday afternoon or evening

11 16.43

12 quinientos

13 el siglo diecinueve

14 primavera

15 el/un setenta y cinco por ciento

Checkpoint 3
Page 44

1 vino m; dentista m/f; problema m; cura m/f; amor m; estación f; pendiente m/f; mano f; casa f; mapa m; calle f; ciudad f

2 las ministras; las conversaciones; los delfines; los gorilas; los cafés; los cocineros; las noches; los profesores; los ciclistas/las ciclistas; los catalanes; las cualidades; los ratones; las excursiones; los cines; las dificultades; las direcciones; los paréntesis; las virtudes; las fotos; los telegramas

3 los tíos

4 la persona/la víctima

5 rana, because it is the only one that does not have a separate word for the female of the species

6 moto f; avión m; lápiz m

7 los peces

8 the first: los coches cama

9 los carnets

10 *a* la biología; *b* el/la fascista; *c* la probabilidad; *d* la diferencia; *e* la nación; *f* la dirección; *g* el feminismo

11 la casita

12 la bailarina

Checkpoint 4
Page 52

1 un tapiz; un análisis; un tigre; una noche; una actriz; un avión; un amor; una dificultad; una virtud; una televisión; un jersey; un ratón; un programa; una madre; una crisis

2 los sistemas; los lápices; los/las estudiantes; las acciones; los/las contables; los camiones; los mapas; los nombres; las costumbres; las manos; las series; los/las terroristas; los/las colegas; las clases; las universidades

3 Me gusta el chocolate; Juan es profesor, un muy buen profesor; trabaja sin ordenador; Quiero ir a la India; El japonés es difícil; Lleva chaqueta; El doctor García es amable; El viernes no trabajo; ¡Qué mujer!; Necesitamos mil libras.

4 unos/algunos

5 lo

Checkpoint 5
Page 62

1 *a* el primer ministro – the Prime Minister; *b* la Casa Blanca – the White House; *c* los juegos olímpicos – the Olympic Games; *d* los gases contaminantes – polluting gases; *e* el turismo verde – green tourism; *f* escrito en tercera persona – written in the third person; *g* el País Vasco – the Basque Country; *h* las Comunidades Autónomas – the Autonomous Communities (self-governing regions in Spain); *i* segunda clase – second class; *j* el sistema universitario – the university system; *k* los recursos naturales – natural resources; el hombre materialista – the materialistic man

2 *a* paciente; *b* simpático; *c* informal; *d* positivo; *e* rápido; *f* necesario; *g* imposible; *h* estúpido

3 *a* informativo; *b* ecológico; *c* voluntario; *d* rígido; *e* generoso; *f* americano; *g* arrogante; *h* evidente; *i* rústico; *j* teológico

4 sano – healthy; educado – polite

5 *a* el blanco; las grandes; el viejo; la verde oscuro; *b* la camisa de seda; el tren de Madrid; la tortilla francesa; la mesa de madera

Checkpoint 6

Page 70

1 *a* absoluto; *b* veloz; *c* simple; *d* raro; *e* típico; *f* normal; *g* profundo; *h* misterioso; *i* severo; *j* dulce

2 *a* pacientemente; *b* fundamentalmente; *c* científicamente; *d* extraordinariamente; *e* regularmente; *f* económicamente; *g* extremamente; *h* indiferentemente; *i* relativamente; *j* lógicamente

3 *a* afortunadamente; *b* justamente; *c* fácilmente; *d* lejos; *e* eficazmente; *f* mejor

4 honestamente – sinceramente; obviamente – evidentemente; cruelmente – brutalmente; despacio – lentamente; finalmente means finally, at last

5 *a* Ese coche es peor que el otro; *b* Ana es mayor que María; *c* Estos bombones son los peores de todos; *d* ¡Nuestro gato es más grande que tu perro!; *e* Carmen es la más pequeña de la clase; *f* Esta película es la mejor de todas; *g* María es menor que Ana.

Checkpoint 7

Page 75

1 *a* ésta; *b* éstos; *c* éste; *d* éste; *e* ésta; *f* éstas

2 *a* ese; *b* esa; *c* esas; *d* esos; *e* ese; *f* ese

3 *a* aquellas; *b* aquellos; *c* aquella; *d* aquel; *e* aquel; *f* aquella

4 esto; eso; aquello

5 éstos; ésos; aquéllos

Checkpoint 8

Page 80

1 *a* sus; *b* nuestro; *c* su; *d* tus; *e* mis; *f* vuestro; *g* sus

2 *a* (el) mío; *b* (los) suyos; *c* (la) suya; *d* (las) nuestras; *e* (los) tuyos; *f* (el) suyo; *g* (la) suya

3 tu, su, vuestro pasaporte; el tuyo, el suyo, el vuestro

4 It's his/her/your (usted and ustedes)/their life.

5 He encontrado las llaves de ella.

6 el coche de la empresa; la casa de mi madre; Muy señor mío

Checkpoint 9

Page 90
1 Hola, soy yo.
2 *a* tú; *b* usted; *c* vosotras;
   d ustedes; *e* tú; *f* usted
3 *a* I give it to her; *b* I prepare it for
   you. (familiar); *c* We don't know
   her; *d* I phone you. (formal); *e* He
   shaves; *f* I haven't seen them. (f);
   g Please excuse us; *h* She did not
   give it to you. (familiar)
4 *a* ¿Qué quiere usted?; *b* Te veo;
   c Se lo explicas; *d* Os laváis;
   e ¿Son ellos?; *f* Nos lo han dado;
   g La he comido; *h* Les gusta.
5 ¿Quieres probarlo?/¿Lo quieres
   probar?
   Tengo que comprarlos./Los tengo
   que comprar.
6 *a* consigo; *b* para ti; *c* cerca de
   mí; *d* de ellas; *e* a él; *f* hasta tú
7 English is spoken here.
8 Lo he hecho yo mismo/misma.
9 the word 'for'
10 les

Checkpoint 10

Page 96
1 *a* de hecho; *b* estoy de acuerdo;
   c ¡Bah!; *d* según yo; *e* ¡Caramba!
   Entonces is left over; it means
   well then, so, right then.
2 *a* that; *b* who; *c* who; *d* which;
   e who(m); *f* who(m); *g* which;
3 cuyos
4 *a* quiénes; *b* cuyas; *c* que/la que;
   d que; *e* que/el que
5 por otra parte
6 en mi opinión/a mi parecer/para
   mí
7 no obstante

Checkpoint 11

Page 108
1 *a* Llegamos al aeropuerto;
   b Carmen es la mujer del pelo
   rubio; *c* Lo hacemos por ella;
   d Las flores son para tu madre;
   e ¿Quiere usted algo de comer?;
   f El tren sale a las siete; *g* Mi
   hermano vive en Alemania.
2 *a* a house by the seaside; *b* a 35
   million euro house; *c* my uncle's
   house; *d* a house for the holidays;
   e a wooden house; *f* a country
   house; *g* a house in the Canaries;
   h a house at the foot of the
   Pyrenees; *i* a house next to the
   park; *j* my grandparents' house;
   k a three-storey house; *l* a house
   between two streets
3 *a* el coche de Paco; *b* un número
   de teléfono; *c* la cáscara de
   naranja; *d* cada uno de nosotros;
   e al final de la película; *f* el primo
   de mi madre; *g* la dirección del
   médico; *h* el tren de las 09.55
4 esperar
5 in the
6 tennis shoes; leather shoes;
   high-heeled shoes
7 Está detrás del banco.
8 en moto; por vía aérea; para las
   dos; pintado por Picasso

Checkpoint 12

Page 120
1 arrival, deep
2 dream
3 -ar, -er, -ir
4 tense
5 yo (I); ellos/ellas (they); ustedes
   (you formal)
6 four: tú, usted, vosotros/as,
   ustedes

7 (el) fumar
8 pull
9 irregular verb; reflexive verb
10 to claim
11 acelerar, ilustrar, separar; commercialise, caramelise, paralyse
12 disconnect, disfigure, disinfect, demoralise, recommence, recycle, recreate

Checkpoint 13

Page 130

1 *a* No trabajan con nosotros; *b* Juan no ha visto la película; *c* No me gusta el té; *d* No he estado en Perú; *e* Nosotros no tenemos hijos; *f* Yo no sé donde viven.
2 nothing; nobody; never; not any; neither … nor; no longer
3 ningún
4 a
5 *a* No me gustan ni las cebollas ni los tomates; *b* María no ha comido nunca el avestruz.
6 ¿cuánto? and ¿cuál?
7 ¿cuál? and ¿qué?
8 *a* ¿Cuándo sale el tren para Barcelona?; *b* ¿Por qué quiere tu hermana hablar conmigo?
9 ¿no? ¿verdad?
10 *a* cuántas; *b* qué; *c* dónde; *d* quién; *e* por qué; *f* cuál

Checkpoint 14

Page 137

1 from left to right: escojo, estoy escogiendo
venís, estáis viniendo
pedimos, estamos pidiendo
encuentra, está encontrando
piensas, estás pensando

construimos, estamos construyendo
dicen, están diciendo
lee, está leyendo
pueden, están pudiendo
oigo, estoy oyendo
duerme, está durmiendo
sienten, están sintiendo
2 *a* Comenzamos mañana; *b* ¿Habla Paco inglés?; *c* ¿Comemos?; *d* Vivo aquí desde hace veinte años.

Checkpoint 15

Page 147

1 *a* el año pasado – Last year we went to Madrid; *b* siempre – When he/she was young, he/she always did his/her homework; *c* con frecuencia – I used to see my friends frequently; *d* anteayer – He/she washed the dishes the day before yesterday; *e* finalmente – They finally visited Seville.
2 *a* jugaba, empezó – Whilst Raul was playing football, it started to snow; *b* veía, llegó – Carmen was watching television, when her boyfriend arrived; *c* era, iba – When she was a child, Dolores used to walk to school; *d* estudiaba, escuchaba – Whilst Paco was studying, he would listen to music.

Checkpoint 16

Page 150

1 llorabas: imperfect, tú → llorar to cry
corrimos: preterite, nosotros/as → correr to run

sufriremos: future, nosotros/as → sufrir to suffer
cociné: preterite, yo → cocinar to cook
ganarán: future, ellos/ellas, ustedes → ganar to win
cerraban: imperfect, ellos/ellas, ustedes → cerrar to close
descubren: present, ellos/ellas, ustedes → descubrir to discover
parecía: imperfect, yo, él/ella, usted → parecer to seem
enviaríais: conditional, vosotros/as → enviar to send
abre: present, él/ella, usted → abrir to open
rompió: preterite, él/ella, usted → romper to break
temíais: imperfect, vosotros/as → temer to fear
obtenemos: present, nosotros/as → obtener to obtain
pagarás: future, tú → pagar to pay
recibirías: conditional, tú → recibir to receive
pintaron: preterite, ellos/ellas, ustedes → pintar to paint
explicarían: conditional, ellos/ellas, ustedes → explicar to explain
salíamos: imperfect, nosotros/as → salir to leave
aplaudíais: imperfect, vosotros/as → aplaudir to applaud
aprendería: conditional, yo, él/ella, usted → aprender to learn
prometerá: future, él/ella, usted → prometer to promise

2 from left to right: llegaré; organizaremos; buscarías; cenamos; crecían; compraré;

abrí; creía; pensaban; escribiríais; compartirás; emigró; ofrecía; bailan

3 Cuando tenía cinco años fui a vivir a Madrid; Pagaría pero no tengo dinero; Cuando cocinaba escuchaba música; Me encantaría ir a Madrid.

Checkpoint 17

Page 160

1 from left to right: comprado; vendido; escrito; roto; comenzado; muerto; trabajado; construido; querido; hecho; abierto; frito; cubierto; venido; tenido; dicho; comido; visto; vestido; decidido; bebido; puesto; vuelto; andado

2 a han; b hemos; c has; d han; e ha; f habéis; g he; h ha

3 a No había entendido nada – He hadn't understood anything; b Habríamos ido al parque – We would have gone to the park; c Raúl ha llegado tarde – Raúl has arrived late; d ¿Cuándo habréis comido? – When will you have eaten? e No se había levantado temprano – He/she hadn't got up early. f ¿Qué has hecho en el colegio? – What have you done at school?; g Habríais organizado una cena – You would have organised a dinner; h Habrán invitado a todos sus amigos – They will have invited all their friends; i ¿Has terminado el libro? – Have you finished the book?; j Se habían vestido con prisa – They had got dressed hurriedly.

Checkpoint 18

Page 164

1 *a* distribuyendo – distributing;
b contraviniendo – contravening;
c maldiciendo – cursing;
d persiguiendo – chasing;
e releyendo – rereading;
f contradiciendo – contradicting;
g sonriendo – smiling;
h contribuyendo – contributing;
i interviniendo – intervening;
j distrayendo – distracting

2 *a* buscando; *b* pagar; *c* nadar;
d tocando; *e* haciendo; *f*
continuar

Checkpoint 19

Page 174

1 "Bueno … no <u>tome</u> la primera a
la izquierda, sino que <u>siga</u> todo
recto hasta los semáforos. <u>Gire</u>
a la izquierda, <u>cruce</u> la plaza
y luego <u>tome</u> la segunda a la
derecha. No se <u>preocupe</u> – no
está lejos."

2 A

3 usted; tú would be: "Bueno … no
<u>tomes</u> la primera a la izquierda,
sino que <u>sigue</u> todo recto hasta
los semáforos. <u>Gira</u> a la izquierda,
<u>cruza</u> la plaza y luego <u>toma</u> la
segunda a la derecha. No te
<u>preocupes</u> – no está lejos."

4 Compraría una casa grande si
fuera rica; Creo que usted está
triste; No puede salir a menos
que termine sus deberes; No creo
que usted esté contento; Habría
comprado el coche si hubiera
tenido el dinero; Espero que
ustedes vengan a la fiesta.

Checkpoint 20

Page 188

1 *a* es; *b* están; *c* es; *d* son; *e* es;
f estoy; *g* es; *h* estás; *i* son; *j* está

2 *a* hay; *b* hay; *c* hace; *d* hay;
e hace; *f* hay; *g* hace; *h* hace;
i hay; *j* hay

3 A Enrique no le gustan los
mariscos – Henry doesn't like
seafood; No te gustaba el
pescado cuando eras joven – You
didn't used to like fish when you
were young; A mis amigos les
gusta esquíar – My friends like
skiing; Os gustaron las cerezas
que compré – You liked the
cherries I bought; Nos gustaban
los caramelos cuando éramos
jóvenes – We used to like sweets
when we were young; Me gustó
mucho la película que vi anoche
– I really liked the film I saw last
night.

Checkpoint 21

Page 196

1 *a* de; *b* a; *c* de; *d* a; *e* a; *f* de;
g a/de; *h* a

2 *a* de la; *b* en la; *c* por el; *d* con la;
e del; *f* al; *g* al

3 *a* Esperan el tren; *b* Me gusta
jugar al golf; *c* Siempre
escuchamos música; *d* Tratáis
de no fumar; *e* Tengo intención
de visitarte; *f* ¿Quieren comer
ahora?; *g* Entramos en el estadio;
h ¿Cuidas del perro del vecino?
or ¿Te ocupas del perro del
vecino? or ¿Cuidas al perro del
vecino?

Index